Arts in Nature with Children and Young People

This novel text brings together research and practice on the intersection between arts and nature and their impact on children and young people's wellbeing, health equality and sustainability.

Existing literature focuses on either the impact of the arts *or* the impact of being in/with nature on children's and young people's wellbeing. However, the intersection between the two – arts *and* nature – and their combined effect on wellbeing has received limited attention. Through five research-based and seven practice-based chapters, this book draws upon arts-in-nature practices that incorporate visual arts, music, movement, drama and poetry, in a range of natural environments, such as forests, beaches, greenhouses, parks, community areas and school playgrounds.

Arts in Nature with Children and Young People will appeal to anyone working with children and young people, including mental health and healthcare professionals, teachers, researchers, artists and art therapists. It is also an accessible guide for parents and families looking for inspiration and ideas for creative and outdoor activities.

Zoe Moula, PhD, is Lecturer in Mental Health at King's College London and the Editor-in-Chief of the *International Journal of Art Therapy*.

Nicola Walshe, PhD, is Pro-Director for Education at the UCL Institute of Education and Executive Director of the UCL Centre for Climate Change and Sustainability Education.

'*Arts in Nature with Children and Young People* is essential reading for all who wish to understand the fundamental connection between human flourishing and the natural environment. Like Zoe and Nicola, I, too, have been inspired and moved by the work of Cambridge Curiosity and Imagination. Through the voices of children, we know that being creative in nature is transformative for their learning and growth. This is a critical field of study in relation to the climate emergency and the ever-growing crisis in young people's mental health.'

Alex Coulter, *Director of the National Centre for Creative Health*

'From the creative programming of practitioners to the empirical findings of researchers, the editors of *Arts in Nature with Children and Young People* have curated a dynamic collection of papers, highlighting the educational, developmental, and therapeutic value of engaging with nature and art. Moula and Walshe have produced a valuable resource for practitioners working with children and youth.'

Nevin J. Harper, *PhD, RCC. Professor, counsellor, author of* Nature-based Therapy *and editor of* Outdoor Therapies

'Bravo to authors Moula and Walshe, who have assembled an outstanding group of authors to demonstrate the healing power of the arts in nature in a variety of natural settings. Grounded in empirical research, this trailblazing book brilliantly synthesizes the interconnectedness between the arts and nature to support the overall well-being of children and adolescents. Beneficially, this book will ultimately inspire readers to personally engage the arts in natural landscapes to deepen their own ecological sense of self.'

Janet A. Courtney, *PhD, Founder FirstPlay Therapy, author and co-editor of* Nature-based Play *and* Expressive Therapies: Interventions for Children, Teens, and Families

'This book brings together an impressive breadth of research and practice showing how creative arts experiences carried out in natural settings can contribute to wellbeing. The authors explore the contribution of a variety of "arts-in-nature" practices toward promoting individual and community wellbeing, social justice, cultural awareness, and personal and environmental sustainability. This is a major contribution of utmost importance to personal and planetary healing for the future of our young people and our Earth.'

Professor Sally Atkins, *Ed.D., REAT, REACE, Founding Director of Expressive Arts, Appalachian State University and author of* Nature-Based Expressive Arts Therapy

Arts in Nature with Children and Young People

A Guide Towards Health Equality, Wellbeing, and Sustainability

Edited by Zoe Moula and Nicola Walshe

Routledge
Taylor & Francis Group

LONDON AND NEW YORK

Designed cover image: 'Fantastical Forest 2023, Cambridge Curiosity and Imagination. Photo by Gerry Weatherhead.'

First published 2025
by Routledge
4 Park Square, Milton Park, Abingdon, Oxon OX14 4RN

and by Routledge
605 Third Avenue, New York, NY 10158

Routledge is an imprint of the Taylor & Francis Group, an informa business

This work was supported by the UK Research and Innovation (UKRI) Arts and Humanities Research Council (AHRC) [grant number AH/S006206/1 and AH/W007819/1].

Trademark notice: Product or corporate names may be trademarks or registered trademarks, and are used only for identification and explanation without intent to infringe.

British Library Cataloguing-in-Publication Data
A catalogue record for this book is available from the British Library

Library of Congress Cataloging-in-Publication Data
Names: Moula, Zoe, editor. | Walshe, Nicola, editor.
Title: Arts in nature with children and young people : a guide towards health equality, wellbeing, and sustainability / edited by Zoe Moula and Nicola Walshe.
Description: Abingdon, Oxon ; New York, NY : Routledge, 2025. | Includes bibliographical references and index.
Identifiers: LCCN 2024036714 (print) | LCCN 2024036715 (ebook) |
  ISBN 9781032412801 (hardback) | ISBN 9781032412795 (paperback) |
  ISBN 9781003357308 (ebook)
Subjects: MESH: Art Therapy—methods | Child Health | Adolescent Health | Nature | Environmental Health | Health Equity
Classification: LCC RJ505.A7 (print) | LCC RJ505.A7 (ebook) | NLM WS 350.25 |
  DDC 615.8/5156083—dc23/eng/20240925
LC record available at https://lccn.loc.gov/2024036714
LC ebook record available at https://lccn.loc.gov/2024036715

ISBN: 978-1-032-41280-1 (hbk)
ISBN: 978-1-032-41279-5 (pbk)
ISBN: 978-1-003-35730-8 (ebk)

DOI: 10.4324/9781003357308

Typeset in Times New Roman
by Apex CoVantage, LLC

For my parents, Evelina and Tasos – for raising me with unconditional love.

(Zoe)

For my wonderful children, Ciara, Emma and Rory – for being the inspiration for all I do.

(Nicola)

Contents

Illustrations

Figures

Tables

Contributors

Alan Cusack is an artist and teacher. His research explores art practice as a social, discursive activity and the potential of individual and shared experience as a space for facilitating productive conflict. He has been working on and collaborating with the Village Project for five years.

Anna Dako is an interdisciplinary artist and a somatic movement educator and therapist with 20 years of experience working with dance, movement and creative arts. Anna's experience stretches from dance research, dramaturgy and site-specific productions. She collaborates internationally and has lived and worked in Poland, the Netherlands, and now in Scotland, UK. Anna is the founder and director of 'Dunami – Movement, Arts, Wellbeing', a platform for ecologically mindful growth, psycho-somatic health and creative development through arts and intercultural dialogue. As a writer, she focuses on practice-based research, ecopsychology and environmental philosophy perspectives. In her private practice she specialises in supporting and working through versatile psycho-somatic imbalances. She also loves guiding experiential walks and working with children and young people, both in therapy and creative education.

Carla van Laar is a creative arts therapist living and working on the unceded lands of the Boon Wurrung/Bunurong people in South-Eastern Australia. Born in Brisbane on Turrbal Country, Carla has European and Nordic heritage. She is one of three children, and mother of two. She brings decades of experience working with people and the arts for wellbeing in community, justice, health, education and private practice contexts. Carla currently provides nature-based arts therapy as part of her work with children, young people and adults who have experienced interpersonal violence.

Debi Keyte-Hartland is an experienced pedagogical consultant, trainer and artist-educator working in early years education both nationally and internationally. She works to amplify opportunities for children to communicate and learn through the arts. She is an associate consultant working with Early Education and teaches and supports masters students researching arts and creativity at the Centre of Research in Early Childhood (CREC). She designs professional learning and development that utilise creative approaches drawing on the arts as languages for learning, which communicate children's thinking about the world. Debi is currently training as a teacher-educator of the Reggio Emilia Approach which continues to shape her thinking.

Dylan Adams is Senior Lecturer in Education at Cardiff Metropolitan University. He worked for many years as a primary school teacher before moving into higher education. His research interests include nature pedagogy; holistic education; contemplative pedagogies; posthumanism; the expressive arts; and hermeneutic phenomenological approaches. He is Vice Chair of The British Education Studies Association, a Fellow of the Royal Society of Arts, and a Fellow of the Higher Education Academy.

Estella Guerrera is a neurodivergent person, an expressive psychotherapist and freelance consultant, based in Bologna, Italy. Through private practice in their studio-atelier, outdoor activities and psycho-social projects, they help people and groups to approach and enhance the connection between personal identity, creativity, environment and collective development of community bonds. As a consultant in mental health and psychosocial wellbeing (MHPSS) and peer-to-peer support, they help organizations in establishing or consolidating inclusive and accessible practices, projects and services for children, adolescents, families and people of every age.

Gary Beauchamp is Professor of Education in the Cardiff School of Education and Social Policy at Cardiff Metropolitan University. His research interests include the expressive arts, outdoor education, and interactive technologies in educational settings. He is Vice Chair of the National Digital Learning Council for Wales and an experienced school governor.

Jane Tarr taught children and young people with social and emotional difficulties before moving into higher education as a teacher trainer/researcher in inclusive education. At UWE, Bristol, she became Director of Teachers' Continuing Professional Development. She is a qualified music therapist, currently working with young people in schools and clinical settings.

Katarina Horrox is an art therapist registered with the British Association of Art Therapists and a psychodynamic organisational therapist registered with the British Psychoanalytic Council. She has studied outdoor therapy in diverse settings and her own practice is strongly informed by Hayley Marshall, Billie Riley and Liz Greenway. She has undertaken specialist trainings with the Tavistock and Portman NHS Foundation Trust and the Anna Freud Centre, and studied trauma practices, such as Somatic Interventions. Her professional experience is in community and institutional settings. Her personal outdoor experience is as a rock climber. Most recently she worked as the senior field clinician on Venture Mor's Wilderness Therapy Programmes and she is now the clinical manager of the Venture Trust Outdoor Therapy Service.

Louise Lowings is the head teacher at Madeley Nursery School in Telford in the West Midlands of the UK. Her pedagogical approach is based on contextual relationships between children, their ideas, and their encounters with the world. She has developed a place where educators and children are researchers. Inspiration from the preschools in Reggio Emilia has led to encounters with other entangled influences, such as the ideas of Gregory Bateson, initially through professional exchange with pedagogues in Stockholm and more recently through the International Bateson Institute. This has transformed her understanding of the place of learning, children, educators, and ecology.

Lucy Tiplady is Senior Research Associate in Education at Newcastle University, UK. Lucy's research interests include children and young people's wellbeing and engagement in learning, outdoor learning and co-produced, participatory and visual research methods. Working collaboratively with schools and the wider education community has led to exploration of how research methods can be used as tools for enquiry to aid practitioner and student learning and in how alternative learning environments can increase wellbeing and address educational disadvantage.

Melissa McDevitt Weston is a Boon Wurrung/Bunurong woman with Yorta Yorta, Waywurru and Dja Dja Wurrung connections. Melissa is one of six children, the mother of five, and grandmother of six grandchildren. She has worked extensively for the community and is a contemporary artist. Melissa's experience as an artist covers 35 years and innumerable exhibitions including a Solo Exhibition in Gondwana Gallery, Alice Springs in the 1990's, and her work has been acquired for the permanent collection of the Bass Coast.

Nick Clough taught in inner urban primary schools before moving into teacher education, first as an LEA advisory teacher and then within the University sector. At UWE, Bristol he became Director of Initial Teacher Education. He currently works as a professional development adviser and community musician. He coordinated the ERASMUS+ LINK Project.

Nicola Walshe is Professor of Education, Pro-Director for Education at IOE, UCL's Institute for Education and Society, and Executive Director of the UCL Centre for Climate Change and Sustainability Education. Her research is predominantly in the field of high-quality teacher education practices in climate change and environmental and sustainability education; her recent AHRC-funded projects, Eco-Capabilities and Branching Out, explore the process by which arts-in-nature practice supports children's connection with the environment and, thereby, their wellbeing. Nicola is co-convenor of the Environmental and Sustainability Education Research network of European Educational Research Association and a UCL Climate Hub Community Expert.

Nomisha Kurian is University of Cambridge Teaching Associate, who specialises in child wellbeing and human-centred design. She recently became the first

Education researcher to win the Cambridge Applied Research Award and is also the recipient of the Cambridge Vice-Chancellor's Award for Social Impact. Previously, as a Yale University Henry Fellow, she used international human rights law to design anti-bullying frameworks for young people. Her work has most recently been published in the Oxford Review of Education, the British Educational Research Journal, and the International Journal of Human Rights.

Penny Hay is an artist, educator, mentor and researcher, Reader in Creative Teaching and Learning, Senior Lecturer in Arts Education, School of Education; Research Fellow, Centre for Cultural and Creative Industries; Bath Spa University and Director of Research, House of Imagination. Signature projects include School Without Walls and Forest of Imagination. Penny's doctoral research focused on children's learning identity as artists. Penny is a National Teaching Fellow and Fellow of the Chartered College of Teaching, with awards from Action for Children's Arts and Creative Bath.

Ruth Sapsed is Director of Cambridge Curiosity and Imagination (CCI) and has led the organisation since it was established as an arts and well-being charity in 2007. Their programmes cultivate creative communities in Cambridgeshire and beyond and aim to help people of all ages foster deep connections with each other and the world on their doorsteps. The work often takes place in communities with particular challenges. They have developed long and fruitful relationships with many Cambridge institutions (including both universities, Addenbrooke's hospital, the city and county councils, many schools, and the region's leading mental health charities for children and young people) and more recently with University College London's new Centre for Climate Change and Sustainability Education.

Sarah Victoria Sharp is PhD Candidate at the University of Cambridge. Her research centres around beyond-anthropocentric stories and their pedagogic potential in environmental education. Sarah uses theories of entanglement and relationality to consider approaches to exploring ways we live with the world in formal education settings. In addition to previously teaching Drama and Theatre Studies for years 9–13, Sarah is a practicing theatre maker and co-founder of the environmental arts organisation, One Step Theatre. She has supported a range of research in the environmental education field and is an Associate Fellow at the Centre for Climate Change and Sustainability Education at UCL.

Zoe Moula is Lecturer in Mental Health at King's College London, and former Research Fellow at Imperial College and University College London. Her research is focused on the impact of arts therapies and arts-in-nature on children and young people's wellbeing and nature connection. Zoe is a member of the Steering Committee of the Arts, Health and Wellbeing Special Interest Group at the Royal Society for Public Health, and the Editor-in-Chief at the International Journal of Art Therapy.

Foreword

Children are spending less time outdoors than ever before. Research shows that children feel less connected to nature and that children from poorer communities are less likely to spend time in nature than those from more affluent areas. At the same time, children and young people are facing unprecedented health challenges, including increased incidence of mental ill-health, rising childhood obesity and associated health challenges such as early onset Type 2 diabetes.

There is growing evidence revealing the benefits of exposure to nature and health. Studies have found links between human health and exposure of the microbiome to the natural environment. Biomedical evidence reveals that these environmental microbiota, also known as microbial biodiversity, play a major role in the development and function of the brain, as well as in the regulation of the immune system. The consequences, therefore, of lack of exposure to nature could be profound. One study found that daily exposure to microbial biodiversity is associated with immune modulation in humans. Another study showed that growing up in urban environments is associated with increased risks of developing psychiatric disorders. A large study involving over 900,000 people showed that children who grew up with the lowest levels of green space had up to 55% higher risk of developing a psychiatric disorder independent from the effects of other known risk factors.

There is a rapidly growing evidence base showing that increased access to green space provides a range of physical and mental health benefits, including reduced blood pressure, reduced stress levels and associated symptoms, lower levels of cardiovascular and respiratory problems, reduced risk of diabetes and obesity, increased wellbeing, including subjective wellbeing, reduced social isolation, increased happiness and resilience wellbeing, a decrease in PTSD symptoms and ADHD.

Similarly, there is an extensive evidence base showing the positive effects of engagement in arts, culture, creativity and heritage (also known as Creative Health). Studies have shown that arts engagement leads to increased social interaction, adoption of healthy behaviours, promotion of physical movement and activity, improved emotional, cognitive and sensory processing and decreased stress, preventing and treating the long-term conditions that are creating pressure on the healthcare system and improvements in outcomes such as employment and skills, economic development, sense of place and social cohesion.

As with green space, there are significant barriers to arts and cultural engagement related to socioeconomic status, geography and accessibility. Removal of arts and creativity from the school curriculum continues to have damaging effects, with significant reductions in the number of art teachers and reductions in the number of students taking art and arts-related subjects in schools. Bearing in mind the complex barriers to access, innovative approaches to overcoming access are required.

The volume presented here provides fascinating examples of novel approaches to tackling the interconnected issues of inequality, wellbeing and sustainability using a 'planetary health' approach, whereby initiatives consider the health of people alongside the health of the environment. This has never been timelier given the growing rates of inequality in our society, with more and more children and young people growing up in poverty. At the same time, the ecological and climate emergency is escalating, and there is an urgent need to engage the whole of society in tackling this crisis. The initiatives described in this volume employ a range of approaches from art-making, music, crafting, performance and storytelling within natural settings to showcase how children and young people can improve their own health, wellbeing and learning, whilst becoming more environmentally aware and better connected to nature. This ecological approach to public health is surely preferable to current systems and structures which have led to structural and systematic inequalities alongside environmental degradation, and this volume provides an excellent starting point to revealing how children and young people can be central in this planetary health solution.

Helen Chatterjee
Professor of Human and Ecological Health, UCL

Bibliography

All-Party Parliamentary Group on Arts, Health and Wellbeing. (2017). *Creative health: The arts for health and wellbeing, inquiry report* (2nd ed.). Retrieved from www.culturehealthandwellbeing.org.uk/appg-inquiry/Publications/Creative_Health_Inquiry_Report_2017_-_Second_Edition.pdf

All-Party Parliamentary Group on Arts, Health and Wellbeing and the National Centre for Creative Health. (2023). *Creative health review: How policy can embrace creative health.* Retrieved from https://ncch.org.uk/creative-health-review

Engemann, K., Pedersen, C. B., Arge, L., Tsirogiannis, C., Mortensen, P. B., & Svenning, J. C. (2019). Residential green space in childhood is associated with lower risk of psychiatric disorders from adolescence into adulthood. *Proceedings of the National Academy of Sciences of the United States of America.* doi: 10.1073/pnas.1807504116

Fancourt, D., & Mak, H. W. (2020). What barriers do people experience to engaging in the arts? Structural equation modelling of the relationship between individual characteristics and capabilities, opportunities, and motivations to engage. *PLoS ONE.* doi: 10.1371/journal.pone.0230487

Mughal, R., Polley, M., Sabey, A., & Chatterjee, H. J. (2022). How arts, heritage and culture can support health and wellbeing through social prescribing. *National Academy for Social Prescribing.* Retrieved from https://socialprescribingacademy.org.uk/read-the-evidence/arts-culture-and-creativity/

Mughal, R., Seers, H., Polley, M., Sabey, A., & Chatterjee, H. J. (2022). How the natural environment can support health and wellbeing through social prescribing. *National Academy for Social Prescribing*. Retrieved from https://socialprescribingacademy.org.uk/read-the-evidence/nature/

Roslund, M. I., Parajuli, A., Hui, N., Puhakka, R., Grönroos, M., Soininen L., . . . Sinkkonen, A. (2022). A Placebo-controlled double-blinded test of the biodiversity hypothesis of immune-mediated diseases: Environmental microbial diversity elicits changes in cytokines and increase in T regulatory cells in young children. *Ecotoxicology Environmental Safety*. doi: 10.1016/j.ecoenv.2022.113900

Seers, H., Mughal, R., & Chatterjee, H. J. (2022). How the natural environment can support children and young people Evidence Information Note EIN067. *Natural England*. Retrieved from https://publications.naturalengland.org.uk/publication/6705674179575808

The Warwick Commission. (2015). *Enriching Britain: Culture, creativity and growth*. Retrieved from https://warwick.ac.uk/research/warwickcommission/futureculture/final-report/warwick_commission_final_report.pdf

Acknowledgements

We share our sincere gratitude to the chapter authors who contributed their time and expertise to this book. We would also like to extend our gratitude to all artists, therapists, teachers and practitioners bringing arts-in-nature experiences to children and young people.

Chapter 1

Introduction

Arts, nature and wellbeing

Zoe Moula and Nicola Walshe

Our inspiration for writing this book

Zoe

The idea behind this book on 'arts-in-nature' (the term we will be using throughout this book) was rooted in 'Artscaping', an arts-in-nature practice developed by the charity Cambridge Curiosity and Imagination (CCI) (Figure 1.1). Artscaping was piloted in schools in areas of high deprivation in Cambridgeshire in a research project led by Nicola entitled *Eco-Capabilities*, which was funded by the Arts and Humanities Research Council (AHRC) in the UK. Shortly after finishing my PhD in school-based arts therapies, I had the privilege of becoming a postdoctoral research fellow in this study. On top of the benefits of this practice for children and young people, which we will be discussing in the following sections, Artscaping had a profound impact on me. Being part of every session as a participant observer, I realised that I had not had access to nature for most of my life. This was mainly because I grew up in Athens (Greece), the city with the least green space per person across Europe. The only park near my neighbourhood, called 'Baroutadiko', was filled with rubbish, and it was notorious for burglaries and violent behaviour when I was growing up in the 1990s, making the only green space both inaccessible and unsafe. Things have changed significantly since then; the park is now well maintained, it feels safer and people use it for leisure activities such as running or walking in nature – a positive sign that people have started to respect and value nature.

In the absence of green spaces, as a child, I was in awe of the sky, my only chance of connecting with nature in a big city. A miracle happened soon after I turned eight when my parents rented a flat to spend our family summer holidays in a seaside town called 'Nea Artaki', the place that I now call my 'home'. It was there, by the sea, that my deep connection with nature started to grow. The sea became my shelter for every happy or sad experiences I was going through as a child. The sounds of the waves, the touch of the water, the smell of the sea – all these senses would stay with me even when I was returning back to Athens until the next summer.

Similar to nature, the arts were what kept me going through my life's happiest and saddest moments or simply to take care of myself. Whether it was singing to

DOI: 10.4324/9781003357308-1

Figure 1.1 'Artscaping', Cambridge Curiosity and Imagination

grieve or singing to celebrate, painting to release my deepest emotions that could not be verbalised, dancing with friends until the early hours or writing a poem as a gift to a loved one, the arts were always an invisible partner supporting me to navigate life and helping me to understand why I am here.

Nicola

Working with CCI has been similarly transformational for me, both personally and professionally. I encountered their practice as an early career academic. At the time, I was a researcher and geography teacher educator grappling with how to engage children and young people with issues of sustainability in the classroom. It had become clear that more traditional, knowledge-based approaches to environmental sustainability education were not providing students with the holistic understanding of and engagement with sustainability that was perhaps required. Many were disengaged and ambivalent and certainly did not have the skills – or indeed motivation – to engage meaningfully with policy and practice at whatever level to effect change. I had started to consider more creative, affective pedagogies when a colleague recommended I look up the practice of CCI, an arts and well-being charity whose creative practice in nature (now termed Artscaping, as Zoe describes) might be just what I was looking for. And indeed it was. Speaking with the artists to understand their practice and how they weave arts and nature together to provide a nurturing space for children and young people to connect with and be part of their local environments was inspirational. Working with them to develop a project (which became *Eco-Capabilities*) to really understand the impact of this on the children and young people was thoroughly rewarding. However, the real impact for me came through being alongside artists working directly with the children in schools across the project – schools that were, frankly, brave enough to see the potential of taking whole classes of children 'off timetable' to become artscapers in a context of busy school days, a crowded curriculum and high stakes account- ability. It was a privilege to be part of those few months in school, to experience the change in the children in response to artscaping, but also to see the transformation in the teachers and other adults in school – their eyes being opened to other ways of being with the children as they witnessed the impact on children's relation- ships, confidence and wellbeing and the way that spilled over into the rest of the school week.

So, from a professional perspective as a teacher educator looking for approaches to support children in better understanding the world around them, this work dem- onstrated that arts-in-nature experiences could be a really significant practice through which to do this. However, I am also acutely aware of the concerning headlines about the mental health and wellbeing of our children; the latest Mental Health of Children and Young People in England report found that 20.3% of eight to 16-year-olds had a probable mental disorder (NHS England, 2023). As a mother of three, I can see how this manifests in children and young people in very different ways, and I understand first-hand the need for a more considered and preventative approach to supporting their mental health and wellbeing in a system which is overwhelmed by need. As such, from a personal perspective, arts-in-nature prac- tice is imperative for schools to support our children and young people. This book is the next small step in the journey towards achieving this because achieve it we must – however long it may take.

Arts, nature and wellbeing

The impact of nature and outdoor environments on the health and wellbeing of children and young people is now widely evidenced. For example, the People and Nature Survey (Natural England, 2020) showed that children who spend more time outside and more time noticing nature/wildlife are more likely to report that "being in nature makes me very happy" (91% and 94%, respectively). Likewise, there is overwhelming evidence from more than 3000 studies globally that arts play a major role in the prevention of ill health, promotion of health and health manage- ment across the lifespan (Fancourt & Finn, 2019). However, what has received scant attention in the literature thus far is the amalgamation and interconnection between the two: arts *and* nature. To our knowledge, there are very few studies con- cerning how access to nature can be facilitated through the arts and how engage- ment with the arts can blossom in nature.

The conception of the idea to write this book started with *Eco-capabilities*, an AHRC-funded study[1] situated at the intersection of three issues: a sharp rise in children and young people's mental health challenges, societal disconnect from nature and a school curriculum that fails to draw on cultural, community and natural assets. The aim of *Eco-capabilities* was to address these challenges and explore how the wellbeing of children living in areas of high deprivation can be supported through arts-in-nature (Walshe, Moula, & Lee, 2022). The arts-in-nature practice, Artscaping, was developed by the arts and wellbeing charity CCI (Walshe et al., 2022), and it was delivered by artists and teachers (in pairs) to 101 children living in areas of high deprivation. In this study, we found that following eight full days of Artscaping, eight (eco-)capabilities were developed: autonomy; bodily integrity and safety; individuality; mental and emotional wellbeing; human and non-human relationality; senses and imagination; and spirituality (Walshe et al., 2022). Children also felt happier with their life as a whole, spending time outdoors and doing things away from home and were more optimistic about what the future holds for them (Moula, Walshe, & Lee, 2023). Arts-in-nature practice not only supported children's wellbeing, but also guided them towards a more entangled relationship with nature and a clearer understanding of themselves as part of it, thereby motivating them to take better care of it. Finally, through an analysis of children's pre-and-post drawings, we found a significant increase in the number of children's drawings which featured nature as a main focus (a 483% increase for plant illustrations and 470% for animal illustrations), suggesting that arts-in-nature experiences contributed towards what we term 'nature visibilisation', an outcome necessary both for human and planetary health (Walshe, Perry, & Moula, 2023).

A second project, *Branching Out*,[2] investigated how arts-in-nature practice can be scaled up through the mobilisation of community assets, including school staff and local volunteers, to reach more children in primary schools (Bungay, Walshe, & Dadswell, 2024). The Branching Out model was piloted in six primary schools across Cambridgeshire with 'Community Artscapers' delivering 1.5-hour Artscaping sessions with children outdoors for eight weeks. Findings indicated how the Branching Out model can provide an opportunity for schools to develop their staff, recruit and support volunteers from the local community and increase their capacity to promote the mental health and wellbeing of their children. Further, the use of Community Artscapers was found to have positive impacts on children, school staff, volunteers and the wider school community (Dadswell, Bungay, Acton, & Walshe, 2024).

Alongside these studies, we also conducted a systematic review of arts-in-nature interventions and practices for children and young people (Moula, Palmer, & Walshe, 2022). Based on 11 studies and 602 participants in total, we found that arts-in-nature can offer an inclusive medium to engage all children and young people, especially those who might otherwise remain disinterested in environmental issues and disengaged with educational programmes. Further, arts-in-nature experiences can provide creative stimuli to increase connection with nature, understand environmental issues and explore ways to prevent environmental disasters, contributing, therefore, to planetary health and sustainability. Nevertheless, in the synthesis of all studies, it became clear that the evidence on the impact of arts-in-nature on health inequities was missing. We consider this a crucial gap in the literature, given that having access to both arts and nature is a privilege in its own right, and children living in areas of high deprivation are nine times less likely to have access to nature (Marmot, 2013). The unequal provision and access to nature means that children who are already at risk of poor health have the least opportunity to reap the health benefits of nature (Allen & Balfour, 2014). Conversely, living in areas with access to nature has been found to reduce income-related health inequalities, counteracting the negative effects of deprivation on health (Mitchell & Popham, 2008).

Through this systematic review, we developed an illustration (Figure 1.2) to explain our understanding of how arts-in-nature can affect both human and planetary health. In all studies, engagement with creative activities increased children's

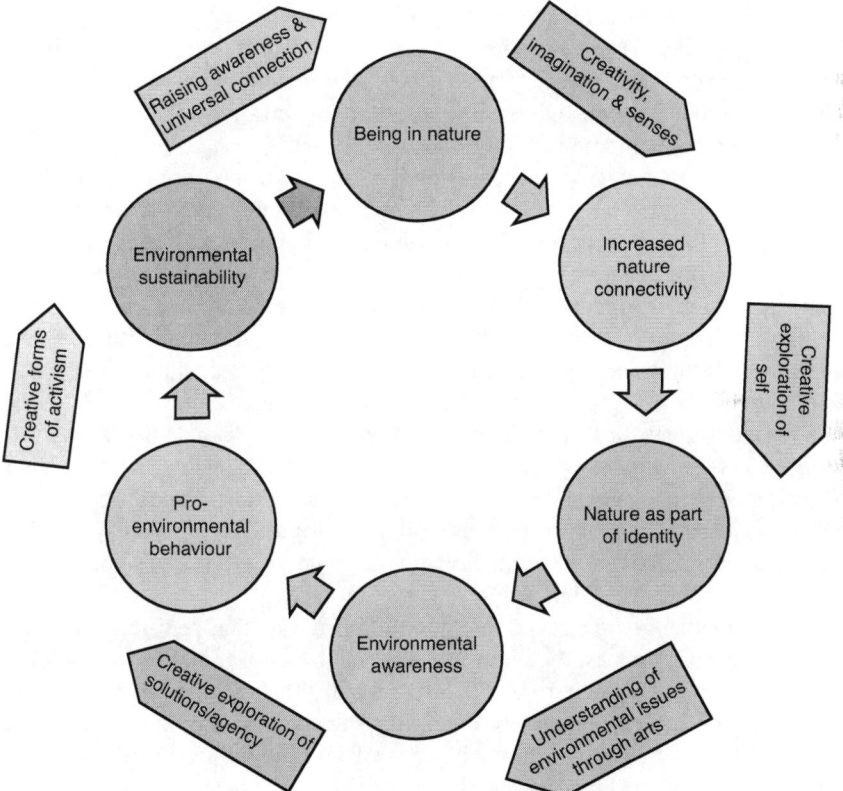

Figure 1.2 Pathways of connecting with nature through the arts

Source: Moula, Z., Palmer, K., & Walshe, N. (2022). A systematic review of arts-based interventions delivered to children and young people in nature or outdoor spaces: Impact on nature connectedness, health and wellbeing. *Frontiers in Psychology*, 13, 858781. doi: 10.3389/fpsyg.2022.858781.

desire to spend more time in nature and they gradually felt more connected to nature. Particularly identity-focused and self-reflective creative activities allowed children to perceive themselves as part of nature slowly and nature as part of themselves (what has been defined as 'pro-environmental identity'; Stets & Biga, 2003). Immersion in arts-in-nature appeared to shape children's appreciation of nature and their motivation to adopt pro-environmental values and attitudes. Furthermore, creative activities focusing on what can be done to prevent future environmental disasters led to an increase in pro-environmental behaviours; behaviours in which children were not only caring for the environment but were also taking protective actions, thereby contributing towards environmental sustainability. The findings of our review echo similar studies suggesting that nature connection cannot be achieved merely through learning in theory about the environment but by being exposed to the beauty of nature, the emotions that arise while being in nature and with sustained contact (Ryan et al., 2010; Rainisio, Boffi, & Riva, 2014; Lumber, Richardson, & Sheffield, 2017). As such, it became increasingly apparent that arts-in-nature practice has significant potential for contributing to planetary wellbeing in its broadest sense, not only through the mental health and wellbeing of children and young people but in nurturing an entangled and reciprocal relationship between the human and more-than-human world.

In response to the environmental and economic crisis, climate change and biodiversity loss, the UK's HM Government environment plan *A Green Future: Our 25 Year Plan to Improve the Environment* (2018) urges for investments in nature-based solutions that provide cost-effective health, socioeconomic and environmental benefits, especially in communities whose health has been disproportionately affected by health inequities. A key target of this plan is the enhanced engagement with nature and the commitment that everyone should live within a 15 minutes' walk of a green or blue space. These priorities echo those identified in the UK Department for Education's *Sustainability and climate change: A strategy for the education and children's services systems* (2022), which is committed to increasing access to and connection with nature in all educational settings. The aim of this book is to link these policies and priorities for a 'Green Future' with current research and practice that illustrate how arts-in-nature can address some of the key health and environmental challenges our society faces.

To our knowledge, this is the first book to bring together research and practice on the interconnectedness between arts and nature as a tool for prevention and wellbeing promotion, their role in addressing health inequities and their contribution towards environmental sustainability. The chapters provide examples from research and practice focused on all types of arts, including visual arts, music, drama, movement and poetry. These have been delivered in a range of natural environments, such as forests, woodlands, parks, beaches, camping sites, school playgrounds and community areas. The first section of the book is research-based (five chapters), authored by academics – sometimes in conjunction with practitioners; the second section is practice-based (seven chapters), so authored by practitioners – artists, therapists and educators.

In the first research-focused chapter, Chapter 2, **Dylan Adams** and **Gary Beauchamp** explore how children from Welsh primary schools benefit from making music in local nature places, such as fields, beaches and woodlands. Within the chapter, Dylan and Gary report that following outdoor music making, children described heightened sensory experiences and a sense of immersion in and with their nature places. This immersion afforded the children an absorption in their music-making that led them to experience feelings of joy and togetherness. The freedom of space outdoors appeared to maximise opportunities for creativity and imagination while also freeing up the institutional normative behaviours expected in the classroom. Furthermore, the children reported feeling an augmented sense of relationship with the more-than-human world involving experiences of transcendence. Dylan and Gary conclude their chapter by discussing how these 'optimal' mind states, such as flow and communitas, can be engendered by music-making in nature and how they are beneficial for children's wellbeing and connection with nature.

In Chapter 3, **Lucy Tiplady** examines the experiences of children over a school year as they engaged with the 'Breeze' Forest School. Focusing on a group of predominantly post-looked-after children, the Breeze project aimed to improve children's emotional wellbeing and their readiness to learn back in the classroom, and to enrich their home lives. Lucy uses the theory of change to explore how children engaged with the natural environment in combination with playful and arts-based activities for their individual development and learning throughout the project. Providing access to nature, arts and bushcraft-based activities and a child-centred pedagogy allowed children to explore and make sense of past experiences and to develop their socio-emotional skills, relationships and self-esteem. Lucy argues that, although schools are well-placed to offer children and young people early wellbeing interventions, they need to be adequately funded to provide non-stigmatising and high-quality mental health provision.

In Chapter 4, **Sarah Sharp** explores how story making and sharing can facilitate the process of imbuing a geographical location with cultural and social significance by drawing upon personal and community experiences with/in it, intertwining physical landscapes with remembered and imagined ones to foster a 'sense of place'. As the co-founder of 'One Step Theatre', Sarah describes the experiences of young people participating in an immersive outdoor performance entitled 'Ears to the Ground', which was part of the AHRC-funded project 'Outside the Box: Open Air Performance as Pandemic Response'. Through posthuman and feminist new-materialist lenses, Sarah's study suggests that outdoor story making and sharing nurtured young people's connection with nature, their sense of confidence, wellbeing and community after the COVID-19 pandemic-induced isolation. Sarah finishes by proposing a model for enhancing environmental consciousness by developing young people's awareness of future wellbeing with/in their local environment and beyond.

In Chapter 5, **Jane Tarr** and **Nick Clough** explore how musical experiences in a woodland environment enhanced connection with nature for children whose social, emotional and mental health difficulties had been exacerbated during and following the COVID-19 pandemic. They report on a project in which, led by a music therapist and a teacher trainer, teachers participated in an action enquiry on 'communicative musicality', which involved children's participation in musical improvisation and dialogic music-making in nature. Their study aimed to address the process by which ecological and musical experiences support children's social and emotional needs and connection with nature. Within their chapter, Jane and Nick identify key observable indicators based on 'Flow' variables (Csikszentmihalyi, 1996), which could be applied specifically to future evaluations of children's ecological and music-making experiences.

In Chapter 6, **Nomisha Kurian** and **Ruth Sapsed** introduce the arts-in-nature practice 'Artscaping' which was designed by the arts and wellbeing charity Cambridge Curiosity and Imagination (CCI) to widen children and young people's access to green spaces through the arts. Using the theoretical frameworks of human-centred design (IDEO, 2015) and Eco-Capabilities (Moula et al., 2023), Nomisha and Ruth explore the experiences of nursery and reception pupils who participate in Artscaping in a nature reserve. Their study suggests that Artscaping improved children's capacities for play, especially schematic and socio-dramatic play. They conclude by suggesting that arts-in-nature experiences also provide an opportunity to practise ecological stewardship through the plethora of sensory-rich experiences and creative stimuli which are present in nature.

In the first practice-based chapter (Chapter 7), **Alan Cusack** describes the Village Project, a week-long residency within the school grounds where students were asked to take responsibility for day-to-day activities, including cooking, cleaning, as well as building their own shelters and making collective decisions. Alan illustrates how building 'communities of practice' through arts-in-nature activities can shape young people's identities and develop their sense of responsibility. Beyond students' sense of independence and interdependence with each other, discussions also involved their interdependence with nature. Alan concludes by arguing that considering the increasingly assessment-driven curriculum, arts-in-nature approaches such as the Village Project may be fundamental for the survival of art education in the UK.

In Chapter 8, **Katarina Horrox** presents a multi-modality outdoor therapy service offering art therapy for young people in Scotland, primarily working with marginalised groups. Katarina outlines the key ethical and practical considerations for working therapeutically outdoors through a composite case study. Based on feedback from service users, Katarina argues that participating in outdoor art therapy facilitated access to therapy as well as access to nature, which further enhanced the development of an ecological sense of self. Outdoor art therapy also harnessed non-verbal communication and elements which may be less accessible to other therapies. As a result, Katarina proposes that outdoor art therapy should be adopted in wider contexts, such as statutory services, in order to increase access to therapy and nature and to reduce the gap in health inequities.

In Chapter 9, **Debi Keyte-Hartland** and **Louise Lowings** introduce an eco-logical curriculum implemented in a nursery school, focusing on learning *with* nature rather than 'about', 'in' or 'for' nature. Within their context, this curriculum approach supported the development of children's ecological identities by exploring, representing and telling the (real and imagined) stories of their environments, thereby facilitating relational learning 'with' nature through the arts. The curriculum also enhanced children's attitudes of care, empathy and attention to the more-than-human. Debi and Louise question whether adding learning 'about' environmental sustainability to an already full curriculum in England is appropriate. Instead, they argue that an ecological curriculum should be at the core of the school culture, leadership and educational practices of schools as a whole.

In Chapter 10, **Penny Hay** presents the Forest of Imagination, an annual participatory contemporary arts and architecture event in Bath, UK. The Forest inspired the public to reimagine familiar spaces through creativity and awareness of nature in an urban context. A multi-modal, in-depth case study in a primary school, the Living Tree Mirror Maze, provided a space for children to discuss their ecological enquiries, debates and thoughts in collaboration with artists. Forest of Imagination exemplified how creative and inclusive placemaking can lead to a higher sense of belonging, wellbeing, connection to nature, sustainability, community engagement and active citizenship. Within her chapter, Penny illustrates the capacity of Forests to inspire creativity, enhance wellbeing and transform lives, communities and economies.

In Chapter 11, **Anna Dako** offers an overview of her eco-somatic 'Felt Thinking', an approach of walking with sensuous presence when working therapeutically with children and young people. The practice of 'Felt Thinking' is based upon the idea of fully engaging the nervous system in an ongoing dialogue with the living environment when walking outdoors and paying attention to listening, smelling, touching and noticing elements of nature. Anna argues that this embodied participation in nature through the senses represents a form of arts-in-nature that is fundamental to young people's self-regulation and emotional wellbeing.

In Chapter 12, **Estella Guerrera** presents the 'Open Studio', an expressive and therapeutic arts approach facilitated by an art therapist and supported by educators in the premises of a greenhouse. This approach was designed to support adolescents in residential and semi-residential care programmes in Imola, Italy. Being fully immersed in the process of creating art in the indoor and outdoor spaces of the greenhouse, young people had the opportunity to find moments of inner peace, process and express their emotions through their artwork and develop a stronger connection with themselves and with nature. Estella notes the absence of judgment on artistic abilities and artworks allowed experiences of acceptance and inclusion within the group to emerge, which was particularly important for adolescents who were used to feeling excluded in other educational, therapeutic and social contexts.

Finally, in Chapter 13, **Melissa McDevitt Weston** and **Carla van Laar** conclude this book by reminding us to be mindful of 'What's beneath our feet' by cultivating cultural awareness, particularly when working with First Nations People.

Melissa is a proud Boon Wurrung woman and contemporary Aboriginal artist, and Carla is a non-Aboriginal woman and creative arts therapist in the Boon Wurrung Country, Australia. Together, they recommend ways to work in culturally respectful ways in nature and with natural materials to understand the connection of Aboriginal people to the Country and the importance of acknowledging the Country and Cultural Heritage. Melissa and Carla argue that cultivating Cultural awareness adds a layer of depth to arts-in-nature practice, which can become a profoundly healing experience for Country, Traditional Owners and their Ancestors, as well as for the practitioners and the young people they work with.

Notes

1 www.ucl.ac.uk/ioe/departments-and-centres/departments/curriculum-pedagogy-and-assessment/eco-capabilities-supporting-childrens-wellbeing-through-participatory-art-nature
2 www.ucl.ac.uk/ioe/departments-and-centres/departments/curriculum-pedagogy-and-assessment/branching-out-tackling-mental-health-inequalities-schools-community-artscapers

References

Allen, J., & Balfour, R. (2014). *Natural solutions for tackling health inequalities*. London: Institute of Health Equity. Retrieved from www.instituteofhealthequity.org/resources-reports/natural-solutions-to-tackling-health-inequalities [Accessed January 3, 2024]

Bungay, H., Walshe, N., & Dadswell, A. (2024). Mobilising volunteers to deliver a school-based arts-in-nature practice to support children's mental health and wellbeing: A modified e-Delphi study with primary school staff. *Cogent Education, 11*(1). doi: 10.1080/2331186X.2023.2298047

Csikszentmihalyi, M. (1996). *Creativity: Flow and the psychology of discovery and invention*. HarperCollins Publishers.

Dadswell, A., Bungay, H., Acton, F., & Walshe, N. (2024). Branching out: Mobilising community assets to support the mental health and wellbeing of children in primary schools. *Frontiers in Public Health, 12*. doi: 10.3389/fpubh.2024.1386181

Department for Education (DfE). (2022). *Sustainability and climate change strategy*. London: Author. Retrieved from www.gov.uk/government/publications/sustainability-and-climate-change-strategy [Accessed January 3, 2024]

Fancourt, D., & Finn, S. (2019). *What is the evidence on the role of the arts in improving health and wellbeing? A scoping review* (Health evidence network synthesis report no. 67). Copenhagen: WHO Regional Office for Europe.

HM Government. (2018). *A green future: Our 25-year plan to improve the environment*. Retrieved from https://assets.publishing.service.gov.uk/media/65fd713d65ca2f00117da89e/CD1.H_HM_Government_A_Green_Future_Our_25_Year_Plan_to_Improve_the_Environment.pdf [Accessed January 3, 2024]

IDEO. (2015). *The field guide to human-centred design. A step-by-step guide that will get you solving problems like a designer*. New York: IDEO.

Lumber, R., Richardson, M., & Sheffield, D. (2017). Beyond knowing nature: Contact, emotion, compassion, meaning, and beauty are pathways to nature connection. *PLoS ONE, 12*(5). doi: 10.1371/journal.pone.0177186

Marmot, M. (2013). *Review of social determinants and the health divide in the WHO European region: Final report*. Copenhagen: WHO regional office for Europe. Retrieved from www.drugsandalcohol.ie/20844/1/WHO_Marmot_final-report-in-english.pdf [Accessed January 3, 2024]

Mitchell, R., & Popham, F. (2008). Effect of exposure to natural environment on health inequalities: An observational population study. *The Lancet, 372*(9650), 1655–1660. doi: 10.1016/S0140-6736(08)61689-X

Moula, Z., Palmer, K., & Walshe, N. (2022). A systematic review of arts-based interventions delivered to children and young people in nature or outdoor spaces: Impact on nature connectedness, health and wellbeing. *Frontiers in Psychology, 13.* doi: 10.3389/fpsyg.2022.858781

Moula, Z., Walshe, N., & Lee, E. (2023). "It was like I was not a person, it was like I was the nature": The impact of arts-in-nature experiences on the wellbeing of children living in areas of high deprivation. *Journal of Environmental Psychology, 90.* doi: 10.1016/j.jenvp.2023.102072

Natural England. (2020). *The people and nature survey.* Worcester: Author. Retrieved from The People and Nature Surveys for England – GOV.UK (www.gov.uk) [Accessed January 3, 2024]

NHS England. (2023). *Mental health of children and young people in England, 2023 – wave 4 follow up to the 2017 survey.* Retrieved from https://digital.nhs.uk/data-and-information/publications/statistical/mental-health-of-children-and-young-people-in-england/2023-wave-4-follow-up [Accessed January 3, 2024]

Rainisio, N., Boffi, M., & Riva, E. (2014). Positive change in environment: Aesthetics, environmental flowability and well-being. In P. Inghilleri, G. Riva, & E. Riva (Eds.), *Enabling positive change: Flow and complexity in daily experience.* Berlin: Walter de Gruyter GmbH & Co KG. doi: 10.2478/9783110410242.6

Ryan, R. M., Weinstein, N., Bernstein, J. H., Brown, K. W., Mistretta, L., & Gagne, M. (2010). Vitalizing effects of being outdoors and in nature. *Journal of Environmental Psychology, 30,* 159–168. doi: 10.1016/j.jenvp.2009.10.009

Stets, J. E., & Biga, C. F. (2003). Bringing identity theory into environmental sociology. *Sociological Theory, 21,* 398–423. doi: 10.1046/j.1467–9558.2003.00196.x

Walshe, N., Moula, Z., & Lee, E. (2022). Eco-capabilities as a pathway to wellbeing and sustainability. *Sustainability, 14,* 3582. doi: 10.3390/su14063582

Walshe, N., Perry, J., & Moula, Z. (2023). Eco-capabilities: Arts-in-nature interventions for supporting nature visibilisation and wellbeing in children. *Sustainability, 15,* 12290. doi: 10.3390/su151612290

Chapter 2

Immersion and transcendence through music making in the more-than-human world

Dylan Adams and Gary Beauchamp

Introduction

The UN's IPCC (2021) report on climate change asserted, "Human influence has warmed the climate at a rate that is unprecedented in at least the last 2000 years" (p. 42). It concluded that it was "code red for humanity" as current levels of emissions from greenhouse gases will result in rising temperatures and sea levels, causing catastrophic devastation for life on our planet (IPCC, 2021). To help avert this, Sobel (2019) argues that children need to love the natural world before they develop a desire to save it. Mackay and Schmitt (2019) and Dickson and Gray (2022) contend that people who have positive experiences of nature connection in childhood are more likely to develop pro-environmental behaviours when they are older. There is also increasing evidence that suggests children's wellbeing can be enhanced through experiences of direct contact with nature outdoors (Chawla, 2015; Gill, 2014; Pirchio, 2021; Owens & Bunce, 2022).

Despite this, it is argued that children in modern industrialised nations increasingly suffer from an impoverished relationship with the natural world (Chawla, 2015); this is only exacerbated by social and financial inequalities (Barrable, 2022). Dodd, FitzGibbon, Watson, and Nesbit (2021) assert that most children's play in the United Kingdom (UK) takes place indoors, reflecting a trend in industrialised societies where it is argued children suffer from a disconnection with nature (Louv, 2012). Malone states children in many Western countries are growing up in a "bubble wrap generation" (2007, p. 513), and Bonnett (2020) describes Western society as having "a kind of autism with regard to nature," caught up in "hyper-consumerism and neophilia" (p. 15). It is argued the dominant culture of these industrialised societies creates a discourse that separates humans from nature and, consequently, the other-than-human is objectified and treated as resource (Evernden, 1999). Abram (1997) coined the term 'more-than-human' as a point of difference from the dominant culture in industrialised societies to highlight the way the other-than-human is framed as *less-than*-human. This framing of nature as less-than-human and an object of resource is significant not only because it has a negative impact on our relationship with the more-than-human, but also because it has a detrimental effect on our wellbeing and our existential understandings. Over 50 years ago, Shepard (1969)

DOI: 10.4324/9781003357308-2

analysed how our relationship with nature is inextricably bound up in our understanding of ourselves and that in the West this entails people suffering from a type of sickness. As a remedy, Shephard (1969, p. 122) stated, "Human sanity requires some less-than-obvious connections to nature as well as the necessities of food, water, energy, and air. We have hardly begun to discover what those connections may be." Perhaps only now, as we begin to be confronted with the realities of the climate crisis and are faced with children's increasing disconnect from the natural world, are we beginning to realise the importance of these 'less-than-obvious connections.'

If a separation from the more-than-human can be detrimental to wellbeing and existential understanding, in contrast, music making can improve wellbeing and enhance human experience. It is argued that joint music making has adaptive value (Mithen, 2009), that our brains are pre-wired for music (Peretz, 2019), and that music is at the core of being human (Hodges, 2019; Levitin, 2008). Regelski (2017, p. 59) states that "music is a primary source of sociality – of all kinds – and, thus, is a key contribution to the health and well-being of society." It is not surprising, therefore, that research shows the positive impact music making can have on people's wellbeing (MacDonald, 2013). In addition, research suggests young people's wellbeing can increase due to music making in schools (Lee, Krause, & Davidson, 2017). Despite this, there is evidence that many young people feel alienated from music making in schools (Cogdill, 2015), in contrast with the positive relationship they have with music outside of school (Welch & MacPherson, 2018). Drawing on Martusewicz et al. (2011) theory of eco-justice education, Smith (2021) calls for a re-visioning of music education away from anthropocentric perspectives and more in tune with "the needs of both humans and other-than-humans in our ecosystem" (p. 5). Smith (2021) argues mainstream music education fails to allow opportunities for children to "maintain their sense of wonder in nature; to fully develop their sensory capacities; to maintain, and if necessary, repair their mental health; and to attune more carefully to their wild nature and soul's purpose" (p. 9). Despite this, there is a wealth of evidence that demonstrates music making and encounters with the more-than-human world enable people to have joyful transcendent experiences that have a significant impact on their wellbeing and existential understandings. These feelings of transcendence have been called 'optimal experiences' and involve "a sense of deep enjoyment" and a sense of feeling in harmony with the world (Csikszentmihalyi, 2002, p. 49).

For the purposes of this study, it is important to identify how optimal experiences share a fundamental element of transcendence as we argue the experience of transcendence is of particular significance when considering how music making and immersion in nature places impact children's wellbeing and their sense of relationship with the more-than-human world.

Transcendence

The word transcendence comes from the Latin *transcendere,* meaning "climb over or beyond, surmount, overstep" based on the Online Etymology Dictionary (https://www.etymonline.com/). Experiences of transcendence move the experiencer beyond everyday reality, allowing them to experience an improved reality. There are various optimal experience theories, yet they all commonly involve an experience of transcendence. Maslow (1968) outlines "peak experience," transcendence of everyday experience where everything feels interconnected and "the whole of the world is seen as unity" (p. 98). Csikszentmihalyi (2002) similarly explains that in a state of consciousness he calls 'flow,' people "stop being aware of themselves as separate from the actions they are performing" (p. 53). In both peak experience and flow, there is a feeling that ordinary reality has been transcended and an augmented reality is perceived. This new or heightened perception, whereby there is a loss of ego and a sense of oneness with the universe, is also an important part of Laski's (1961) theory of 'ecstasy,' during which people experience a reality that is "outside the normal course of events" yet felt to be "derived from a praeternatural source" (p. 5).

Turner's theory of communitas, an experience of a heightened sense of community, also involves similar feelings of transcendence. Turner positions communitas in the context of Csikszentmihalyi's flow theory, claiming that "Flow may induce communitas, and communitas flow" (Turner, 1974, p. 80). He explains, however, that whereas an individual experiences flow, communitas is a type of shared flow (Turner, 1977). Turner conceptualised that communitas is preceded by an experience of liminality, a time when people "act and feel in ways opposite to or different from their standardized modes of behaviour" (1970, p. 200). It is during liminality that people experience wide-open wonder, paving the way for the joy of communitas (Turner & Turner, 1970).

A fundamental aspect of all these optimal experiences is complete absorption in the moment that allows transcendence from everyday concerns and identities to an ego-less state. Turner (2012) describes how musical activity can induce communitas as "the musicians' eyes may be open but are unseeing because they have become the music" (Turner, 2012, p. 45). There is also evidence claiming that outdoor nature spaces enable people to experience communitas (Ashworth, 2017; Sharpe, 2005; Sudmann, 2018). In all these optimal experience theories, artistic experiences and experiences of nature are highlighted as common activities that are particularly potent at causing transcendence from everyday reality (Csikszentmihalyi, 2002; Laski, 1961; Maslow, 1968). Although differences have been identified between these optimal experience theories (Bassi & Delle Fave, 2016), this study focusses on how the children's responses relate to the experience of transcendence, which is a common feature of all these theories.

Existential understanding

The experiences of transcendence espoused by these different optimal experience theories are not only described as being an elevation above everyday reality that brings about an increased sense of wellbeing, but also as providing an existential understanding of the true nature of reality. During these times, "the authentic human essence" (Turner, 1974, p. 77) is revealed, and people "are closest to their real selves" (Maslow, 1968, p. 115). Experiences of engagement with music and with nature are seen as being particularly powerful at inducing profound existential insights. Bonnett (2015) argues that nature's inherent mysteriousness and integrity "have the power to shape our perception, understanding and existence and in so-doing connect us to the cosmos as a whole" (Bonnett, 2015, p. 48).

The study

This research analysed the experiences of children aged 7 to 10 years of age from six different primary schools making music in outdoor rural locations. The sampling was purposive (Bryant, 2017) as schools were chosen, at least partly, due to their close proximity and accessibility to rural locations surrounded by nature. The participating children (n=161) all undertook the same task: to create music in a rural location using the same resources (drums, wooden flutes, didgeridoos, vocal sounds, and movement). Choosing instruments that could be played easily without the need for prior practising or training was important as it allowed all children to be able to make music easily. The rural locations were either fields, woods, or beaches (see Table 2.1).

Ethical approval was gained from the university ethics committee before beginning research. All participants (including the children and their parents/ guardians) completed letters of informed consent, which noted that children were able to withdraw from taking part at any time (BERA, 2018). In addition, as Groundwater-Smith, Dockett, and Bottrell (2015) highlight, ethical decisions are continually made throughout the research process. This meant adopting what Guillemim and Gillam (2004) call a reflexive research process as research ethics "is more than the linear application of specific rules" (Punch & Oancea, 2014, p. 75).

After informed consent was obtained from all the participants, the research methods in each school followed the following procedure:

Day 1 – The children created and performed their music in the outdoor rural locations.
Day 2 – The children were interviewed about their experiences of music making outdoors.

Table 2.1 Sample of schools, pupils, and locations

	School 1	School 2	School 3	School 4	School 5	School 6
Sample size	30	25	48	28	28	28
Number of pupils interviewed	5	5	6	6	6	6
Age (in years)	9–10	9–10	7–9	7–8	8–9	9–10
Location	Field	Beach	Beach	Woodland	Woodland	Field

On the first day, one of the researchers set the task, but they did not interfere once the children began composing their music. The other member of the team was not present but provided an external perspective in the later analysis. The aim was to create a setting that would allow the children to freely express themselves both in their music making and in their descriptions of their experiences. It was the children's choices and the children's ideas that were sought. In this sense, the aim was that the children were the custodians of power and knowledge regarding their musical experiences. In addition, their responses would show how their autonomy during their music making had impacted their experience. This is in line with Kincheloe's (2012) assertion that critical teacher researchers should focus "on the relationship between knowledge and power" and conduct research and formulate pedagogy "in ways that open this relationship to the sunlight of analysis" (p. 202).

On the second day, a random sample of children (n=34) from across all the schools were asked about their experiences and how they felt when they were making their music in group interviews to reflect the group music making. Qualitative data was gathered in order to "enter the child's world and meanings to get the child's perspective from the inside out" (Greig, Taylor, & Mackay, 2007, p. 54). The interviews were recorded, transcribed, and analysed. This analysis was not an attempt to discover an objective reality "but an attempt to secure an in-depth understanding of the phenomenon in question" (Denzin & Lincoln, 1994, p. 2). Each interview was analysed before merging the data sets 'into one overall interpretation' (Punch & Oancea, 2014, p. 345). The data gathering and analysis was an inductive "bottom-up," not a "top-down" procedure and prioritised gathering data and "examining potential patterns amongst the data produced" (Greig et al., 2007, p. 50). This ensured no preconceived categories or codes (Morse et al., 2009).

Findings and discussion

The analysis provided a number of common themes, described in turn in what follows.

Freedom

Children described an enhanced sense of 'freedom' when making music in nature places. All the children interviewed felt that a combination of making music in the outdoors allowed them to feel more freedom in comparison to being in school. This is expressed by School 5, Pupil 3 (S5P3): "I think it was the setting that made it. When you're in school, it's just like in a prison, but when you're outdoors, you feel, I can do whatever I want."

The children's responses consistently described being absorbed in their music making and that nothing else seemed to matter. For example, School 2, Pupil 4 (S2P4) said: "It felt like the only thing I needed to concentrate on when we were there was just making the song."

The importance of freedom was highlighted by P4S5:

Music, I felt . . . I love music and all, but I thought 'it's going to be the same thing.' We went to the woods, and it was different. We felt close to nature. Then, we started playing and everything felt free, and you could feel the sounds. . . . That's when you really just go along with it. When you're inside the music, it feels like it's changed.

Senses

The children consistently highlighted the impact of a heightened sensory awareness gained from music making outdoors in rural locations. For example, one theme that kept on returning as a reason why experiencing nature through the senses may have positively impacted the music making was because it made the children more easily get ideas – it helped their music 'flow.' This is exemplified in the following interview extract:

S3P1:   Down the beach, there's different scenery and, like, at school it's, like, just one sound. It's like just one sound because you're in a room. But, in the beach, it's like lots of different sounds. It's in the air; there's loads of sounds, and it kind of helps your music go with flow.
Interviewer: So how does that help?
S3P1:   I think it's easier down the beach because there's lots of different sounds. Like . . . at school, it's harder because you can't get the right note. There's lots of sounds in school, but sometimes you can't hear properly, and there's not the right one that you need.

Similarly, another pupil noted, "The environment and the sounds of nature like help you concentrate and it just to takes you to a completely different level . . . of sound and music . . . just makes it sound very good" (P5S3).

Immersion in nature

The children's responses from the interviews suggested a sensory immersion in nature had positively affected their music making and wellbeing. Throughout the children's responses, this sense of being absorbed in their music making due to a sensory immersion in nature is repeated. For example, P2S2 stated, "I liked playing the music because of the waves and the birds and the echoes helped the music to flow, so it's like part of all around us."
Similarly, P2S6 stated that:

It's like going to a different world, like entering different worlds. You just put all your worries aside, and you don't really care, almost like what anyone thinks or what everyone does. You're just yourself, and there's almost nobody there, and you're just there in a happy place, and you're just doing whatever you want to do.

Enhanced wellbeing

Aligning with Csíkszentmihályi 's (1990) flow theory, Laski's (1961) theory of ecstasy, Maslow's (1970) theory of peak experience, and Turner's (1969) theory of communitas, the children describe their music making as involving intrinsic pleasure. The pleasure was not experienced afterwards or as a result of some end goal. It was experienced because of the immersion in the music making and during their music making. In other words, it was autotelic (Csíkszentmihályi, 1990). This example from P2S6 exemplifies this:

> You forget everything, and you get really into the music. It feels like you've got to stick with it; you've got to have the amazing time. You're not thinking, 'Oh, when is this over.' You've got to go, and you've got to keep playing because it feels great. You're thinking . . . 'Oh, I don't want this to end.' You've got to do the music, and it makes me feel happy that you're doing it, and it makes me feel like I don't want to stop doing the music.

The responses from the children consistently expressed how they felt their music making had helped their feelings and made them feel better. This response from P2S3 was typical when stating, "Playing the music made me happy just because the sun was reflecting on me. It makes my heart go stronger because I'm brave enough to sing out." P4S6 reported that "Playing my music changed me and made me feel happy to just go out and do something, just feel free."

Similarly, P2S1 said, "It feels, like, more just enjoyable, like, if it's just doing its own thing and you're not making it do everything. The music just takes over and kind of does it." P1S6 also emphasised the enjoyment and union that's felt with the music:

> When we were playing music . . . it's just like a dream, and everyone is just like happy, and you're in like a fairy tale like X said you're just it . . . just makes you feel really like happy and you don't want it to ever stop.

Transcendence

The interviews showed that the children seemed to have experienced a sense of transcending their sense of self. In other words, experiencing freedom from the identities of the ego, creating "a sense of deep enjoyment" (Csikszentmihalyi, 2002, p. 49). Maslow (1968) explains how peak experiences allow perception to be "ego-transcending, self-forgetful, egoless" (p. 90). Laski (1961) similarly describes the experience "in which the ecstatic and what is believed to be encountered become more or less one" (Laski, 1961, p. 122). This is perhaps more aptly described as freedom from the ego self rather than a loss of the ego self as it is a positive experience. This is reflected in the children's responses. For example, P5S4 said:

> I felt like I was someplace else playing a bit of music . . . I felt a bit different. It didn't feel like me; it felt like someone else. . . . I felt like I was in a different place where nothing else mattered, a whole different world of music.

The idea of being teleported to a different world, where anything could happen, resonates with Turner's liminality (1969). Turner and Turner (1970) describes liminality as a "fructile chaos, a fertile nothingness, a storehouse of possibilities, not by any means a random assemblage but a striving after new forms and structure" (pp. 11–12). He argues that this enables people "to act and feel in ways opposite to or different from their standardized modes of behaviour" (Turner & Turner, 1970, p. 200). In all the interviews, there was evidence that the children experienced states or modes of behaviour during their music making, that were different from their normal ways of behaving. This included responses that suggested they felt that their sense of identity had been changed, albeit momentarily, during their music making. For example, "I didn't feel like me. I felt like a different person, but I didn't know who. I just felt like a made-up person and not me. . . . I just felt not like myself."

Transcendence occurs even though these liminal experiences are described as being different, even 'wild' ways of feeling. For example, P1S6 said:

> I think when the music is playing, I do transform into a different person, to a different world. We see it as different stuff. When you transform into that different world, it is calm, but it doesn't always have to be calm. You can change it. Sometimes you can feel happy and wild, and you can just imagine when you turn and transform into that world. . . . You don't always have to be calm; you can be wild.

This is supported by P6S4, who stated, "When they were all bashing the drum all quickly, I quickly started playing the drum quickly. I was like a crazy person! Then we were all together, and nothing else mattered. Everything felt happy and smooth."

We can see the progression to communitas here as the pupil goes from feeling like a "crazy person" to feeling "together and nothing else mattered" and then feeling "happy and smooth." This was supported in all the responses. For example, P1S5 stated:

> I felt like I was just going with the rest of them. They were all doing the same thing. We were communicating but not talking. We were talking to get ideas, but when it was time to perform, we all got our heads in it, and we all thought, yeah . . . then when we were playing . . . it was like blowing in the wind, really. . . . Just being together.

The effortless nature of the experience, "like blowing in the wind," can be related to Turner's (1977, p. 50) description of communitas being like a "shared flow," where there is intrinsic pleasure gained from feeling and being together. In all the interviews, the children stated that they had experienced a sense of feeling at one with their fellow music makers and that this was a pleasurable experience.

Implications for policy, practice, and research

It is claimed that music education is in decline as fewer students are choosing to study music when they are given a choice (Aróstegui, 2016; Bath, Daubney, Mackrill, & Spruce, 2019; Cooper, 2018; Savage, 2021). Lamont and Maton (2010) suggest that pupils choose not to study music because they view it as an elite option, accessible only to those who have a talent for music. This perspective is perhaps being perpetuated by the way music is framed in mainstream education (Bath et al., 2019), as it is seen as less of a priority for pupils compared to other subjects (Savage, 2021). Csikszentmihalyi (2002) states that in music education, "too much emphasis is placed on how they (children) perform, and too little on what they experience" (Csikszentmihalyi, 2002, p. 112). Such views imply that music education needs to be made more relevant to students and allow them opportunities to explore music making and experience the potential of their own music making, particularly in settings outside of school. The results of this study suggest that children's music making can be a powerful experience when taking place outdoors and immersed in natural environments, especially when children are given the freedom to create their own music together in groups. There was no expectation of an aesthetic standard that the children's music needed to reach. The combination of this sense of freedom and the impact of the natural environments allowed the children's music making to instigate transcendent optimal experiences that positively affected their wellbeing and existential understandings. This has significance for music education policies and curricula that currently present a conception of music and an aesthetic standard that is unattractive to many pupils.

Conclusion

The previous analysis suggests that the children's music making in nature places afforded the children experiences that were beneficial to their sense of wellbeing. The music making in the nature places allowed the children to access states of being that relate to optimal experience theories (Csikszentmihalyi, 2002; Laski, 1961; Maslow, 1968; Turner, 1974). These experiences involved an immersion in nature and a sense of transcendence, whereby the children felt elevated above their everyday reality. The children's responses consistently expressed that they not only felt close to nature and part of the more-than-human world but that this felt like a natural experience. For example, P6S6 said: "It just felt like I was natural, I was something natural, like a tree or something. It felt like I did it every day."

This is significant, as it is claimed that children in 'Western societies' are increasingly separated from the natural world (Louv, 2012). It is argued that enabling children to feel an augmented connection with the more-than-human world through making music in natural settings is more likely to lead to more pro-environmental attitudes and behaviours in the future (Mackay & Schmitt, 2019; Dickson & Gray, 2022). Moreover, the music making activities undertaken by the children require no previous musical training or musical knowledge. Therefore, the resulting wellbeing benefits are potentially accessible to all children if teachers are willing to engage children with nature places in this way. We suggest that as well as the musical experiences, which are valuable in and of themselves, this also has significance in terms of helping to address health and wellbeing inequities that exist due to impoverished socio-economic circumstances.

References

Abram, D. (1997). *The spell of the sensuous: Perception and language in a more-yhan-human world.* New York: Pantheon.

Aróstegui, J. L. (2016). Exploring the global decline of music education. *Arts Education Policy Review, 117*(2), 96–103. doi: 10.1080/10632913.2015.1007406

Ashworth, D. (2017). Can communitas explain how young people achieve identity development in outdoor adventure in light of contemporary individualised life? *Journal of Adventure Education and Outdoor Learning, 17*(3), 216–226.

Barrable, A. (2022). *Independent thinking on nature-based learning: Improving learning and well-being by teaching with nature in mind.* Carmarthen: Crown House Publishing Ltd.

Bassi, M., & Delle Fave, A. (2016). Flow in the context of daily experience fluctuation. In L. Harmat, F. Ø. Andersen, F. Ullén, J. Wright, & G. Sadlo (Eds.), *Flow experience: Empirical research and applications* (pp. 181–196). Springer International Publishing/Springer Nature. doi: 10.1007/978-3-319-28634-1_12

Bath, N., Daubney, A., Mackrill, D., & Spruce, G. (2020). The declining place of music education in schools in England. *Children & Society, 34*(5), 443–457. doi: 10.1111/chso.12386

BERA. (2018). *Ethical guidelines for educational research* (4th ed.). BERA. Retrieved from https://www.bera.ac.uk/publication/ethical-guidelines-for-educational-research-2018

Bonnett, M. (2015). The powers that be: Environmental education and the transcendent. *Policy Futures in Education, 13*(1), 42–56.

Bonnett, M. (2020). *Environmental consciousness, nature and the philosophy of education: Ecologizing education.* London: Routledge.

Bryant, A. (2017). *Grounded theory and grounded theorizing: Pragmatism in research practice.* Oxford: Oxford University Press.

Chawla, L. (2015). Benefits of nature contact for children. *Journal of Planning Literature, 30*(4), 433–452.

Cogdill, S. H. (2015). Applying research in motivation and learning to music education: What the experts say. *Update: Applications of Research in Music Education, 33*(2), 49–57.

Cooper, B. (2018). *Primary schools: The decline of arts education in primary schools and how it can be reversed.* London, UK: Fabian Society, Children & the Arts, Musicians' Union.

Csikszentmihalyi, M. (2002). *Flow: The classic work on how to achieve happiness.* New York: Random House.

Denzin, N. K., & Lincoln, Y. S. (1994). *Handbook of qualitative research.* Thousand Oaks, CA: SAGE.

Dickson, T. J., & Gray, T. L. (2022). Nature-based solutions: Democratising the outdoors to be a vaccine and a salve for a neoliberal and COVID-19 impacted society. *Journal of Adventure Education and Outdoor Learning, 22*, 1–20.

Dodd, H. F., FitzGibbon, L., Watson, B. E., & Nesbit, R. J. (2021). Children's play and independent mobility in 2020: Results from the British children's play survey. *International Journal of Environmental Research and Public Health, 18*(8), 4334.

Evernden, L. L. N. (1999). *The natural alien: Humankind and environment.* Toronto: University of Toronto Press.

Gill, T. (2014). The benefits of children's engagement with nature: A systematic literature review. *Children Youth and Environments, 24*(2), 10–34.

Greig, A., Taylor, J., & MacKay, T. (2007). *Doing research with children* (2nd ed.). London: Sage.

Groundwater-Smith, S., Dockett, S., & Bottrell, D. (2015). *Participatory research with children and young people.* SAGE Publications Ltd. doi: 10.4135/9781473910751

Guillemin, M., & Gillam, L. (2004). Ethics, reflexivity, and "ethically important moments" in research. *Qualitative Inquiry, 10*(2), 261–280. doi: 10.1177/1077800403262360

Hodges, D. (2019). *Music in the human experience: An introduction to music psychology.* London: Routledge.

IPCC. (2021). *Climate change 2021: The physical science basis* (Contribution of working group I to the sixth assessment report of the intergovernmental panel on climate change). Cambridge: Cambridge University Press. Retrieved from www.ipcc.ch/report/sixth-assessment-report-working-group-i/ [Accessed August 10, 2021]

Kincheloe, J. L. (2012). *Teachers as researchers (classic edition): Qualitative inquiry as a path to empowerment.* London: Routledge.

Lamont, A., & Maton, K. (2010). Unpopular music: Beliefs and behaviours towards music in education. In R. Wright (Ed.), *Sociology and music education* (pp. 63–80). London: Ashgate.

Laski, M. (1961). *Ecstasy; A study of some secular and religious experiences.* London: Cresset Press.

Lee, J., Krause, A. E., & Davidson, J. W. (2017). The PERMA well-being model and music facilitation practice: Preliminary documentation for well-being through music provision in Australian schools. *Research Studies in Music Education, 39*(1), 73–89.

Levitin, D. J. (2008). *The world in six songs: How the musical brain created human nature.* Canada: Penguin Books.

Louv, R. (2012). *The nature principle: Reconnecting with life in a virtual age.* New York: Algonquin Books.

MacDonald, R. A. (2013). Music, health, and well-being: A review. *International Journal of Qualitative Studies on Health and Well-Being, 8*(1), 20635.

Mackay, C. M., & Schmitt, M. T. (2019). Do people who feel connected to nature do more to protect it? A meta-analysis. *Journal of Environmental Psychology, 65*, 101323.

Martusewicz, R. A., Edmundson, J., & Lupinacci, J. (2011). *EcoJustice education: Toward diverse, democratic, and sustainable communities.* New York: Routledge.

Maslow, A. (1968). *Toward a psychology of being* (2nd ed.). New York: Van Nostrand.

Maslow, A. H. (1970). *Religions, values, and peak experiences.* New York: Penguin Books Limited.

Mithen, S. (2009). The music instinct: The evolutionary basis of musicality. *Annals of the New York Academy of Sciences, 1169*, 3–12. doi: 10.1111/j.1749-6632.2009.04590.x

Morse, J. M., Stern, P. N., Corbin, J., Bowers, B., Charmaz, K., & Clarke, A. (2009). *Developing grounded theory: The second generation.* Walnut Creek, CA: Left Coast Press Inc.

Owens, M., & Bunce, H. L. (2022). Nature-based meditation, rumination and mental well-being. *International Journal of Environmental Research and Public Health, 19*(15), 9118.

Peretz, I. (2019). *How music sculpts our brain.* Paris: Odile Jacob.

Pirchio, S., Passiatore, Y., Panno, A., Cipparone, M., & Carrus, G. (2021). 'The effects of contact with nature during outdoor environmental education on students' wellbeing, connectedness to nature and pro-sociality. *Frontiers in Psychology*, *12*, 648458.

Punch, J. P., & Oancea, A. (2014). *Introduction to research methods in education*. London: Sage.

Regelski, T. A. (2017). *Social observations for why teach music?* Topics for Music Education Praxis. https://topics.maydaygroup.org/articles/2017/Regelski_2017.pdf

Savage, J. (2021). Teaching music in England today. *International Journal of Music Education*, *39*(4), 464–476. doi: 10.1177/0255761420986213

Sharpe, E. K. (2005). Delivering communitas: Wilderness adventure and the making of community. *Journal of Leisure Research*, *37*(3), 255–280.

Shepard, P., & McKinley, D. (1969). *The subversive science; Essays toward an ecology of man*. London: Houghton.

Smith, T. D. (2021). Music education for surviving and thriving: Cultivating children's wonder, senses, emotional wellbeing, and wild nature as a means to discover and fulfill their life's purpose'. *Frontiers in Education*, *6*. doi: 10.3389/feduc.2021.648799

Sobel, D. (2019). *Beyond ecophobia: Reclaiming the heart in nature education*. Northampton, MA: Orion Reader.

Sudmann, T. T. (2018). Communitas and friluftsliv: Equine-facilitated activities for drug users. *Community Development Journal*, *53*(3), 556–573.

Turner, J. (2012). *Communitas: The anthropology of collective joy*. New York: Palgrave Macmillan.

Turner, V. (1969). *The ritual process: Structure and anti-structure*. Chicago, IL: Aldine Publishing.

Turner, V. (1974). Liminal to liminoid, in play, flow, and ritual: An essay in comparative symbology. *Rice Institute Pamphlet-Rice University Studies*, *60*(3).

Turner, V. (1977). Chapter III: Variations on a theme of liminality. In S. Mooreand & B. Myerhoff (Eds.), *Secular ritual* (pp. 36–52). Assen: Van Gorcum.

Turner, V., & Turner, V. W. (1970). *The forest of symbols: Aspects of Ndembu ritual*. New York: Cornell Paperbacks.

Welch, G. F., & McPherson, G. E. (2018). Commentary: Music education and the role of music in people's lives. Music and music education in people's lives. In G. E. McPherson & G. F. Welch (Eds.), *An oxford handbook of music education* (Vol. 1). Oxford: Oxford University Press.

Chapter 3

The Breeze Forest School Project

Child-centred support for development and wellbeing

Lucy Tiplady

Introduction

In England, increasing numbers of young people are experiencing mental health difficulties. NHS Digital reported that in 2022, 18% of children aged 7 to 16 years and 22% of young people aged 17 to 24 years had a probable mental disorder; in children aged 7 to 16 years, the rates of a probable mental disorder have risen from 1 in 9 in 2017 to 1 in 6 in 2022, whilst in young people aged 17 to 19 years, the rates have risen from 1 in 10 in 2017 to 1 in 4 in 2022 (Newlove-Delgado et al., 2022). The COVID-19 pandemic is widely believed to have caused additional difficulties for children and young people (Crawley et al., 2020). The increased demand, together with severe disruption to already over-stretched and underfunded NHS services, has created extremely long waiting lists with many young people's needs remaining unmet.

Poor mental health impacts upon many areas of a young person's life, including educational disadvantage and increased risk of school exclusion (Ford et al., 2018). We also know that health inequalities are widespread: children experiencing social and economic disadvantage are more likely to experience mental health difficulties (Reiss, 2013), and research in the UK reports that the socioeconomic mental health gap has not reduced over the past 20 years but may be widening (Collishaw, Furzer, Thapar, & Sellers, 2019). If given appropriate funding and time, schools are well placed to support children and young people and whilst there has been some critique of "the therapeutic turn in education" (Ecclestone & Hayes, 2019), overall there is widespread evidence that mental health interventions in schools can have a wide range of benefits for children, families and communities (Weare & Nind, 2011). Nevertheless, it is also the case that stigmas associated with school-based interventions continue to be a barrier to accessing services (Bowers, Manion, Papadopoulos, & Gauvreau, 2013; Gronholm, Nye, & Michelson, 2018). This chapter argues that there is an urgent need for a range of non-stigmatising, child-centred approaches to support children and young people's wellbeing and development.

The Breeze Forest School Project was developed by Harriet Menter, the education manager at Scotswood Garden, in response to a local need from schools struggling to support children and young people's mental health and engagement

DOI: 10.4324/9781003357308-3

in education. Whilst in no way replacing specialist mental health services, Menter believed that schools could provide support for students experiencing social and emotional difficulties through a forest school approach. At the time of the project's development (2016–2017), research had shown contact with nature to impact the behavioural development of children, including symptoms of ADHD (Amoly et al., 2014), and to moderate the impact of stressful life events for children (Wells & Evans, 2003). However, there was little research on how forest school could support children's wellbeing. Menter had been delivering forest school and forest school training and had observed the power of the approach, particularly for young people with additional needs. She believed that children and young people with social and emotional needs would benefit from small groups with high adult ratios delivered on a regular and long-term basis. These parameters are embedded within the six forest school principles advocated by the Forest School Association (2022), but the competing priorities of schools often mean that these are not fully realised. Whilst forest school practice continues to grow throughout the UK and internationally, there are concerns that this expansion has led to a dilution of the principles (Sackville-Ford & Davenport, 2019), with McCree (2019) referring to "Full Fat FS," "FS Lite," and "FS Ultra Lite" (p. 4).

The Breeze Project has worked with schools since 2017, including first and primary mainstream schools, a primary age additionally resourced centre, secondary special schools, and pupil referral units. This chapter will focus on Park View First School,[1] a mainstream school located in an urban area of the North East of England which, at the time of engagement, had a high number of care-experienced children who were struggling within the classroom environment:

> Our initial participation in the Breeze Forest School Project came about as a result of wanting to support a number of post looked-after children in the school, both adopted and those under special guardianship orders, who due to their early life experiences were finding it difficult to settle in a classroom, displaying hypervigilance, distressed behaviours and a lack of self-belief and self-worth.
>
> (Park View First School)

The majority of children and young people taken into care have experienced abuse and/or neglect (National Society for the Prevention of Cruelty to Children [NSPCC], 2021), which are associated with poorer educational, mental and physical health outcomes (Rahilly & Hendry, 2014). Wilkinson and Bowyer (2017) state that "there is strong evidence to suggest that maltreatment is associated with social, emotional, behavioural and mental health difficulties, which can continue throughout childhood and beyond" (p. 27). McAuley and Davis (2009) also highlight the extensive research which shows that care experienced children and young people are more likely to display disorganised attachment behaviours due to their earlier experiences. Educationally, in 2019, 27% of looked-after children were classified as Special Educational Needs (SEN) compared to 3.1% of the general child population, with the average Attainment 8 score[2] for looked-after children in England

19.1, compared to 44.6 for non-looked-after children (Department for Education [DfE], 2022a, 2022b). Schools are crucial in supporting care experienced children and young people and the support necessary to be 'ready to learn' often goes far beyond academic support.

This chapter will explore how the children at Park View used the natural environment in combination with playful and arts-based activities embedded in the forest school approach to support their development and emotional wellbeing. Forest School research has experienced recent growth, with some studies evidencing the impacts on wellbeing (McCree, Cutting, & Sherwin, 2018; Coates & Pimlott-Wilson, 2019; Tiplady & Menter, 2021a); however, we are still learning what the full impacts of such approaches might be and under what conditions (McCree, 2019; Sackville-Ford, 2019). Beyond forest school, Moula, Palmer, and Walshe (2022) have highlighted the scarcity of research evidence of health and wellbeing interventions for children and young people that combine both arts and nature. In exploring the interconnection of such approaches through forest school, we are not only contributing to the understanding of forest school but to the wider field of how arts in nature can support the wellbeing and mental health of children and young people.

Methods

Study design

The researcher took an ethnographically inspired participatory approach in researching with participants and using the ongoing research to inform the development of the Breeze Project. The researcher was an embedded member of the project, attending approximately half of the sessions; this ensured that she could witness and experience the project firsthand and engage in knowledge exchange throughout whilst also retaining intellectual integrity and utilising robust research methods to ensure the rigour and validity of findings. Theory of change (Dyson & Todd, 2010) was used to work with the school and forest school practitioner to clearly articulate the desired outcomes of the Breeze Project, together with the steps of change that were anticipated to lead towards those outcomes; these steps of change were informed by practice, research, and theory. Participatory and visual methods were used to maximise the variety of ways in which the children could contribute to the research and convey their experiences. Full details can be seen in the Breeze Forest School 2018–2021 evaluation report (Tiplady, 2022).

Participants

This chapter focuses on data from nine children, aged 5 to 9 years, from Park View First School who engaged with Breeze during the 2018–2019 school year. The research also sought feedback from the children's families, school staff, and the forest school practitioner.

Intervention description

The Breeze Project was designed to use a forest school approach to support the social and emotional development of children currently struggling to engage fully in their education. Forest school is based within a natural environment with trees and uses a range of learner-centred processes to support the holistic development of individuals. Learners choose their own activities, with no pre-determined curriculum or programme; typical activities might include exploration of nature, den building, role-play and games, fire lighting and cooking, and arts and bushcraft activities (including whittling and the use of tools). Practitioners support learners to take risks, appropriate to their own development and the environment, and to build resilience and self-confidence. Forest school should maintain regular sessions over a sustained period of at least two seasons. Breeze was designed to take place weekly over a minimum of a school year and included a plan-do-review cycle to ensure that sessions were designed to meet the needs and interests of each child in the group. Menter began by leading sessions herself in partnership with the school and was involved in the weekly planning, delivery, and reviewing of sessions (with the researcher also participating approximately every other week); school staff concurrently engaged in forest school training (one at Level 3, which qualifies a person to lead forest school sessions, and a second at Level 1) with the intention that they would gradually take over responsibility by the end of the school year.

Data collection and analysis

A data collection plan was co-designed in relation to the school's theory of change, with school staff, the forest school practitioner, children, and the researcher all participating in data collection as detailed in Table 3.1.

For the purposes of the Breeze evaluation, data was analysed in relation to the theory of change, with multiple sources of data being used to assess whether a particular step of change had been "substantially evidenced," "partly evidenced," "not evidenced," or whether there had been "evidence to refute" (Tiplady, 2022). Beyond this, the data was analysed thematically using Braun and Clarke's six-phase process to look for any unanticipated processes and impacts of the project (Braun & Clarke, 2006). This chapter will explore an aspect of this thematic analysis related to the questions: what contribution does the natural environment combined with arts and bushcraft-based activities make within the forest school approach; how do children respond to these opportunities and utilise them in their learning and development; and what outcomes are experienced?

Ethics

The research was reviewed and granted ethical approval by Newcastle University. Participants gave informed consent, and it was made clear that they could withdraw from the research at any time during the research project without

Table 3.1 Methods of data collection for Park View First School

Data	Person responsible for data collection
Observations of Breeze sessions (17)	Researcher
Planning and evaluation meetings and documents for weekly Breeze sessions	School and/or forest school practitioner
Interviews with school staff (5)	Researcher
Interviews with the forest school practitioner (2)	Researcher
Children's reflections during sessions	Researcher, school staff, and forest school practitioner
Individual forest school diaries (9)	Children and school staff
Individual interviews with children using visual methods (e.g., photographs, artefacts, and/or pupil views templates; Wall, Higgins, & Packard, 2007) (9)	Researcher
Parent/carer questionnaires (7)	Researcher
Interviews with parents/carers (3)	Researcher

adverse consequences. The research was designed in co-production with the school and forest school practitioner to ensure that it sat comfortably within the project and did not detract from the project aims and objectives. As the researcher often attended Breeze sessions, she explained her role to the group, gained consent at the start of the project, and checked that individual children were happy to take part in the research during any given encounter, asking: "Is it ok if I join you? Would you like to tell me about what you are doing?" If a child either verbally or non-verbally communicated that they did not want to engage at that time, the researcher would always respect that and move away. It was also important that the research was not unduly time-consuming for school staff, practitioners, or the children but that there was a reciprocal transfer of knowledge that everyone benefitted from. In these ways, the researcher was mindful of the 'everyday ethics' often involved in community-based participatory research, with responsibilities to relationships in addition to ethical principles of consent (Banks et al., 2013).

Findings and discussion

Park View First School engaged with Breeze because they recognised that, for a number of their children, the classroom could be an extremely challenging environment. As such, there was an immediate need to support their holistic development and self-belief in order for them to develop the skills to engage fully in their education. Whilst schools in England are obliged to follow a tightly packed curriculum (DfE, 2014), forest schools have no pre-determined curriculum, with learners encouraged to make their own choices, supported by a trained practitioner. Research has shown that, when given the opportunity, children and young people can 'take what they need' from their forest school experience and develop in ways important to them as individuals (Tiplady & Menter, 2021a). In addition to the learner-centred pedagogy, the Park View data demonstrates the importance of the natural environment in combination with arts and bushcraft-based activities that the children utilised in their forest school experiences. Here, we discuss how the environment and activities can support children in their development and wellbeing, firstly through imaginative play and performance and secondly through whittling and bushcraft.

Imaginative play and performance

At the start of their engagement in Breeze, a number of the children found it difficult to interact with one another, and disagreements and emotional outbursts were common. Over time, the children were given the opportunity to develop social and emotional skills, supported by skilled adults who modelled and scaffolded new skills, gradually reducing involvement as learners developed (Bruner, 1977). These skills were often developed through games and play, which the children chose to engage in, and so were especially motivated to persevere when disagreements occurred. For some of the children, imaginative play and performance became a recurring focus, as exemplified by the case of Peter.

Peter

Peter is a lively 6-year-old who immediately enjoyed the space available at forest school; this included playing in trees, bushes, and the mud, making dens and engaging in imaginative play, as well as relaxation and engagement with nature, such as spending time in a hammock and watching the birds, "I love lying in things. . . . I'm watching the birds". Peter is care experienced and was adopted after being taken into care due to neglect. Initially, Peter found it difficult to take the other children's ideas on board and would try to control the rules and narrative of games and play; this would often lead to conflict if he was challenged. However, over time, Peter learnt to compromise with his friends and to be more flexible in welcoming others into games if they asked. Peter's mum shared that whilst she had worried at first that being taken out of class might be stigmatising, forest school had been a "saving grace, it really helped him to see school in a different light . . . a place where he can feel good about himself". Peter took delight in telling his mum the names of plants and bugs that he learnt and talked to her about the other children in the group. His mum commented on how she believed that Breeze had provided a space for Peter to develop friendships which he had previously found difficult:

> He seems more confident now, there's that level of maturity in his relationships, he's had issues with emotional regulation, but he's been allowed to work through that at forest school . . . the main benefits are in terms of his relationships with other children. He used to be quite scared of other children. Forest school has provided a safe space to work at friendships.
>
> (Peter's mum)

Over the year, Peter used these developing social and emotional skills to engage in imaginative play and performances with other children; a common narrative which was returned to regularly over a six-month period was that of rescuing a 'rock baby.' Engaging in this role-play sometimes involved firefighters, the police, or family members who would rescue the baby from fire or some imminent danger. Family situations would often be enacted; homes would be made in the bushes, and a bed would be made for the rock baby. Peter would sometimes invite adults into the game, "You look after the baby," and at other times, he would invite the adults to watch a performance, "Come and see, you sit there," as he and the other children enacted the latest storyline.

Learner-centred play is an important part of the pedagogical approach at forest school (FSA, 2022). This enables children to choose to explore and make sense of their experiences and has similarities with child-centred play therapy, which is based on the belief that children have the "ability to be beneficially self-directing" (Porter, Hernandez-Reif, & Jessee, 2009, p. 1028). Unlike play therapies, forest school does not have the aim of engaging in therapy, but its holistic approach to supporting children's development means that children may engage in some of these processes with appropriate adults close at hand where needed; within the Breeze Project, there was always specialist trained school staff to support the children in addition to the forest school practitioner.

Children's play can have many outcomes, including working through trauma and exploring emotions (Andrews, 2012); by enabling children to direct their own activities, there is a greater likelihood of reducing stigma and working at a child's individual pace. It is further thought that the natural environment encourages creativity and exploration; drawing on Nicholson's "theory of loose parts" that an environment rich in open-ended resources, such as sticks, stones, mud, and water, facilitates inventiveness, creativity, and discovery (Nicholson, 1971). Forest school pedagogy recognises the natural environment as particularly beneficial for creative processes as natural objects may be used to represent innumerable things; for example, a stick may be used as a support structure, a barrier, a pen, a wand, a sword, a conductor's baton, etc. This enables children to be much more self-directed in their games and play as many more possibilities are available in comparison with more structured environments common in schools.

Whittling and bushcraft

Another common activity at forest school is whittling and bushcraft, where children are encouraged to use the materials they find to create artefacts. Learners are supported to create objects of their own choosing with no expectations from the adults beyond using the equipment safely; this can be a very different experience for children who are often used to engaging in activities that have pre-defined outcomes. A number of the children from Park View developed a love of whittling and bushcraft; the process appeared calming and rewarding for the children, and school staff and parents believed that it contributed to improved self-esteem, as in the case of Luke.

Luke

Luke is 9 years old and in the final year of first school. He was adopted as a baby, and his parents shared that:

> During the last 18 months or so (since the age of about 7), he has been trying to come to terms with what it (being adopted) means in terms of his background, identity, family relationships, and self-esteem. This has translated into difficult behaviour at times – especially at home when he regularly questions authority and shows insecurity around attachments.

Luke was also finding it difficult to settle in class, and there were concerns that he had not made expected progress during the previous school year. Forest school was an entirely different environment for Luke compared to the classroom, and the school staff commented on how calm and relaxed he was compared to school. Luke was particularly interested in whittling and crafting and, over the school year, he learnt how to use a sheath knife, bow saw, loppers, and bill hook. Luke used these skills to create a range of artefacts, including wands, lightsabres, a gnome, toadstool, animals, medals, and a marble run; these would sometimes be developed over a session but often over a number of weeks. Adults would praise Luke's efforts during sessions, supporting him in internalising positive dialogues, and his creations would also be celebrated back at school and home. Luke expressed feelings of satisfaction at anticipating a whittling project turning out well, "this is going to look really good" and his parents commented:

> He looked forward to every Wednesday morning (when Breeze took place) and was really proud of his achievements (e.g., crafts/drawings/wood handiwork) during his time at forest school. We have kept a lot of these as mementos of his time at forest school. The whole experience at forest school, we think, helped to build up his self-confidence and self-esteem, making him more resilient, content, relaxed, understanding, and patient.

Research has shown that the environment at forest school can be experienced as both physically and pedagogically very different to school (Tiplady & Menter, 2021b); this is also true of the types of activities that learners engage in as there are no expectations about how something will be crafted, how long it will take or what will be produced. This departure from past experiences that have often been negative for children who struggle within the classroom can open up new possibilities as they see themselves succeed and create new self-narratives. Luke's parents and teachers believed that the positive experiences he had at forest school helped him to develop self-esteem and enabled him to have more positive experiences at school and home:

> Luke really shines at forest school and is doing better in the classroom. We've seen it with his self-esteem; he's able to say, "I'm good at climbing or whittling," and that's really boosting his self-esteem.
>
> (Park View First School)

The children from Park View all expressed their enjoyment of Breeze and were keen to talk about the activities they enjoyed and, in particular, the freedom they experienced: "You can relax and do things you want to do," "You have a lot more freedom at forest school, you're allowed to run a lot," and "You get to play for the whole morning!" School staff and parents spoke of the children's enthusiasm for forest school:

> They all love forest school.
>
> (Park View First School)

> She says she loves forest school and that forest school is 'her thing.' . . . Martha has had a lot of therapeutic support in the past (four months of therapy and two years of child psychotherapy), and this has definitely been the most effective. . . . Martha is definitely happier on forest school days. She says it is the best day of the week.
>
> (Parent/carer)

Enjoyment and engagement are important elements in supporting children and young people's development and wellbeing.

Implications for policy, practice, and research

The Breeze research has shown that forest school can support children and young people's development and wellbeing, particularly in regard to developing the social and emotional skills essential to relationships and engagement in learning. Combining access to the natural environment, arts and bushcraft-based activities, and child-centred pedagogy through forest school appears to be particularly powerful in disrupting negative narratives that young people may have formed about themselves and school and instead encourages creativity and exploration. We have seen how children have utilised these processes to explore and make sense of past experiences and to develop social and emotional skills, relationships, and self-belief. Schools and practitioners need to carefully consider the broad outcomes that they hope their children and young people will achieve and to plan and resource forest school accordingly. Some key aspects that have been seen to be important in supporting children and young people with social and emotional needs include selecting appropriate young people according to the intention of the group; maintaining consistent staff and young people; high adult-to-young person ratios; ensuring forest school is not conditional on behaviour in school (unless there are safeguarding concerns); establishing long term programmes of at least two and a half hour sessions; enabling freedom with some structure as appropriate to the group; and locating within a suitable wooded site (Menter & Tiplady, 2023). Future research and policy need to address how school-based interventions such as Breeze can reach more children and young people whilst still retaining the key aspects, such as long-term and high staffing ratios, that make programmes both enjoyable and effective.

Conclusion

We know that increasing numbers of children and young people are experiencing mental health difficulties and that those already facing disadvantage are more likely to experience poor mental health, exacerbating existing health inequalities. Current services are not meeting the needs of many, and alongside increased NHS services, schools are in urgent need of support to address the needs of children and young people struggling to engage in education. It is essential that schools are funded to provide non-stigmatising provision that takes a child-centred approach. By combining access to the natural environment, arts and bushcraft-based activities, and child-centred pedagogy, forest school has been shown to be particularly effective in supporting children and young people's wellbeing and development. Research shows that schools are well placed to offer early interventions around mental health and wellbeing, given their close relationships with and access to the children who need them. However, this can only be achieved with additional funding and support for schools.

Notes

1 The name of the school and participants are pseudonyms.
2 Attainment 8 measures pupil attainment across eight government approved subjects at GCSE level and is used to judge school performance (DfE, 2022a).

References

Amoly, E., Dadvand, P., Forns, J., López-Vicente, M., Basagaña, X., Julvez, J., Alvarez-Pedrerol, M., Nieuwenhuijsen, M. J., & Sunyer, J. (2014). Green and blue spaces and behavioral development in Barcelona school children: The breathe project. *Environmental Health Perspectives*, *122*(12), 1351–1358.
Andrews, M. (2012). *Exploring play for early childhood studies*. Exeter: Sage.

Banks, S., Armstrong, A., Carter, K., Graham, H., Hayward, P., Henry, A., Holland, T., Holmes, C., Lee, A., McNulty, A., Moore, N., Nayling, N., Stokoe, A., & Strachan, A. (2013). Everyday ethics in community-based participatory research. *Contemporary Social Science*, *8*(3), 263–277.

Bowers, H., Manion, I., Papadopoulos, D., & Gauvreau, E. (2013). Stigma in school-based mental health: Perceptions of young people and service providers. *Child and Adolescent Mental Health*, *18*(3), 165–170.

Braun, V., & Clarke, V. (2006). Using thematic analysis in psychology. *Qualitative Research in Psychology*, *3*(2), 77–101.

Bruner, J. S. (1977). *The process of education*. Cambridge, MA: Harvard University Press.

Coates, J. K., & Pimlott-Wilson, H. (2019). Learning while playing: Children's forest school experiences in the UK. *British Educational Research Journal*, *45*(1), 21–40.

Collishaw, S., Furzer, E., Thapar, A. K., & Sellers, R. (2019). Brief report: A comparison of child mental health inequalities in three UK population cohorts. *European Child & Adolescent Psychiatry*, *28*, 1547–1549.

Crawley, E., Loades, M., Feder, G., Logan, S., Redwood, S., & Macleod, J. (2020). Wider collateral damage to children in the UK because of the social distancing measures designed to reduce the impact of COVID-19 in adults. *BMJ Paediatrics Open*, *4*, e000701.

Department for Education [DfE]. (2014). *The national curriculum in England framework document*. (The national curriculum in England – Framework document). Retrieved from publishing.service.gov.uk [Accessed December 29, 2022]

Department for Education [DfE]. (2022a). *Secondary accountability measures: 2022 guide for maintained secondary schools, academies and free schools*. Retrieved from publishing.service.gov.uk [Accessed December 29, 2022]

Department for Education [DfE]. (2022b). *Outcomes for children looked after by local authorities in England*. Retrieved March 31, 2019, from https://assets.publishing.service.gov.uk/government/uploads/system/uploads/attachment_data/file/884758/CLA_Outcomes_Main_Text_2019.pdf [Accessed December 29, 2022]

Dyson, A., & Todd, L. (2010). Dealing with complexity: Theory of change evaluation and the full service extended schools initiative. *International Journal of Research and Method in Education*, *33*(2), 119–134.

Ecclestone, K., & Hayes, D. (2019). *The dangerous rise of therapeutic education*. London: Routledge.

Ford, T., Parker, C., Salim, J., Goodman, R., Logan, S., & Henley, W. (2018). The relationship between exclusion from school and mental health: A secondary analysis of the British child and adolescent mental health surveys 2004 and 2007. *Psychological Medicine*, *48*(4), 629–641.

Forest School Association. (2022). *Full principles and criteria for good practice*. Retrieved from https://forestschoolassociation.org/full-principles-and-criteria-for-good-practice/ [Accessed December 29, 2022]

Gronholm, P. C., Nye, E., & Michelson, D. (2018). Stigma related to targeted school-based mental health interventions: A systematic review of qualitative evidence. *Journal of Affective Disorders*, *240*, 17–26.

McAuley, C., & Davis, T. (2009). Emotional well-being and mental health of looked after children in England. *Child and Family Social Work*, *14*, 147–155.

McCree, M. (2019). When forest school isn't forest school. In M. Sackville-Ford & H. Davenport (Eds.), *Critical issues in forest schools* (pp. 3–20). London: Sage.

McCree, M., Cutting, R., & Sherwin, D. (2018). The hare and the tortoise go to forest school: Taking the scenic route to academic attainment via emotional wellbeing outdoors. *Early Child Development and Care*, *188*(7), 980–996.

Menter, H., & Tiplady, L. (2023). *Forest school for wellbeing: Supporting children and young people with social and emotional needs*. Newcastle: Newcastle University.

Retrieved from https://scotswoodgarden.org.uk/learn/forest-schools-research [Accessed March 23, 2023]

Moula, Z., Palmer, K., & Walshe, N. (2022). A systematic review of arts-based interventions delivered to children and young people in nature or outdoor spaces: Impact on nature connectedness, health and wellbeing. *Frontiers in Psychology*, *13*, 858781.

National Society for the Prevention of Cruelty to Children [NSPCC]. (2021). *Statistics briefing: Looked after children*. Retrieved from https://learning.nspcc.org.uk/media/1622/statistics-briefing-looked-after-children.pdf [Accessed December 29, 2022]

Newlove-Delgado, T., Marcheselli, F., Williams, T., Mandalia, D., Davis, J., McManus, S., Savic, M., Treloar, W., & Ford, T. (2022). *Mental health of children and young people in England, 2022*. Leeds: NHS Digital.

Nicholson, S. (1971). How not to cheat children: The theory of loose parts. *Landscape Architecture*, *62*, 30–34.

Porter, M. L., Hernandez-Reif, M., & Jessee, P. (2009). Play therapy: A review. *Early Child Development and Care*, *179*(8), 1025–1040.

Rahilly, T., & Hendry, E. (2014). *Promoting the wellbeing of children in care: Messages from research*. London: National Society for the Prevention of Cruelty to Children.

Reiss, F. (2013). Socioeconomic inequalities and mental health problems in children and adolescents: A systematic review. *Social Science & Medicine*, *90*, 24–31.

Sackville-Ford, M. (2019). What does 'long-term' mean at forest school? In M. Sackville-Ford & H. Davenport (Eds.), *Critical issues in forest schools* (pp. 33–44). London: Sage.

Sackville-Ford, M., & Davenport, H. (2019). *Critical issues in forest schools*. London: Sage.

Tiplady, L. S. E. (2022). *The breeze forest school project 2018–21 evaluation report*. Newcastle: Newcastle University. Retrieved from https://scotswoodgarden.org.uk/learn/forest-schools-research [Accessed December 29, 2022]

Tiplady, L. S. E., & Menter, H. (2021a). Forest school for wellbeing: An environment in which young people can 'take what they need'. *Journal of Adventure Education and Outdoor Learning*, *21*(2), 99–114.

Tiplady, L. S. E., & Menter, H. (2021b). The breeze project: Supporting children and young people through forest school. In M. Jayman, M. Ohl, & L. Jewett (Eds.), *Supporting new digital natives: Children's mental health and wellbeing in a Hi-Tech age* (pp. 78–96). Bristol: Policy Press.

Wall, K., Higgins, S., & Packard, E. (2007). *Talking about learning: Using templates to find out pupils' views*. Southgate: Publishing Devon.

Weare, K., & Nind, M. (2011). Mental health promotion and problem prevention in schools: What does the evidence say? *Health Promotion International*, *26*(1), 29–69.

Wells, N., & Evans, G. (2003). Nearby nature: A buffer of lie stresses among rural children. *Environment and Behavior*, *35*(3), 311–330.

Wilkinson, J., & Bowyer, S. (2017). *The impacts of abuse and neglect on children; and comparison of different placement options: Evidence review*. London: Department for Education.

Chapter 4

Performing with/in place
Exploring sense of place through story making and sharing

Sarah Victoria Sharp

Introduction

> You can be inspired by all your different surroundings, it's kind of interesting how it can go from just a place to a *story*.
>
> (Participant audio recording)

All places are full of stories – echoes of the past, becomings of the present, and whispers of futures yet to be made. Stories entangle local and global experiences, weaving together endless encounters into a collaborative tapestry of place. They are the constructed narratives through which we understand the world (Basso, 1996). We are all entangled in this world-story, intricately and inextricably enmeshed in the time/space/matter of the universal web. We are infinitely engaged in an ongoing process of mutual affect, both affecting and affected by the multiplicity of connections. The stories we tell simultaneously express and shape what we learn and know about this experience, but as Donna Haraway (2019) tells us, "It matters what stories tell stories" (p. 565). So, how do we make and share stories with the world around us? What might the process of creating them reveal about our relationships with the world or our 'sense of place'? And how might this sense of place impact our wellbeing? These were the questions that motivated the launch of a new participatory drama project by One Step Theatre (Figure 4.1).

One Step Theatre is an environmentally focussed arts organisation founded by Sarah Victoria Sharp and Florence Taylor (hereafter "we"/"us"/"our", etc.). One Step produces participatory performances and creative experiences with and for young people, providing opportunities to include their voices in environmental dialogues within their local communities. Our work combines live and digital art to platform accessible and relatable conversations about the environment while facilitating young people to develop their creativity by collaborating with professional theatre makers. In 2021, One Step created an immersive audio and physical performance entitled *Ears to the Ground (ETTG)*, commissioned as part of the Arts and Humanities Research Council (AHRC), a part of the United Kingdom Research and Innovation (UKRI), funded project 'Outside the Box: Open Air Performance

DOI: 10.4324/9781003357308-4

Figure 4.1 'Ears to the Ground', One Step Theatre, Exeter 2021. Photo: Rhodri Cooper. Commissioned by Outside the Box

as Pandemic Response' (see O'Malley & Turner, 2021). *ETTG* brought together five teenagers aged 14–17 years in Belle Isle Park, Exeter, for a workshop week culminating in a show created and performed by them *in situ*. Through participatory drama activities we recorded responses that the young people had to their local environment, making a verbatim audio track which they paired with collaboratively devised physical movements in an immersive outdoor performance.

The aim of *ETTG* was to explore the ways that story making and sharing with/in place might help us to understand our relationships with the more-than-human world or our 'sense of place'. Our understanding of a sense of place was initially inspired by Ursula Heise's *Sense of Place, Sense of Planet* (2008), which considers ways that developing relationships with our local place or environment can impact our understanding of our entanglement with the global environment. 'Place' in this context can be understood not simply as a fixed geographical location but as an ensemble of co-constitutional relations across time/space/matter. A sense of place, therefore, moves beyond *connecting* people with place as if they are separate fixed entities in need of a communication link and towards exploring how embodied experiences *shape* both people and place through reciprocal agentic encounters. Thus, *ETTG* foregrounded embodied encounters to develop an understanding of relationality and entanglement with/in place. I draw on feminist post-human and new-materialist interpretations of 'entanglement' and 'relationality' to articulate the knotted way in which everything is interconnected and interdependent through the affective process in which things exist in constant relationships. Quantum physicist and philosopher Karen Barad (2003) explains how all matter exists only through and because of its relationship with all other matter, making existence a state of *becoming-with* everything else through mutual relationality. During our encounters *with* place, therefore, we cannot ignore the way in which we are implicated *in* place; as Greg Mannion (2020) explains, "people and places are reciprocally enmeshed and co-emergent" (p. 1357). My use of 'with/in' denotes the complexity of emergent encounters through their entangled relationality. Understanding ourselves as implicated in the world's becoming, always already existing in relation to our more-than-human environment, suggests possibilities for ways to develop a sense of place. Ecological philosopher Anna Tsing explains why an understanding of relationality is vital in our approach to environmental education as it is "the beginning of appreciation for multi-species interactions" (2012, p. 142). Tsing suggests that it is this appreciation which is necessary in our time of climate crisis to imagine better ways of living together on our damaged planet.

Much of current environmental education is predominantly focussed on scientific knowledge transmission about climate change and conservation, perpetuating ideas of human exceptionalism by separating human activity from 'nature' by teaching *about* the environment rather than acknowledging how we live *with/in* it (Dunlop & Rushton, 2022b). Understanding ourselves as entangled entities, deconstructing human exceptionalism, and resisting anthropocentric philosophies which implicitly justify the exploitation and destruction of multi-species ecologies is the imagining required to develop a pedagogy for living in a changing world (Haraway, 2016; Tsing, Bubandt, Gan, & Swanson, 2017). *ETTG* proposes a model of participatory story-making practice to facilitate such imaginings through the development of a sense of place. This model could help inform pedagogic strategies to address the needs of young people, including their wellbeing, as they learn to live in a changing world.

Methods

ETTG was a week-long participatory project with a group of young people in August 2021, which included multiple days of creative activities prompted by facilitators Sarah Victoria Sharp and Florence Taylor. The project adhered to BERA Guidelines (2018) for research with young people, and informed consent for participation was obtained from the young people and their guardians.

Participants

Participants were recruited through an opportunistic selection process (Cohen, Manion, & Morrison, 2017) via an open call on social media and targeted advertisement at local schools through drama departments. The project was described to potential participants as a free-of-charge opportunity to create an original outdoor performance for those interested in the environment. Recruitment resulted in five participants, four girls and one boy, aged 14–17 years. All those who expressed an interest took part in the project. Four of the participants came from the same school, which has 21.5% of students receiving free school meals (FSM). In 2019, Devon County Council reported a wide range of deprivation, with areas in both the most and least deprived 10% nationwide; Exeter was ranked 193 out of 317 local authorities in England for deprivation. However, we did not collect any specific information on the socio-economic background of our participants as it was not relevant to their participation in the project.

Location

The entirety of the on-site delivery (stages 1, 3, and 4 outlined further on) took place in a small coppice in Belle Isle Park, Exeter, an area the young people had passed by/through before but did not report a relationship with at the start of the project. The coppice was in a public park without restricted access during the project, and whilst we were somewhat secluded under the trees, passers-by did occasionally stop to watch or walk directly through the area, thereby becoming part of the entangled encounter of performance and place.

Activity

We guided participants through creative activities on-site from 10 a.m. to 4 p.m. each day in a variety of weather conditions. *ETTG* was evaluated by an external evaluator provided by the 'Outside the Box' umbrella project (Faull, 2021). Alongside observations throughout the project, a core part of the evaluation was informal interviews with participants and audience members who shared their experiences of the process. One Step also undertook an internal review following the project, including practitioner reflection and a short follow-up survey with audience members and participants. The survey encouraged a reflection on the impacts of *ETTG* on their relationships with outdoor spaces and performances, their enjoyment of the project, and their personal development through the process (participants only). The evaluation helped inform the development of One Step's subsequent work.

Findings and discussion

Four key findings supported the project aim: participants experienced heightened observation of their environment; the activities instigated a recall of memories and creation of imagined stories inspired by place; participating in the project improved participant wellbeing; and finally, possibly as a result of the above three, participants reported an increased understanding of, and appreciation for, their relationships with/in the environment – their sense of place.

Stage 1: audio collection. (2 days)

The project started with activities to develop a connection between the participants and practitioners with/in the park. These activities progressed towards exploring the place in further detail, drawing on activities to engage both imagination and memory. Activities included opportunities for a combination of individual creation and response as well as group collaboration. All activities were audio-recorded by participants on separate devices, generating over 30 hours of content.

Attentive exploration

Our launching point for the audio collection activities was through the encouragement of close attentiveness to place. Close attention to place can facilitate an awareness of relationality with/in it as it encourages a noticing of the many and complex entanglements that are already and always unfurling (Taylor & Pacine-Ketchabaw, 2015). Attending to the details of place is vital in story-making as it is from these encounters that stories of relationality can flow:

> [Looking at leaf] It's yellow, you know what the yellow reminds me of? Cause I can see that it's the same colour as my hair, maybe a bit more, yeah, pretty much is the same colour as my hair, actually. And it reminds me of the – of 'Thank you for the Music' by ABBA where they're like '[singing] I am the girl with golden hair, I want to sing it out to everybody'.
>
> (Participant audio)

Attentiveness was facilitated by prompts given in the workshop activities, the first of which was to 'explore the space'. Initially, we prompted them to explore the place through walking, inspired by Sarah Pink's (2009) suggestion that walking is an "experiential process through which understanding, knowing and (academic) knowledge are produced" (p. 8). Walking allows for an embodied, sensory understanding of place when undertaken with the practice of close attentiveness. Stephanie Springgay (2011) advocates for walking as a performative practice to promote 'emplacement', in which one becomes aware of "the bodily encounters that happen along the way, the shared experience of affective relations", claiming that "it is these moments that create the art" (p. 653). And so it was for our participants, the process of exploring facilitated careful attentiveness, which allowed for an experience of encounters with/in place:

> Everything just, like, amazes me, like, woooaoah grass! I normally spend my time inside, so going outside is like, "wowww, I've never seen this before". Maybe I should invest in going outside more.
>
> (Participant audio)

Within the exploring stages, participants were encouraged to find stillness in place to create and respond individually. Rosemary Lee (2006) promotes stationary exploration in her article, *Expectant Waiting*, in which she examines the profound connection between environment and character invoked by attending to place through stillness. Such stillness allows for a consideration of self in relation to place, a moment to explore the embodied experience of being still with/in place and consider its affective potential. Facilitating extended stillness turned out to be a core aspect of the improved wellbeing experienced by participants, suggesting a connection between an awareness of relationality with/in place and improved wellbeing:

> It's nice to just sit here, I think. . . . I feel quite comforted talking to you [a tree]. It's just enjoyable to be next to you. Maybe someone before me, like years ago, maybe like a hundred years ago, ranted to the very same tree. That would be cool.
>
> (Participant audio)

Fictioning

The close attentiveness developed through detailed exploration was then used in the story-making process. Our approach to story-making was informed by Burrows and O'Sullivan's (2019) writing on 'fictioning'. They explain fictioning as a playful imagining of stories informed by attentiveness to sensory information from the surrounding physical world. We incorporated this with our understanding of story-making from feminist writer and philosopher Ursula Le Guin (1986), who proposed that it is "an active encounter with the environment by means of posing options and alternatives and an enlargement of present reality by connecting it to the unverifiable past and the unpredictable future" (p. 44–45). Our interpretation of story-making, or fictioning, articulates an embodied experience of encounters across temporal scales by sharing imaginings of unmemorable pasts and possible futures. Imaginings here can be understood not merely as make-believe but as the creative process of folding possibilities for alternative worlds into the present. Through *ETTG,* we discovered that fictioning can be a way to express an understanding of relationality and can unlock experiences that work towards the development of a sense of place:

> What if a tree decided things? What decisions would a tree make?
>
> (Participant audio)

> I'm drawn to this tree because it has an aura of knowledge and omniscience. I think it could tell me a lot about the future and the past, what might happen and what might not. . . . It will remind me a lot of the lessons I've learned, how these sort of places can become home. . . . I think this place has helped me regain my creativity, and I really appreciate that. I'm leaving a little bit of what I'm receiving.
>
> (Participant audio)

We followed the idea of fictioning to draw attention to the relationality and precarity of life through story-telling activities. Our activities collapsed together sensory information from our physical world with imagined worlds and used this combination to explore the ways in which we respond, and are responded to by, our Earthly companions:

> Like, there's a woodlouse here, and I'm not going to kill it instantly because, like, I'm scared of it. I'm not scared of it, but if I was, I'm not just gonna kill it because, like, it has a life, and it has a job to play in this, like, role.
>
> (Participant audio)

> We should believe ourselves to be equal to everything around us. . . . We need to learn how to live harmoniously.
>
> (Participant audio)

Through the process of storying sensory encounters, narratives of possible "future-images (of people and worlds) are manifested within the present" (Burrows & O'Sullivan, 2019, p. 17). By engaging with this story-making process, *ETTG* encouraged a sensory attentiveness to place and allowed for collaboratively imagined futures to weave through encounters of relationality:

> Unchartered territories within charted territories. An oasis of life within a corrupted world. Filtered light speckles on overgrown land. A colony of species rebelling against one. A silent war brought about the oppression of the senses. Stories fly around.
>
> (Participant audio)

Our experience of story-making with/in place suggests possibilities for learning to understand the ways in which we continue to become *with* the more-than-human world.

Stage 2: audio compilation. (2 days)

Once all the audio content had been generated, the practitioners worked through it without participants to compile a 30-minute audio track. The audio editing was a creative process, cropping and compiling the audio recordings using our skills as theatre makers and story-crafters. It required an attunement to the possibilities of audio assemblages as they formed and fell away in the editing process. Guided by the new-materialist writing of Mannion (2020) on the curative role of creating artistic assemblages, we retained an awareness of the multiplicity of opportunities afforded by different audio combinations, embracing their affective potential and allowing that to guide curation. Therefore, our process of cutting the participant's material was a generative one that created the audio experience, actively entangled with the encounters of place experienced by the participants in the preceding two days to co-create the final audio track. The audio track was compiled on Logic Pro and downloaded into an MP3 file format that could be shared with participants and audience members for the performance (see Stage 4).

Stage 3: physical development. (2 days)

After a few days' rest while practitioners compiled the audio, the participants returned to the site to engage in a series of physical activities, developing a live performance which accompanied the audio track. We drew on our experience as physical theatre practitioners to facilitate the creation of movements that took inspiration from ideas that had emerged through the audio. The focus of the exploration was the participants' relationship with/in the place and with each other. For example, we encouraged participants to experiment with gestures and poses that embodied some keywords (including 'lively', 'connected', and 'peaceful') that had been expressed in the audio. We then used drama techniques of patterning (e.g., repeating movements in different orders), staggering (e.g., different people starting movements at different times), and synchrony (e.g., finding one movement to all do simultaneously) to create sequences of movement with the group.

We also played with multiple ways to move through the area to create an ensemble performance. For this exploration of moving, we drew on the principles of Laban Movement Analysis (LMA), which identifies human bodies as moving according to four components: direction, speed, weight, and flow (Laban, 1950). Thinking with LMA, we folded through aspects of the physical Viewpoints Method (Bogart & Landau, 2005), exploring bodily relationships in time and space. We experimented with the shoaling exercise, where participants move together through the space as an ensemble (a collaborative group) whilst exploring different ways of moving the body following the leader style, for example, moving slowly low to the ground (in response to the word 'grounded') or waving arms whilst tall in the air (in response to "space to breathe"). Another exercise was grid formation movements, where participants imagine the space as a grid that directs channels of movement along which they explore encounters with place, for example, what happens when they collide with an obstacle such as a tree, hear a noise, come face to face with each other, and how these moments of tension are resolved (i.e., what movement is taken). These approaches to considering movement encouraged participants to explore their bodies *in relation*, thus creating a performative encounter of place by experiencing time, space, and bodies (including more-than-human bodies) through and with movement (which can, of course, include stillness). These sequences made up the physical part of the performance.

The performative encounter through the body draws on ecological artist Susan Finley's (2010) proposition that "performance is a way of knowing and of being. . . . Knowledge is located *in* the body" (p. 3). Movement allows us to experience how "cognition, action, and the senses are intertwined" (Powell, 2010, p. 541), both within and across bodies – including nonhuman bodies. Thinking with such philosophies, environmental awareness can be achieved by understanding the moving body as intricately connected with both the internal and external environment, which simultaneously make and shape each other. Therefore, movement is part of the process of becoming-with place. We encouraged participants to use their bodies to perform their experiences with/in place as ways of learning *with* their embodied encounters of entanglement, which helped them build a greater sense of relationship with place:

> I'm leaving a gift of presence, but I'm leaving a burden of a footprint.
>
> (Participant audio)

Stage 4: performance. (1 day)

Audience experience

At the end of the week, participants shared their work in a public performance. There were three performances across one day with an average audience size of 11. The audio track was distributed to the audience, who listened to it whilst immersed in the place of the performance with the participants moving around them. Audience members noted an increased level of observation of the space throughout the performance, which developed their sense of relationship with the environment:

> It made you look around you more. I've never thought to stop and look at the trees in such detail before.
>
> (Audience member)

> It made me look at the trees in a new way. I know the area and have been through it many times, but this time, I stopped and *looked*.
>
> (Audience member)

This heightened observation could be attributed to being encouraged to spend an extended period in place whilst watching the performance. This time spent *in situ*, combined with listening to the audio recording, highlighted details they might have missed without the encouragement of such close attention. The format of the performance also allowed audience members to feel like contributors, adding to the sense of relationality engendered by the performance:

> It was really very interesting. A bit different to other audio performances I have experienced. These have been very solitary walking tours. This was more of a gathering with performers in front of us. It was more social – as if we are witnesses; onlookers, but also part of it.
>
> (Audience member)

Perhaps then, both the form and content of the performance engaged the audience in developing a relationship with the environment (which included the participants and each other). Heise (2008) articulates that a sense of place is deeply interwoven with an understanding of environments as shared spaces that transcend immediate human physical and temporal barriers. In *EETG*, this could be seen in the audience's experience of the participants' performed encounters of place, both current in the physical performance and historical in the audio track, which the audience experienced simultaneously with their own encounters of place. The performances collapsed together multiple scales of memory and imaginings within more-than-human encounters to encourage an experience of the co-constituting environment, or as Heise would have it – a sense of place.

Impact on wellbeing

From discussions with the young people over the week, after the final performance, and from talking to their families, the external evaluator concluded that the project had a strong impact in developing participant's confidence, resilience, creative and performing skills, and improved their social and emotional wellbeing:

> This space has brought me peace. It's let me express myself, my thoughts, my interests. It's let me have a distraction without actually being distracted – having a focus point.
>
> (Participant audio)

All participants commented on improved confidence and resilience as a result of the project:

> I feel more confident and can express myself better.
>
> (Participant feedback)

> I'm more confident interacting with others. That's a big change for me.
>
> (Participant feedback)

This was also noticed by a number of parents of participants who commented on benefits to the wellbeing of their child as a result of their involvement with the project:

> [Name] is so much more confident because of this. They loved the autonomy – It was so young-person-led, which was excellent.
>
> (Parent of participant)

Due to our collaborative project design, participants all commented they felt they were '100%' co-creators in the project, and using their own ideas and being treated as collaborators were regularly mentioned positively:

> It's a place to be creative. Freedom to be yourself.
>
> (Participant feedback)

> It's not like school. Here, you are listened to. Here, we are treated more like equals.
>
> (Participant feedback)

During the week, confidence within the group grew, so they were more willing to take risks and explore performance strategies they hadn't encountered before. The external evaluator concluded that by the end of the week, there was a strong sense of collaboration and understanding within the group, which was evident not only when speaking to them for feedback but also within the performance itself. These impacts on the personal development of participants contributed to their reports of improved wellbeing as a result of the project. They noted that increased provision of creative activities outdoors such as this would benefit them and their peers, and they did not feel this was something they were currently receiving through the school curriculum or extra-curricular activities.

I wish we had more things like this.

(Participant feedback)

Implications for education

Despite commitments by the Department of Education in England to "put climate change at the heart of education" (DfE, 2021), young people still desire a reformation of the national curriculum to include more substantial teaching about the ecological emergency we currently face (Teach the Future, 2022). Further, 92% of surveyed teachers think more needs to be done to address climate change in schools (Teach the Future, 2021). The demand for more effective environmental education in British schools is apparent, leading to the challenging question of what that education looks like. In *Theatre Ecology,* Baz Kershaw (2007) suggests that art and the environment are both so enmeshed in daily life that engaging with one without the other is paradoxical since they are not ontologically distinctive. An active awareness of the role of each in relation to the other, therefore, increases the efficacy of learning as a fuller understanding of entanglement can be attained. Indeed, Hilary Inwood (2008) advocated for integration of creative activities with place-based education as a "dynamic way to increase the power and relevancy of learning about the environment" (p. 30). This is in line with the demands of young people represented by groups like Teach the Future for a revised approach to environmental education.

ETTG provides an example of the pedagogic potential of story making as a way to experientially learn about our entangled relationships with/in our local environment. Exploring these relationships can encourage the development of a sense of place, which might inspire young people to think critically about their affective role in the worldwide environment and be aware of the interconnected ways all actions, encounters, and decisions are part of the world's becoming. From this mindset of relationality, we can take a hopeful interpretation of individual agency, we are part of a changing world and are co-authors of that change as it continues to unfold. Young people often report feelings of powerlessness when engaging with environmental education, leading to fear or anxiety (Hickman et al., 2021). Considering individual agency through relationality could combat this by empowering young people to understand themselves as affective authors of the world's changing story.

It enacts the pedagogic shift from learning *about* the environment to learning how we are always and already becoming *with/in* it. Such a shift could facilitate imagining ways to live better on a changing planet to emerge.

But that's just my view. You don't have to predict the future, for hope.

(Participant audio)

Conclusion

ETTG adds to the body of evidence that outdoor creative activities provide opportunities for young people to build relationships with their more-than-human environments (Taylor & Pacine-Ketchabaw, 2015). Such opportunities have a positive impact on participants' wellbeing and can improve their confidence and capacity for creative expression. *ETTG* contributes that creative activities which encourage close attention offer embodied experiences of being with/in the world by exploring everyday encounters as possibilities of relational knowledge exchange. The process of *ETTG* enabled us to explore ways that story-making, through interactive drama activities, can facilitate such relational encounters by co-creating an outdoor, immersive, and participatory performance with a group of young people. It demonstrates a practice for creative engagement with a place that can encourage an awareness of entanglement by developing a sense of place. The implications of such practice are significant as it proposes possibilities for ways that an ontological shift towards learning to become with the world can be undertaken, a process which may be vital for multi-species survival in our time of planetary crisis.

References

Barad, K. (2003). Posthumanist performativity: Toward an understanding of how matter comes to matter. *Signs: Journal of Women in Culture and Society, 28*(3), 801–831.

Basso, K. (1996). *Wisdom sits in places: Landscape and language among the Western Apache*. Albuquerque: University of New Mexico Press.

Bogart, A., & Landau, T. (2005). *The viewpoints book: A practical guide to viewpoints and composition*. London: Theatre Communications Group.

British Educational Research Association (BERA). (2018). *Ethical guidelines for educational research* (4th ed.). London: Author.

Burrows, D., & O'Sullivan, S. (2019). *Fictioning: The myth-functions of contemporary art and philosophy*. Edinburgh: Edinburgh University Press.

Cohen, L., Manion, L., & Morrison, K. (2017). *Research methods in education* (8th ed.). London: Routledge.

Department for Education (DfE). (2021). *Education Secretary puts climate change at the heart of education* [online]. Retrieved from www.gov.uk/government/news/education-secretary-puts-climate-change-at-the-heart-of-education–2#:~:text=National%20Insurance%20record-,Education%20Secretary%20puts%20climate%20change%20at%20the%20heart%20of%20education,at%20the%20heart%20of%20education [Accessed July 13, 2023]

Dunlop, L., & Rushton, E. A. C. (2022b). Putting climate change at the heart of education: Is England's strategy a placebo for policy? *British Educational Research Journal, 48*(6), 1083–1101.

Faull, E. (2021). Ears to the ground external evaluation report [Unpublished internal report]. *'Outside the Box: Open Air Performance as Pandemic Response', Supported by the Arts and Humanities Research Council and the University of Exeter.*

Finley, S. (2010). Ecoaesthetics: Green arts at the intersection of education and social transformation. *Cultural Studies ↔ Critical Methodologies, 11*(3), 306–313.

Haraway, D. (2016). *Staying with the trouble: Making kin in the Chthulucene.* Durham, NC and London: Duke University Press.

Haraway, D. (2019). It matters what stories tell stories; It matters whose stories tell stories. *a/b: Auto/Biography Studies, 34*(3), 565–575.

Heise, U. K. (2008). *Sense of place and sense of planet.* New York: Oxford University Press.

Hickman, C., Marks, E., Pihkala, P., Clayton, S., Lewandowski, R. E., Mayall, E., Wray, B., Mellor, C., & van Susteren L. (2021). Climate anxiety in children and young people and their beliefs about government responses to climate change: A global survey. *The Lancet Planetary Health, 5*(12), 863–873.

Inwood, H. (2008). At the crossroads: Situating place-based art education. *Canadian Journal of Environmental Education, 13*(1), 29–41.

Kershaw, B. (2007). *Theatre ecology: Environments and performance events.* New York: Cambridge University Press.

Laban, R. V. (1950). *The mastery of movement on the stage.* London: MacDonald & Evans.

Le Guin, U. (1986). Carrier bag story of fiction. In U. Le Guin (Ed.), *Dancing at the edge of the world: Thoughts on words, women, places* (pp. 165–170). New York: Grove Press.

Lee, R. (2006). Expectant waiting. In C. Bannerman, J. Sofaer, & J. Watt (Eds.), *Navigating the unknown: The creative process in contemporary performing arts.* Enfield: Middlesex University Press.

Mannion, G. (2020). Re-assembling environmental and sustainability education: Orientations from New Materialism. *Environmental Education Research, 26*(9–10), 1353–1372.

O'Malley, E., & Turner, C. (2021). Outside the box: Open air performance as pandemic response. *AHRC Award Number, AH/V015230/1.* Retrieved from https://openairperformance.com/ [Accessed July 17, 2023]

Pink, S. (2009). *Doing sensory ethnography.* Thousand Oaks, CA: Sage.

Powell, P. (2010). Making sense of place: Mapping as a multisensory research method. *Qualitative Inquiry, 16*(7), 539–555.

Springgay, S. (2011). 'The Chinatown Foray' as sensational pedagogy. *Curriculum Inquiry, 41*(5), 636–656.

Taylor, A., & Pacine-Ketchabaw, V. (2015). Learning with children, ants, and worms in the Anthropocene: Towards a common world pedagogy of multispecies vulnerability. *Pedagogy, Culture & Society, 23*(4), 507–529.

Taylor, A., Pacini-Ketchabaw, V., Blaise, M., & Silova, I. (2020). Learning to become with the world: Education for future survival. In *Common worlds research collective. Paper commissioned for the UNESCO futures of education report.* Retrieved from https://unesdoc.unesco.org/ark:/48223/pf0000374032

Teach the Future. (2021). *New research shows nearly three quarters of teachers haven't received enough training on climate change* [Online]. Retrieved from www.teachthefuture.uk/blog/new-research-shows-nearly-three-quarters-of-teachers-havent-received-enough-training-on-climate-change [Accessed July 13, 2023]

Teach the Future. (2022). *The launch of curriculum for a changing climate* [Online]. Retrieved from www.teachthefuture.uk/blog/the-launch-of-curriculum-for-a-changing-climate. [Accessed July 13, 2023]

Tsing, A. L. (2012). Unruly edges: Mushrooms as companion species. *Environmental Humanities, 1*(1), 141–154.

Tsing, A. L., Bubandt, N., Gan, E., & Swanson, H. (Eds.). (2017). *Arts of living on a damaged planet: Ghosts and monsters of the Anthropocene.* Minneapolis, MN: University of Minnesota Press.

Chapter 5

Exploring restorative connections with nature through communicative musicality

Nick Clough and Jane Tarr

Introduction

This chapter explores how children's experience of music-making enhances the healing power of their connections with nature. David Orr, in writing about ecological literacy and human interaction with nature, noted that:

> The form and structure of any conversation with the natural world is that of the discipline of ecology as a restorative process and a healing art.
>
> (Orr, 1992, p. 90)

This chapter focuses on musical dimensions that can add to such ecological conversations with nature. It describes how a teacher, a Forest School (FS) practitioner, a music therapist and a teacher trainer participated in a small-scale action enquiry within an Academy Trust in Southwest England. Together, they explored the contributions of 'communicative musicality' (Malloch & Trevarthen, 2009) in establishing restorative connections with nature for primary-aged school children whose social, emotional and mental health had been identified as a cause for concern (DfE & DoH, 2015, p. 98). Their social and emotional difficulties manifested in many ways, including anger, aggression, anxiety, attention difficulties, bullying and vulnerability to bullying, communication difficulties, lack of empathy, obsessive tendencies, panic attacks, stress, unstable relationships and withdrawal (Clough & Tarr, 2022).

The study is pertinent considering that incidences of self-harm, attempted suicide and anxiety have become more frequent in young people since the COVID-19 lockdown (Commission on Young Lives, 2022). Whilst young people may not generally have experienced severe physical symptoms when contracting COVID-19, they remained highly susceptible to its psychosocial effects (Power, Hughes, Cotter, & Cannon, 2020). Moreover, COVID-19 has compounded the anxieties of young people with vulnerabilities arising from other adversities (Young Minds, 2020). One in six children aged 6–16 were identified as having a probable mental health problem in July 2021, a huge increase from the already troubling one in nine in 2017 (NHS Digital, 2021). These phenomena are reflected in subsequent

DOI: 10.4324/9781003357308-5

discussions of psychosocial damage to children's wellbeing that have occurred as a result of COVID-19 (Howard-Jones et al., 2022) and form the basis for exacerbating children's health inequities that are discussed in this chapter.

The enquiry reported here represents a sequel to recommendations made in our earlier study that encouraged ongoing collaborations between teachers and music therapists (Clough & Tarr, 2022). The intention in this study was to promote safe, inclusive and interactive practices that can facilitate vulnerable children's social and emotional access to learning and also address health inequities within the school environment. Building on emerging evidence that forest schools can support young people's wellbeing (Tiplady & Menter, 2020), the inter-professional discussions that have informed this enquiry have drawn attention to the restorative potential of musical engagement and interaction within the forest school context. It was understood that insights from the field of music therapy may complement the practices of the participating teacher and FS practitioner within a local designated woodland environment of natural beauty. Thus, the action enquiry was inter-professional in its intent, exploring the application of improvisation, dialogic engagement and connectivity (as they relate to communicative musicality) within an ongoing nature-based wellbeing programme. The enquiry also addresses timely questions about how nature itself is valued as a relational human resource while the UN Decade on Ecosystem Restoration (2021–2030) is in progress.

The enquiries were shaped by addressing the following research questions:

1. To what extent did the ecological and musical experiences address children's social and emotional needs?
2. What new professional capacities were required to enhance children's wellbeing through the experience of music-making within nature?

Methods

Participatory action research (PAR) was chosen as a framework that could engage the teacher, the FS practitioner, the music therapist and the teacher trainer collaboratively in the intervention and research process that took place over two months. The imagery of Chevalier and Buckles writing about PAR was invoked as a basis for the invitation to participate and as justification for gathering the inter-professional team together.

Those who accept the invitation meet at agreed crossroads and choose to interact according to shared rules. But they do so with many other considerations in mind. The gathering is like a nexus – a focus point where lines and paths intersect for a period of time. All those taking part spend time at this junction, but the way that they interact, the things they do and the rules they follow are directly affected by their respective origins and destinations.

(Chevalier & Buckles, 2019, p. 29)

This study gained ethical approval from the Bath Spa University Ethics Committee in March 2022. It was agreed the children themselves would not participate directly as respondents in the PAR process. Nonetheless, an information sheet and consent form were signed by their parents or carers, the teacher and the FS practitioner, including information about confidentiality, anonymity, and the right to withdraw at any time. Children themselves assented enthusiastically to participating in the modified forest school programme that included music-making,

Study design

As we gathered together, it was accepted that sharing the knowledge and skills of the trained music therapist could be pivotal in developing new approaches that can address the identified needs of children. Thus, the themes of communicative musicality, improvisation and dialogue were prioritised in the study design as transferable points of focus.

Communicative musicality (Malloch & Trevarthen, 2009) has been recognised as a fundamental theme in the field of music therapy. Engaging with communicative musicality as a concept, music can be seen as the foundation of human expression and communication. For example, the vocalising between a baby and their carer uses the musical elements of timbre (quality of sound), pitch (high and low sounds), duration (short and long sounds) and loudness or dynamics (volume of sound) to communicate. This is a vital part of building secure attachments between parents or carers and their children (Papousek & Papousek, 1981). Malloch, Sharp, Campbell, Campbell, and Trevarthen (1997) conducted close auditory analyses of the interactions between babies and their carers, documenting all musical elements within these communications. Malloch named this process 'communicative musicality', specifying it as an art of companionable communication that draws on innate human abilities to move sympathetically with the other and acts as a vehicle which, through the participants' use of voice, gesture and movement, carries emotion from one to the other (Malloch, 1999, pp. 48–50). Together with Trevarthen, he later published a comprehensive collection of materials related to communicative musicality (Malloch & Trevarthen, 2009).

This understanding of communicative music-making provided a practical focus in the teacher training described in what follows through encouraging the replication of these kinds of interactions in a forest school setting. Teachers we have worked with previously have recognised this as a restorative process and have adopted similar approaches using musical instruments (and occasionally their voices) to stimulate socialising musical responses from young people (Clough & Tarr, 2022, pp. 44–69). We have observed that communicative music-making frequently starts, as conversations do, from moments of paired interaction. On hearing two players making music together, other participants will often join in, synchronising their playing with the original pair. Such communicative group music-making can include a range of active and physical responses referred to as 'musicking', a term originally coined by Small (1998) as 'the art of taking part in any capacity in a musical performance' (p. 9). In this chapter, the term musicking is used to convey this wider understanding of group music-making and listening. It is reflected by Stensaeth (2015), a music therapist and researcher, writing that 'musical improvisation refers not only to composing in the moment but includes joyful playing on musical instruments and everything that is understood as musically intended within the situation (body language, gestures, mimicry, etc.)' (p. 210). The inclusion of gesture and body language further supports the notion of musical improvisation as a holistic form of communication that involves reflecting, grounding, dialoguing and accompanying (Wigram, 2004).

The notion of dialogic interaction was relevant to this inter-professional enquiry, having complementary applications within music therapy and education. 'Joint focused attention' and 'answerability' are two elements of a dialogic process identified by Stensaeth (2015, pp. 213–222) that were applied within this study. Wegerif (2019) also argues for a broader definition of dialogue, drawing on earlier propositions of Bakhtin (1984) that dialogue is not limited to spoken words but includes personality and tones of voice. This broader definition of dialogic interaction, which could potentially include dialogic interaction with natural phenomena, influenced the design of this study.

Intervention outline and ethical approval

This intervention was a pilot to explore the potential of communicative musicking for enhancing children's restorative connections with nature. Due to high instances of COVID-19 across the school, we chose (as the music therapist and teacher trainer who were orchestrating the intervention) to restrict our engagement to direct contact with the teacher and FS practitioner. They were both working one afternoon every week in a woodland with 12 children following referrals from an Academy Trust overseeing educational provision across a range of primary schools in southwest England. Over a period of two months, the teacher and FS practitioner engaged with us in five two-hour training and enquiry sessions immediately following their work in the woodland with the 12 children. This was an opportunity to explore skills related to communicative musicking, to share their experiences on the woodland activities that had just occurred and to discuss plans for their next session. During each training session, we recorded the conversations with the teacher and FS practitioner and developed verbatim narrative accounts that included their photographs and musical recordings. Selected photographs from the woodland activities were converted into graphic sketches to protect the identities of all participants (Figure 5.1).

The programme was organised over the five-week period around these ecological and musical themes:

- communicative musicality (Malloch & Trevarthen, 2009);
- earth walking for earth keeping (Van Matre, 2019);
- dialogic experience (Stensaeth, 2015; Wegerif, 2019);
- making wider connections (Carmichael, 2022); and
- listening to nature, ecotones, soundscapes of trees (Bayley, 2022).

The newly accessed blowing instruments supported the development of the previous week's activities involving conversations with birds. The children took to this straight away and went off to their own spots that they had identified and visited previously. T1 observed that C2 was completely engrossed in chatting away with the bird on her musical instrument_ As T1 observed other children, she recognised that the blowing instruments supported these bird conversations in new ways and that the children's engagement in the activity was more sustained. Later in the session, C2 was observed lying in a hammock playing the newly accessed autoharp. She spent 3-4 minutes making sounds to call in the birds with her playing.

Figure 5.1 An example of a reflexive product based on the teacher's original photograph and verbal account. Sketches by Jane Tarr

The programme emphasised the significance of structuring musical spaces and experiences in ways that allowed time for attentive listening; the sensory exploration of phenomena, including the instruments themselves and relational activities that involved turn-taking, dialogic pair work, group improvisation and opportunities to take the lead as a conductor of sounds in nature. A collection of small and portable instruments was loaned to the project, which was carefully selected to reflect a range of natural sounds, such as seed and nut rattles, egg shakers, small carved soft-sounding drums, frog guiros and coconut shell kalimbas.

Data collection and analysis

We used three approaches to address the research questions. Throughout data collection and analysis, the teacher and FS practitioner were coded as T1 and T2 and children as C1, C2, C3, etc.

Approach 1. Data collection that drew on the teacher's/FS practitioner's narrative and graphic accounts of children's encounters with nature through musical experiences in the woodland. Photographs, sketches and musical artefacts from the activities, together with verbal descriptions, were refashioned as 'reflexive products' (Clough & Tarr, 2022, pp. 38–39) to stimulate the participants' further shared recall, self-reflections and theorising (see Table 5.1). Chevalier and Buckles (2019) have termed such methods as 'interfacing' arguing that these may 'create genuine dialogue and break open the private turfs and bunkers of disciplinary data collection, analysis and theory' (p. 27).

Approach 2. Data collection from observable indicators related to music-making in natural environments. They were derived from five identified 'flow' variables (Csikszentmihalyi, 1996) – focused attention, clear-cut feedback, clear goals, control of situation and pleasure – that were seen as relevant to the social and emotional needs of the children. These observable indicators, presented in what follows, stimulated the teacher's and FS practitioner's reflections on children's ecological and music-making experiences in the woodland.

- **Focused attention**: noticing the ways that the child looks carefully at aspects of the natural environment or musical instrument; explores textures or sounds of the natural environment; listens attentively to own musical productions and productions of the partners.
- **Cut feedback**: noticing the ways that the child listens carefully and reacts to the instrument or natural environment through smiling, showing expressions of puzzlement, joy, surprise, saying something and moving in response.
- **Clear goals:** noticing the ways that the child aims to explore the sounds of the instrument or natural environment; developing a musical response or movement within the natural environment; discovering the rules of interaction and musical dialogue with the natural environment and partners.
- **Control of situation**: noticing the child's movements within the natural environment and with the musical instruments that are well controlled, both during listening and playing. The child listens to the partner(s) or the natural environment and responds by repeating or changing musical ideas, engaging in collaborative playing or movements, respecting turn-taking and natural phenomena.
- **Pleasure**: noticing the ways that the child is smiling or laughing, is calm, shows no displeasure, repeating musical actions and environmental explorations; speaks to the teacher or partners and shares the joy of music-making in the natural environment.

Approach 3. A professional competence framework (UNESCO, 2015, p. 39) supported the collaborative identification and naming of new inter-professional competencies. These comprised knowledge, skills and ways of being and living alongside others that could enhance future practices on communicative musicality. New emerging competencies were recognised as the teacher and FS practitioner reflected on their interactions with children.

Findings and discussion

Following the first session with children in the woodland, T1 and T2 expressed that they valued the practical introduction to the instruments that they received during the first training session with the teacher trainer and music therapist, which allowed them to facilitate simple musical exchanges with the group. The examples reported here are distilled from discussions with T1 and T2 that were stimulated by their own photographs, musical recordings and verbal narrative accounts that were subsequently presented back to them as reflexive products (Table 5.1).

Reflecting further on children's level of engagement, T1 and T2 reported that the non-verbal aspect of playing music made it accessible to children who were hesitant to engage and that the open woodland space provided opportunities for paired and group work that was quite loud and animated. Some of this work was trans-modal, allowing one partner to play rhythmically and another to dance. They also reported that as subsequent sessions included activities that drew attention to sensory aspects of trees (drawing on the work of Van Matre, 2019), children began to relate their playing to natural phenomena, such as answering birdsongs.

Table 5.1 Twelve professional competencies that have emerged as teachers supported children's restorative journeying in nature through musical experiences

Professional competences	Learning how to know	Learning how to do	Learning how to be	Learning how to live alongside others
Supporting children's restorative connections with nature through musical experiences	Understanding phenomena in the natural environment alongside the qualities of the selected musical instruments.	Making music alongside children to encourage non-verbal expression within the natural environment.	Being playful with the social opportunities of musical interactions in the natural environment.	Recognising the power of sitting in a circle and participating in music-making together with other children.
	Understanding how one's own musical capacities can support children's musical communications with others and with nature.	Encouraging children's dialogic musical responses within the natural environment.	Valuing children's own strategies for connecting with nature through music-making.	Recognising the restorative value of dialogic musical exchanges with/between children within natural environments.
	Exploring how group music-making in the natural environment impacts on children's wellbeing.	Documenting the impact of children's sensory and relational musical experiences in nature through Flow criteria.	Recognising how freedom of movement within the natural environment contributes to children's wellbeing.	Sharing curiosity about phenomena in the natural environment during group musical walks and music-making.

The discussions regarding the extent to which the ecological and musical experiences addressed children's social and emotional needs were enriched through the five selected observable indicators from Csikszentmihalyi's theory of Flow (1996). As T1 and T2 became familiar with these indicators, they supported their decision-making about future session planning. T1 and T2 also gained confidence in identifying how each observable indicator was relevant to the musical woodland activities. For example, they noted that the Flow indicator 'focused attention' was very high when children stopped to study the tracks of birds in soft mud during a musical group walk and when individual children identified their own spots where they could converse musically with birds.

While this feedback from T1 and T2 indicated that the ecological and musical experiences were addressing children's social and emotional needs, it was also apparent that they themselves were developing new professional capacities and awareness around children's wellbeing. The iterative process of describing, representing and reflecting on the experiences of the children provided opportunities for T1, T2, the music therapist and the teacher trainer to explore how their professional knowledge, skills and values may be extended to counter the social and mental health inequities that the children were facing.

Our starting point as leaders of this study was that 'competencies cannot be taught but have to be developed by the learners themselves. They are acquired during action, on the basis of experience and reflection' (UNESCO, 2017, p. 10). We adopted a form of experiential professional learning identified by Kolb (1984), arguing that acquiring new knowledge, skills and values derives from the transformation of experience. We tried to establish a cycle of learning that moved from concrete experience to reflection and encouraged forms of theorising that stimulated abstract experimentation (Kolb, 1976, p. 24). Within the framework of participatory action research, this cycle of learning provided opportunities for the inter-professional team to explore how to know and act and how to adapt their ways of being and living alongside others in the context of the woodland classroom.

During an early interaction in session 2, in response to two short texts that T1 and T2 had chosen for themselves (Wall Kimmerer, 2020, pp. 9–10; Carmichael, 2022, pp. 25–29) they reflected on their ongoing learning about the contributions that nature itself can make to children's restoration. T1 commented:

I would love to be able to help the children get access to her (Wall Kimmerer's) sense of the sacred space of nature, to be able to have a dialogue with nature and to receive the learning from nature.

Carmichael's account (2022) stimulated T1 to report how an interaction with a spider in the woodland prompted one child to recognise that his initial aggressive response had been triggered by his fears. T1 reported that through discussion:

He learned something about himself that he had not been able to learn in the classroom with his peers. He got it through the spider. It was magic to me, like a native American cultural view that nature speaks to us and that animals are holders of knowledge.

For both T1 and T2, it was a new experience to consider the contributions of music-making/listening within the natural environment to children's wellbeing. The discussions were focused on the 12 categories listed in Table 5.1. Each competence statement emerged through the weekly shared reflections by T1 and T2 immediately following their weekly woodland sessions. As a group of 12 professional competence statements, they provide an informative summary of the proceedings.

Implications for policy, practice and research

Our study highlights the need to develop policies and school-based practices to address the health inequities experienced by children with social, emotional and mental health concerns. Even within this small-scale enquiry, the contribution of inter-professional collaboration was evidenced as the participating teacher and FS practitioner developed the confidence to introduce new interactive, inclusive and restorative music practices within the natural woodland environment as part of school provision. The findings indicate it may be fruitful to consider the inclusion of such practical inter-professional knowledge and skill sharing within initial teacher education programmes and music therapy training.

With respect to ongoing enquiries in the workplace, there is evidence that the iterative process of reflection about music- and nature-based actions has fed the teachers' capacity for transformation with respect to enhancing children's wellbeing. The participatory action research approaches that were adopted were effective in capturing the efforts and reflections of the practitioners. The systematic documentation informed their subsequent discussions about how to improve the way that health inequities experienced by children may be addressed. The dialogic exchanges between the participants within the enquiry were also instrumental in creating new opportunities for children to experience music-making and listening in natural woodland settings; they have opened spaces for new inter-professional conversations and critical thinking about how natural learning environments can also be restorative.

Conclusion

This chapter has outlined ways in which the combination of cultural and professional approaches (including music therapy practices) and ecological resources (local natural environments) which are readily available can contribute to teacher training and subsequently to children's wellbeing. It has been noted that communicative musicality is understood by music therapists as a means through which secure connections between parent/carer and child are built. An implied subtext to the discussions in this chapter is that children's connections with nature are themselves vulnerable and that their health inequities arise in part because of human separation from nature. Recognition of the effects of these disconnections has been fundamental to the arguments that have been rehearsed. Recognition that music-making/listening can support children's restorative connections with nature is also significant to the development of holistic approaches to environmental protection. The sensitising of teachers and children to the beauty and restorative effect of intertwining musical and ecological experiences is an opportunity open to policy-makers as they promote awareness of the interdependence of humans with the natural world. It is one small but feasible step towards restoring the health of human communities and ecosystems together.

References

Bakhtin, M. (1984). *Mikhail bakhtin: The dialogical principle* (Vol. 13, T. Todorov, Trans.). Manchester: Manchester University Press.

Bayley, A. (2022). *Ecotones: Soundscapes of trees*. Retrieved from https://acoustics.ac.uk/ecotones-soundscapes-of-trees/ [Accessed September 16, 2023]

Carmichael, M. (2022). The wasp lesson. *Resurgence & Ecologist, 330*, 25–29.

Chevalier, J. M., & Buckles, D. J. (2019). *Participatory action research: Theory and methods for engaged inquiry*. London: Routledge.

Clough, N., & Tarr, J. (2022). *Addressing issues of mental health in schools through the arts: Teachers and music therapists working together*. London: Routledge.

Commission on Young Lives. (2022). *Thematic report 4: Heads up – rethinking mental health services for vulnerable young people*. Retrieved from https://thecommissionon-younglives.co.uk/wp-content/uploads/2022/07/COYL-Heads-Up-Report-July-2022.pdf [Accessed December 30, 2022]

Csikszentmihalyi, M. (1996). *Creativity: Flow and the psychology of discovery and invention*. New York: Harper Collins.

Department for Education, Department of Health (DfE, DoH). (2015). *Special educational needs and disability code of practice: 0 to 25 years* (Statutory guidance for organisations which work with and support children and young people who have special educational needs or disabilities). London: Crown Copyright.

Howard-Jones, A. R., Bowen, A. C., Danchin, M., Koirala, A., Sharma, K., Yeoh, D. K., Burgner, D. P., Crawford, N. W., Goeman, E., Gray, P. E., Hsu, P., Kuek, S., McMullan, B. J., Tosif, S., Wurzel, D., & Britton, P. N. (2022). COVID-19 in children: I. epidemiology, prevention and indirect impacts. *Journal of Paediatrics and Child Health, 58*, 39–45.

Kolb, D. A. (1976). On management and the learning process. *California Management Review, 18*(3), 21–31.

Kolb, D. A. (1984). *Experiential learning: Experience as the source of learning and development*. Englewood Cliffs, NJ: Prentice-Hall.

Malloch, S. N. (1999). Mothers and infants and communicative musicality. *Musicae Scientiae, 3*(1), 29–57.

Malloch, S. N., Sharp, D., Campbell, D. M., Campbell, A. M., & Trevarthen, C. (1997). Measuring the human voice: Analysing pitch, timing, loudness and voice quality in mother/infant communication. *Proceedings of the Institute of Acoustics, 19*(5), 495–500.

Malloch, S. N., & Trevarthen, C. (Eds.). (2009). *Communicative musicality: Exploring the basis of human companionship*. Oxford: Oxford University Press.

NHS Digital. (2021). *Mental health of children and young people in England 2021: Wave 2 follow up to the 2017 survey*. Retrieved from https://digital.nhs.uk/data-and-information/publications/statistical/mental-health-of-children-and-young-people-in-england/2021-follow-up-to-the-2017-survey [Accessed May 29, 2023]

Orr, D. W. (1992). *Ecological literacy*. New York: State University of New York Press.

Papousek, M., & Papousek, H. (1981). Musical elements in the infant's vocalisations: Their significance for communication, cognition and creativity. In L. P. Lipsitt (Ed.), *Advances in infancy research* (Vol. 1, pp. 163–224). Norwood, NJ: Ablex Publishing Corporation.

Power, E., Hughes, S., Cotter, D., & Cannon, M. (2020). Youth mental health in the time of COVID-19. *Irish Journal of Psychological Medicine*, *37*(4), 301–305.

Small, C. (1998). *Musicking: The meanings of performing and listening*. Hanover: Wesleyan University Press.

Stensaeth, K. (2015). 'Musical dialoguing': A perspective of Bakhtin's dialogue on musical improvisation in asymmetric relations. *Nordic Research in Music Education, Yearbook*, *16*, 209–225.

Tiplady, L. S. E., & Menter, H. (2020). Forest school for wellbeing: An environment in which young people can 'take what they need'. *Journal of Adventure Education and Outdoor Learning*, *21*(2), 99–114.

UNESCO. (2015). *Rethinking education: Towards a common global good?* Paris: Author.

UNESCO. (2017). *Education for sustainable development goals: Learning objectives*. Paris: Author.

Van Matre, S., & Associates. (2019). *Earth walks: An alternative nature experience*. Greenville, WV: The Institute for Earth Education.

Wall Kimmerer, R. (2020). *Braiding sweetgrass: Indigenous wisdom, scientific knowledge and the teaching of plants*. London: Penguin.

Wegerif, R. (2019). *Dialogic education*. Oxford: Oxford Research Encyclopaedia of Education. doi: 10.1093/acrefore/9780190264093.013.396 [Accessed May 14, 2023]

Wigram, T. (2004). *Improvisation: Methods and techniques for music therapy clinicians, educators, and students*. London: Jessica Kingsley.

Young Minds. (2020). *Coronavirus: Impact on young people with mental health needs*. London: Young Minds. Retrieved from https://youngminds.org.uk/media/3904/coronavirus-report-summer-2020-final.pdf [Accessed May 14, 2023]

Chapter 6

Pocket adventures

Nurturing young children's wellbeing and development through art-in-nature early childhood education

Nomisha Kurian and Ruth Sapsed

Introduction

> Under the canopy: the bent heads of snowdrops in spring, the lilt of the robins, the juniper green of a leaf-trail swinging back and forth. The children seem alive to every sound, every sight, every touch.
>
> (Extract from Nomisha's observational notes)

In this chapter, we introduce the work of Cambridge Curiosity and Imagination (CCI), an arts and wellbeing charity that works locally, nationally and internationally to build creatively healthy communities. Children and their communities are at the heart of CCI's work. CCI explores how ideas and questions can lead the way in creative explorations supported by artists. Each programme aims to help individuals become more deeply connected to the world on their doorstep, often in socio-economically disadvantaged communities.

The first author of this chapter is a CCI Community Ambassador who researches children's wellbeing (Kurian, 2022, 2023). The second author is CCI's Director, bringing over 15 years of practitioner experience furthering CCI's vision of an inclusive, accessible and creative society (Ayliff, Sapsed, Sayers, & Whitley, 2020).

Human-centred design and eco-capabilities

We adopted a two-part theoretical framework in our arts-in-nature practice described in what follows. One element is the human-centred design, used to explore the aesthetic and embodied dimensions of children's lived experiences. The other element is the eco-capabilities framework (Walshe, Moula, & Lee, 2022) to understand how the programme impacted creativity, play and wellbeing.

Human-centred design is an approach that prioritises the needs and voices of service users in emotionally-intuitive services that promote human wellbeing (IDEO, 2015). It helps place-based arts praxis achieve participatory, grassroots, collective creativity. For example, Derby Museums ('Designated' by Arts Council England as having a nationally significant collection) launched its human-centred design approach to "expand perspectives of what a museum is and can be", and

DOI: 10.4324/9781003357308-6

became the UK's first major museum designed entirely through co-production with the local community (Butler, Fox, & MacLeod, 2018).

The eco-capabilities framework pioneered by Walshe, Moula, and Lee (2022) offers a structured pathway for exploring the impact of nature on human well-being. Eight eco-capabilities can be developed in children through arts-in-nature: autonomy; bodily integrity and safety; relationality (both human and nonhuman); senses and imagination; mental and emotional wellbeing; spirituality; and identity.

CCI's design

When viewed through a human-centred design lens, CCI's ethos to designing arts-in-nature programmes can be understood, in part, as a response to a creative and spatial *design challenge*: local communities' struggles to access green spaces for creativity, health and wellbeing. On the one hand, time in green spaces has been shown to promote feelings of contentment and pleasure for individuals across varied ages, races, genders and socio-economic origins (Capaldi, Passmore, Nisbet, Zelenski, & Dopko, 2015; Richardson, Passmore, Lumber, Thomas, & Hunt, 2021). While assessing the nature-wellbeing link is beyond the scope of this chapter, we note the rich literature proposing varied mechanisms for the link between nature and wellbeing. Theoretical explanations include "biophilia" – the idea that individuals are born with an innate attraction to nature (Wilson, 1984); attention-restoration theory, which holds that nature provides complex yet appealing shapes and patterns that have a restorative effect upon mental capacity (Kaplan & Kaplan, 1989); and stress-reduction theory, which proposes that nature has a calming effect upon the body's physiological systems (Ulrich, 1983). The link between nature and enhanced health and wellbeing has thus been demonstrated.

On the other hand, inequalities in young people's access to green spaces and its subsequent health benefits are increasingly widening. The Natural Childhood Report (2012) found that, in the last 30 years, the number of children regularly playing in wild places in the UK has fallen by 90%. Given the well-documented nature-wellbeing link, it is concerning that contemporary youth may be less supported in engaging meaningfully with nature. Youth in low-income households may be still more disadvantaged, since children living in deprived areas are nine times less likely to have access to green space (National Children's Bureau, 2012). Since there is already a strong link between poverty and ill health, this means that children already at risk of poor health have the least opportunity to reap the health benefits of green space (Allen & Balfour, 2014). Tackling inequalities in access to nature thus goes hand-in-hand with addressing health inequalities more broadly.

CCI seeks to address these issues by helping people trust in their own creativity, learning from artists' creative practices and creating spaces in nature for children to flourish. The organisation was founded in response to concerns about the stripping away of children's freedoms, particularly in the UK education system and the impact on their future. CCI projects involve people of all ages. They take place in various spaces, including schools, nature reserves, hospitals and playgrounds. The

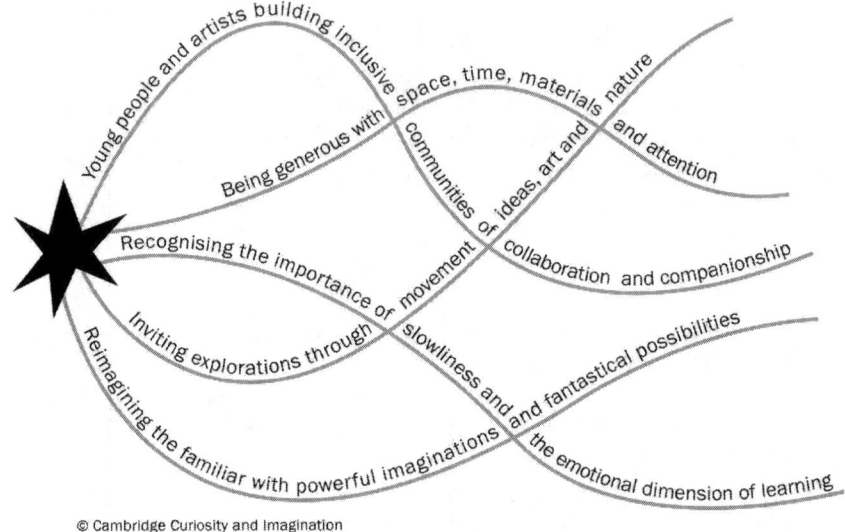

© Cambridge Curiosity and Imagination

Figure 6.1 Cambridge Curiosity and Imagination (CCI) core design principles/
threads of practice

charity prioritises recruiting socio-economically disadvantaged families and young people for its programmes, as they are less likely to have access to green space. As part of the Fullscope consortium, the charity works collaboratively to support children and young people's health and wellbeing in Cambridgeshire and Peterborough.

Much of CCI's work is grounded in green spaces. However, well-structured design principles govern *how* CCI supports communities in engaging with green spaces. Figure 6.1 captures the principles/threads of practice which underpin all CCI's programmes. Taken together, these principles embody an approach to working locally to make art in the outdoors that CCI calls 'Artscaping', defined as to affect and be affected by art, nature and space; to create a response from materials and feelings in order to express new ideas; and to enhance the environment in ways that delight (Figure 6.1). These ways of working are woven into everything from how projects are planned at the outset to every experience and invitation that those involved are offered through to how the work is documented and shared at the end.

Pocket adventures: methodology

CCI's interest in learning from and with children sits at the heart of the design for the project 'Pocket Adventures' that we describe here. Cambridgeshire County Council's 'Talking Together' team was commissioning innovative approaches to support the "50 things to do before you're five" app, a free resource they provide to help parents develop their home learning environment. The app shares a wide range of low-cost and no-cost local activities and CCI's aim was to bring some of these to life, led by local young children. CCI had begun to work with a local primary school (given the pseudonym of the "Abbey School" in this chapter) back in 2019 through the Eco-Capabilities programme (Walshe et al., 2022), where two classes of eight- and nine-year-olds had spent eight sessions with artists and their educators discovering a small and tangled nature reserve on the back fence of their school (the reserve has been given the pseudonym 'Hawthorne' in this chapter). They had grown to love and cherish this space and a small number from this original group then worked with artist Sally Todd to support children from the nursery and reception classes on this new project.

The project aimed to co-create a series of 'Pocket Adventure' cards showcasing children's explorations of their local green space. Educators, CCI volunteers, 12 four and five-year-old Nursery and Reception pupils and four Year 5 pupils joined Sally for the project. The older children were encouraged to work as peer mentors. There were six sessions out in Hawthorne Nature Reserve, all following CCI's core design principles.

In our findings, we draw on three sources of data: observational notes created by Nomi, who was acting as a CCI community ambassador during her ethnographic immersion in the field-site; exploratory interviews with Sally Todd as the lead artist-educator leading the project; and interviews with teachers and families to assess the outcomes of the project. Consent was gathered from all families and children through official CCI forms signed prior to the commencement of the project. Pseudonyms have been used for all children and families.

We used deductive coding to identify patterns and themes within the data and draw conclusions based on the theoretical frameworks of human-centred design and eco-capabilities. This meant that our data analysis connected the socio-material design elements of CCI's practice to children's social, emotional and intellectual experiences in the nature reserve. We note that the eco-capabilities framework contains a range of possible abilities that can be nurtured in a natural environment. Given the multiple dimensions of Pocket Adventures – from rapport-building with the children to co-creating cards – numerous opportunities for analysis emerge. However, we focus specifically on dimensions of children's lived experiences that proved particularly relevant to the aims of this book: autonomy and play, identity and relationality.

Findings and discussion

Autonomy and play

The nature reserve was part of a forest space, which was chosen for its capacity to offer children a more intense sense of expansiveness than they were used to – a novelty that could be both daunting and liberating, as the lead artist-educator attests:

> The environment holds us; it provides a framework. Hawthorne is not the wildest place, but it is beyond the school gates and has a sense of wildness. It's actually a very small space. If you look at it on a map, you can sense its parameters.

But a place like this, it does some alchemy to our minds. It's a bit like a Tardis; it feels expansive. To a four-year-old, this must feel enormous. The bendiness of the trees, the wildness. The freedom may even be a bit uncomfortable at times. But the children became so emboldened.

(Sally)

Accessing this spatial contrast to school helped children reclaim the autonomy to play. Our previous research has shown young children thriving in joyful play (Kurian, 2023). Yet, as noted by a pioneering early years educationalist, play comes under threat when children enter formal schooling and find their free time restricted:

For five years, an intuitive program called play has worked so well. . . . Then the children enter school and find, strangely enough, that this natural theatre they have been performing, this playfully deep fantasy approach to life is no longer acceptable, is no longer valid. Suddenly they begin to hear, "Do that playing outside, after your work". This is a serious problem, for when play is eliminated, the model for story making is eliminated as well.

(Paley, 1997, p. 122)

CCI aims to reclaim this "natural theatre". In contrast to the overly prescriptive schooling that Paley (1997) critiques, Pocket Adventures was designed to provide more mindful engagement with time and space. Whilst site-checks of Hawthorne were always conducted prior to artscaping so that health and safety hazards were cleared by adults, natural formations (e.g., rocky outcrops, trailing brambles, leafy trails) were embraced as spaces for the children to discover and explore freely. Adults were continually on standby as a friendly, safe, but non-directive presence. The programme was thus designed to embrace the sensory abundance of the forest in a safe yet exploratory way, a balance that triggered rich, complex play behaviour.

For example, being surrounded by objects of varying sizes, shapes and states of motion (from a still leaf to a fast-moving stream) stimulated children to engage in schematic play. This is a type of play that involves repetitive action; in the early years, children often feel a powerful drive to repeat actions, such as moving in circles, jumping up and down, throwing objects or moving them from one point to another (Louis, Featherstone, Macgraw, Hayes, & Beswick, 2013). Schematic play can be seen as disruptive, nonsensical or futile. Indeed, amidst the fast pace of mainstream classrooms, young children are often chastised for engaging in repetitive actions that look non-productive (Grimmer, 2021). However, schematic play is valuable for learning through repetition, helping children to represent and develop their ideas about the world and developing their creativity and intellectual curiosity.

A strength of Pocket Adventures was that, by abandoning the timetabling and prescribed routines of a typical lesson, the design of the programme allowed multiple forms of schematic play to emerge by enfolding children in natural stimuli in free-flowing, unstructured time and space. Table 6.1 below offers a glimpse into these spontaneous play behaviours.

Table 6.1 Types of schematic play observed in Pocket Adventures

Type of schematic play	Examples observed in Pocket Adventures
Transporting	Carrying leaves to build a house.
Trajectory	Watching the movement of the nearby stream and the flight path of nearby magpies and robins.
Enveloping	Covering soil with petals.
Vertical and circular movement	Jumping, brandishing twigs, swinging back and forth on a leaf trail.
Collecting	Gathering 'treasure-troves' – a tarpaulin sheet was spread on the forest floor and children were instructed to collect objects they found memorable or special. These collections included magpie feathers and heart-shaped leaves.
Hiding	The children called nooks and crannies they found in the nature reserve 'secret tunnels'.

Hawthorne also differed from more regulated play spaces, as Sally said:

If you offered a prescribed space like a playground, the children would not react that way. They began to move independently through those spaces from week to week. A relaxing of their body, a sense of being so preoccupied with exploring this wonderful distraction of the space. They would move beyond clinging to the adults or the children that they normally hung out with in school.

(Sally)

One mother made a similar point about space and agency:

The thing about Hawthorne is that it is quite a wild space. It is not a playground. It is quite organic. There are spaces in it to really explore. He (my son) liked the untamed elements and seeing an odd animal. He'd come home and say, "I saw a deer". You're out of the classroom environment; you're out of the school grounds. Letting them feel they are experiencing something different. Elements of light and shade. They need a space where they're not observed, where they can jump out of places. . . . Not being prescribed . . . that's the important part of being in the natural world. It sparks their imagination. Children are always drawn to the margins, spaces they have freedom. Climbing over something, making their way over something, especially if they get muddy. They need to explore freely to be able to have those challenges.

(Mother of child-participant)

These narratives prompt reflection on the possibilities of different spaces opening up (or closing down) for autonomy as an eco-capability, depending on whether spaces are designed to convey messages of restraint and restriction or exploration and privacy. Human-centred design practitioners have pointed out that even play-ful designs that claim to foster fun and enjoyment can become "a prison" if they set out to prescribe exactly how, what and where to play (Köknar, 2019, p. 11). This reflects our interviewees' objections to restricted spaces. Children's responses to the wilderness of Hawthorne support growing calls in human-centred design research for playful designs to honour "blank spaces" where individuals derive their own meanings from the play space (Köknar, 2019, p. 11).

In addition to enabling the type of free-flowing play marginalised in traditional schooling, the autonomy that children gained in Hawthorne may have encouraged growth in confidence.

> One of the nursery children, from week to week, took ownership of that little bit of woodland and became independent rather than watching peripherally. He moved material, picked up sticks and mapped out a place for himself. I felt he was emboldened through this offer of an open invitation rather than me say-ing, "We're going to this place to do this and this". His teacher remarked on his behaviour as being quite distinct as he began talking very animatedly about Hawthorne. His mother also remarked on the change in her son, a sense of con-fidence, something being unleashed, a physical expansion.
>
> (Sally)

Our previous research has found that being given opportunities to make choices and exercise agency (even in seemingly small actions) can support children's confidence that they matter as full individuals (Kurian & Cremin, 2023). Sally's testimony suggests how a blend of natural stimuli and unstructured playtime can support the eco-capability of autonomy. In Hawthorne, children's creativity and wellbeing were nurtured in environments free of rebuke, censure and restriction.

Senses and imagination

Another eco-capability that proved to be closely connected to free play and auton-omy was senses and imagination. Human-centred design considers sensory-rich design to be an effective tool for fully engaging the user through multiple modali-ties, from sight to smell to touch (IDEO, 2015). The eco-capabilities framework places similar value on developing one's senses and imagination (Walshe et al., 2022).

In Pocket Adventures, children frequently utilised their senses and imagina-tion through their abundant opportunities for socio-dramatic play. This is a type of 'make-believe' play that involves children using objects, language, space or move-ment to represent something else; it has long been identified as crucial for social, linguistic, cognitive and emotional development, as it develops key skills such as meta-cognition, self-regulation, literacy, planning and problem-solving (White-bread, Coltman, Jameson, & Lander, 2009). The design of the Pocket Adventures played an important role in promoting socio-dramatic play; the following snippets of peer dialogue suggest how physical elements of the reserve became transformed into fantastical spaces in the children's imaginations.

Tim:	*spotting a hollow in the ground* "That's a bear cave".
Arabella:	*jabbing twig back and forth and manoeuvring smaller stick on top of it* "This is my pet horse and I'm feeding him a carrot".
Laura, Tania and Makis:	*poking sticks into the ground in carefully coordinated unison* "We're digging for diamonds".
Arabella:	*spotting branches significantly bigger than her* "We need to run! This is a giant's garden!"
Paula:	*touches hair ribbon to leaf, puts leaf on hair* "I've got fairy hair, you know. The woods make me a fairy".

Our previous research has found that fantastical stories carry the unique power to captivate young children's imaginations, fuel their curiosity and foster their emotional and cognitive development (Kurian, 2023). Indeed, in Hawthorne, children's journeys of discovery included numerous fantastical stories and imaginings:

When we sat around in a circle with the children and asked them to describe Hawthorne, the words that emerged were hairy fields, strawberry fields, tweety fields, bramble bush . . . brambleforest. It has 1,000 trees, a jungle swing, the boot eater tree, the unicorn boat house tree, heart-shaped leaves, furry leaves, spiky leaves, stripy leaves, a secret tunnel . . . and a bear cave.

(Sally)

Many of these imaginings evoke what early years psychologists have called "dizzy" play – when the conventional rules of reality are subverted in favour of surreality and humour (Wood, 2014). Hawthorne became more than a physical site. In line with the participatory nature of human-centred design, children became symbolic *co-designers* of the space, reshaping it through their imagination. These musings even included frightening or disturbing meanings.

The children said they saw "ghosts in the tree" – maybe they'd heard a ghost story. Many children said they were the monster; some chased the others. I think this is primal for us as humans; we need to be able to build up strategies for dealing with fear. That is the important role of fairytales in our life. There is a need for us to be emboldened by facing up to things that frighten us. I saw this rippling through their play. As humans, we are shaped by these fears, and we come up with strategies.

(Sally)

Socio-dramatic play in the forest could thus include pretend play to process anxieties and fears, turning Hawthorne into a site of emotionally complex mythmaking.

Identity and entangled eco-capabilities

Walshe et al. (2022) allude to eco-capabilities potentially being entangled and interconnected (p. 19). This section develops this notion, using the term 'entangled eco-capabilities' to capture abilities that grow together in overlapping ways. To this end, we examine identity, which the framework defines as the qualities, beliefs, personality and expressions that characterise an individual; and how identity is shaped by relationality, which the framework defines in both human and nonhuman terms as expressing care and concern for fellow humans and for nature respectively (Walshe et al., 2022). A striking example of entangled eco-capabilities emerged from nine-year-old Rob's acts of selfhood and mythical identity-making:

Rob: Pan is God of the Wild. He has goat legs and a horn.
Nomi: Have you ever seen Pan?
Rob: Yes. I am Pan.
Nomi: Does Pan live near you?
Rob: Very near. Because I am him.

Rob's roleplay as Pan included safeguarding flowers and foliage:

Rob: *holding up snowdrop he tucked into his coat pocket on the way home* This one died because somebody trampled near it. So I'm keeping it. I hate the human world because some people throw rubbish around in nature. People do bad things. I'm Pan, God of the Wild. So look, I put the snowdrop here in my coat pocket. I'm going to protect it. I have a snowdrop charm.

In setting out to protect fragile nonhuman life, Rob's socio-dramatic play developed his identity as a steward of nature. Rob became known as the 'Snowdrop Guardian' by other children. Eventually, he chose to embody this identity visually while artscaping (Figure 6.2).

Rob's self-depiction affirms his sense of ecological stewardship. His guardian-avatar wields a staff confidently, connoting strength and protectiveness. Tree and sky blur together and hover above Rob, bigger than the human figure, suggesting that Rob sees himself not as dominating nature but harmoniously ensconced *within* it. Hawthorne seems to have transmitted 'place-responsive pedagogy' – that is, empowering children like Rob to nurture human-environment relationships in organic, spontaneous ways (Mannion et al., 2012, p. 792). Simultaneously, Rob's sketch suggests how art provides "the space to do, see, be and believe in children's real and imagined worlds' and 'understand the ways children do, see, be and believe in themselves" (Hickey-Moody, Horn, Willcox, & Florence, 2021, p. 3). His mingling of senses, imagination and identity suggests the potential of designing for *entangled* eco-capabilities: eco-capabilities that grow together in overlapping and symbiotic ways, like trees with shared roots.

Figure 6.2 The 'Snowdrop Guardian': A Forest Guardian for Bramblefields Nature Reserve, co-created by Sally Todd with Shirley Primary School community for the Fantastical Forest

Implications for practice

Foregrounding the voices of artists, children and their families, this chapter explored how an art-in-nature environment was mindfully designed to promote imaginative play and autonomy and develop children's sense of identity and engagement with their senses and imagination. The following implications for practice should be considered by practitioners offering arts-in-nature experiences to children and young people:

1. Offering children a sense of expansiveness and novelty in their play environments is key. A natural space can provide this, even if it is relatively small.
2. Recognise the value of play in children's development and be mindful of how schooling can sometimes limit it.
3. Consider how the natural environment differs from more regulated play spaces, such as playgrounds. Recognise that children may react differently to each type of space and consider the benefits of offering a more organic, untamed space for play.
4. Create opportunities for play that are free-flowing, unstructured and not overly prescriptive. Allow children to feel agency. Let them stretch their imagination.
5. Embrace the sensory abundance of a natural space, while conducting site-checks to ensure health and safety hazards are cleared. Achieving a balance of safety and freedom is possible, even with very young children.
6. Be a friendly and safe but non-directive presence. Allow children to discover and explore freely.
7. Recognise the value of schematic play, which involves repetitive action, and encourage it in natural environments. Schematic play is valuable for learning through repetition and can help children develop their creativity and intellectual curiosity.
8. Giving children creative tools (e.g., drawings about their time in green space) can allow them to express and process their evolving relationship with the environment. It can also be a chance to express positive roleplays through socio-dramatic play (e.g., expressing a new identity as a protector, steward or friend of nature).

While these recommendations are child-centred, they can also be adapted for adults in age-appropriate ways.

Conclusion

We close with a practitioner's words that sum up CCI's desire to provide creative refuge through ways of being and learning in nature that are multi-sensory, exploratory, embodied and emplaced:

> The children we work with are very vulnerable – many don't have a place they feel they can go in their community where they feel safe. Many spend little or no time outside. Many speak regularly about death and sadness. Yet the children

who have joined projects we've run with CCI often say that these are their favourite two hours of the week, that they notice how happy they feel outside. This work is therapeutic, but not therapy.

(*Matt Edge, CEO and Therapeutic Practitioner,*
Cambridge Acorn Project, June 2022)

Integrating a human-centred design and eco-capabilities lens has helped us stress the value of designing playful environments in nature. In the words of CCI patron and award-winning author Robert Macfarlane, it appears timely to "tip a little wonder back into the world" (CCI, 2022).

References

Allen, J., & Balfour, R. (2014). *Natural solutions for tackling health inequalities*. London: UCL Institute of Health Equity. Retrieved from www.instituteofhealthequity.org/resources-reports/natural-solutions-to-tackling-health-inequalities/naturalsolutions-to-tackling-health-inequalities.pdf [Accessed February 11, 2022]

Ayliffe, P., Sapsed, R., Sayers, E., & Whitley, D. (2020). *Artscapers: Being and becoming creative*. Cambridge: Cambridge Curiosity and Imagination.

Butler, T., Fox, H., & MacLeod, S. (2018). Placing citizens at the heart of museum development: Derby Silk Mill – Museum of making. In S. MacLeod, T. Austin, J. Hale, & O. Hing-Kay (Eds.), *The future of museum and gallery design* (pp. 160–174). London: Routledge.

Capaldi, C. A., Passmore, H. A., Nisbet, E. K., Zelenski, J. M., & Dopko, R. L. (2015). Flourishing in nature: A review of the benefits of connecting with nature and its application as a wellbeing intervention. *International Journal of Wellbeing, 5*(4), 1–16. doi: 10.5502/ijw.v5i4.449

CCI. (2023). *Trustee recruitment pack*. Retrieved from https://cambridgecandi.org.uk/sites/default/files/2023-11/CCI%20Board%20pack%20Nov%202023.pdf

Grimmer, T. (2021). *Developing a loving pedagogy in the early years: How love fits with professional practice*. London: Routledge.

Hickey-Moody, A., Horn, C., Willcox, M., & Florence, E. (2021). *Arts-based methods for research with children*. London: Springer Nature.

IDEO. (2015). *The field guide to human-centred design. A step-by-step guide that will get you solving problems like a designer*. New York: Author.

Kaplan, R., & Kaplan, S. (1989). *The experience of nature: A psychological perspective*. New York: Cambridge University Press.

Köknar, C. (2019). Who is at the center? Designing playful experiences by using player-centred approach. In *International Conference on Human-Computer Interaction* (pp. 11–21). Cham: Springer.

Kurian, N. (2022). School as a sanctuary: Trauma-informed care to nurture child well-being in high-poverty schools. In A. Green (Ed.), *Springer international handbook of education development in Asia-Pacific*. London: Springer.

Kurian, N. (2023). Building inclusive, multicultural early years classrooms: Strategies for a culturally responsive ethic of care. *Early Childhood Education Journal*, 1–16. doi: 10.1007/s10643-023-01456-0

Kurian, N., & Cremin, H. (2023). Helping young people feel that they matter: Promoting students' eudaimonic wellbeing and agency to build peace. In P. Trifonas (Ed.), *Springer handbook of curriculum theory and practice*. London: Springer.

Louis, S., Featherstone, S., Macgraw, L., Hayes, L., & Beswick, C. (2013). *Understanding schemas in young children: Again! again!* London: Bloomsbury Publishing PLC.

Mannion, G., Fenwick, A., & Lynch, J. (2012). Place-responsive pedagogy: Learning from teachers' experiences of excursions in nature. *Environmental Education Research*, *19*(6), 792–809. doi: 10.1080/13504622.2012.749980

National Children's Bureau. (2012). *Environmental inequalities and their impact on the health outcomes of children and young people: Policy and evidence briefing* [online]. Retrieved from www.ncb.org.uk/sites/default/files/uploads/files/Environmental%2520Inequalities.pdf [Accessed February 11, 2022]

Natural Trust. (2012). *Natural childhood report* [online]. Retrieved from https://nt.global.ssl.fastly.net/documents/read-our-naturalchildhood-report.pdf [Accessed February 11, 2022]

Paley, V. G. (1997). *Story and play: The original learning tools*. Cambridge, MA: Harvard University Press.

Richardson, M., Passmore, H.-A., Lumber, R., Thomas, R., & Hunt, A. (2021). Moments, not minutes: The nature-wellbeing relationship. *International Journal of Wellbeing*, *11*(1), 8–33. doi: 10.5502/ijw.v11i1.1267

Ulrich, R. S. (1983). Aesthetic and affective response to natural environment. In I. Altman & J. F. Wohlwill (Eds.), *Behaviour and the natural environment* (pp. 85–125). Boston, MA: Springer.

Walshe, N., Moula, Z., & Lee, E. (2022). Eco-capabilities as a pathway to wellbeing and sustainability. *Sustainability*, *14*(6), 3582.

Whitebread, D., Coltman, P., Jameson, H., & Lander, R. (2009). Play, cognition and self-regulation: What exactly are children learning when they learn through play? *Educational and Child Psychology*, *26*(2), 40–52.

Wilson, E. O. (1984). *Biophilia*. Cambridge, MA: Harvard University Press.

Wood, G. (2014). *Surreal things: Surrealism and design*. UK: V&A Publishing.

Chapter 7

The Village Project

A community of relational creativity

Alan Cusack

Introduction

At 9 a.m. on a Monday morning in the third week of June, 50 Year 8 students enter a small screened-off wooded area behind the tennis courts where they will live together for a week. For the rest of the year, it is an underused area of the school. A liminal space that has escaped the formal occupation of classrooms, labs, and gyms typical of the school institution. A quiet place where the canopy of tall syca-more trees dampens the noise of the nearby playground and tennis court. It is only 50 meters from the main school grounds but could not be further away. The site reveals little of what took place the previous year. Disappearing desire lines still crisscross rhizomatically through the forest floor, faintly mapping the movements of last year's Village and connecting sites once deemed important. By this evening, the site will be transformed when this small stretch of woodland will once again be shared with 50 12-year-old students. In small groups of four or five, they will have built huts from sustainable materials and will be cooking their first meal together on an open fire, nervously speculating on the days ahead when they will be given more responsibility than they have possibly ever experienced. They will have no electronic devices or contact with the outside world. They will establish their own rules and govern themselves. They will have the opportunity to work alongside creative practitioners or initiate their own activities. They may do nothing at all. The site will be one of a number of transformations that will take place this week.

A brief history of the Village Project

King Alfred School is an informal independent day school in North London. It was founded in 1898 by a group of liberal parents and intellectuals who were concerned with conventional Victorian educational practices at the time. The school aimed to provide a progressive education by adopting child-centred learning theories, privileged outdoor education, and a hands-on approach to learning. It was originally intended to be a 'demonstration' school where innovative approaches to pedagogy could be developed with a view to contributing to the wider educational debate. With increasingly similar concerns today, the Village Project has become

DOI: 10.4324/9781003357308-7

an integral part of the school's curriculum and a unique opportunity to explore theories of teaching and learning through practice.

The project was established in 1990 by the head of Design and Technology at the time, Stephen de Brett. A somewhat radical figure, de Brett had previously trained as a person-centred psychotherapist under the leading psychologist Carl Rogers. A series of personal experiences, including facilitating cross-cultural workshops across Europe and accidentally stumbling into Woodstock, contributed to de Brett's ideas about education. He wanted to give students greater control over their learning and provide an opportunity to explore what it means to be part of a community. The first Village consisted of thatched huts made from straw, willow, and hundreds of saplings, felled by the students themselves. Initially, the scale of the project meant it was only feasible biannually. Two further Village Projects took place in 1992 and 1994, exploring various hut-building techniques, but due to the construction time and its impact on the wider curriculum, it was eventually deemed unsustainable. However, reflecting on the value of these early experiences and recognising the potential, a revised Village Project was reintroduced as an annual event in 2012 and continues to be a vital part of the King Alfred School narrative.

The project was initially developed from the psychological ideas of Carl Rogers, who believed that therapeutic practices could be more effective, and more positive, if understood as 'client-centred'. Rogers' 'humanistic psychology' would later inform his contributions to education and student-centred learning. In both contexts, Rogers believed that the quality of the relationship between the client and psychologist or teacher and student is of most significance. He believed this relationship should be underpinned by three core conditions: Empathy, Congruence, and Unconditional Positive Regard. When these conditions are met, individuals have the natural capacity towards growth and reaching their full potential in a process he referred to as the *actualising tendency* (Rogers, 1995). These core conditions would form the bedrock upon which the Village Project was established. It addressed concerns over the diminishing agency found in schooling at the time and provided an opportunity for what de Brett (2022) describes as *experiential citizenship;* one that investigated ideas of democracy while cultivating a sense of ownership over one's own learning.

The project has also focussed on a particular age group, which has been noted for its own concerns. A Government report published in 2015 described Key Stage 3 as the 'wasted years' of education, suggesting more priority should be given to "timetabling, assessment, and monitoring of pupils' progress" (OFSTED, 2015). Year 8, in particular, is often regarded as lacking purpose or a "clear and compelling identity" and is defined by a dip in both attainment and motivation (Galton, Gray, & Rudduck, 2003, p. 93). This can often result in behavioural issues in which many teachers may find an unconditional positive regard difficult to maintain. While numerous factors have been attributed to this decline, including poor teaching and inconsistent homework, it seems unlikely that more assessment and monitoring would contribute positively to the wellbeing of most 12-year-olds. A heightened awareness of emerging adulthood can sometimes be at odds with the lived reality in Year 8 where there is a "widespread failure to acknowledge pupils' social maturity and their readiness to take on more responsibility" (Galton et al., 2003, p. 95). Research carried out in the US by Eccles and her colleagues argue that the apathy often assumed by adolescents is "less a consequence of students' developmental stage than of the mismatch between students' needs and the opportunities afforded them" (Eccles et al., 1993, p. 567). The Village Project is an opportunity to provide greater autonomy and creative freedom in a bid to re-imagine the potential of the 'wasted' year of education.

A community of relational creative practice

Although originally underpinned by Rogerian ideas of the self and community, the Village Project affords a unique opportunity to explore how we learn. It has become increasingly informed by pedagogical theories such as Jean Lave and Eteinne Wenger's ideas around "situated learning" and "communities of practice" (Lave, 1991; Wenger, 2008) in which learning is understood as "a social phenomenon constituted in the experienced, lived-in world, through legitimate peripheral participation in ongoing social practice" (Lave, 1991, p. 64). A crucial aspect of Lave and Wegner's model is the legitimacy of the practice taking place. For example, the Villagers spend a considerable amount of time learning how to design and build huts from sustainable materials, not to demonstrate an abstract notion of knowledge but to have somewhere to sleep. During the week, the students work alongside highly skilled practitioners to collaboratively produce artworks and artefacts that have utility in the Village. These makers and doers are not necessarily teachers, not in any formal sense at least, and so different kinds of learning can take place. The dialogue between material, process, and participants offers rich opportunities for sensory and embodied learning and questions teacher/student relationships. It also clearly reveals teaching and learning as a social enterprise. In his plea for a communalist teaching, Sennet argues that "Innovation is collective activity" occurring through "dialogic conversation" (Sennet in Geilen & Bruyne, 2012, p. 40). This social aspect is something Carl Rogers also deemed important. Despite being written in the 1950s, his theories of creativity included a concern for the relational:

> My definition, then, of the creative process is that it is the emergence in action of a novel relational product, growing out of the uniqueness of the individual on the one hand, and the materials, events, people, or circumstances of his life on the other.
>
> (Rogers, 1954, p. 251)

Rogers recognised the impact creativity has on wellbeing and self-actualisation. However, collaborative approaches to creativity can often be at odds with a prevailing perception of the artist as an individual genius. As a secondary school art teacher, I witnessed a decline in artistic engagement during early adolescence, often accompanied by the phrase "I can't draw". Fear of failure at this stage of development can have a negative impact on wellbeing and lead to "possible self-schemata that define life goals and life tasks in terms of present failure, rather than future possibilities" (Anderman & Maehr, 1994, p. 292). Artistic practices have the capacity to offer alternative and arguably more inclusive ways of knowing through embodied and affective learning experiences. These opportunities can become quickly effaced in the school setting where the criteria are often structured around measurable individual achievement. These assessment-based regimes have sustained a misalignment between contemporary art practice and what is taught in schools. Recent developments in contemporary art have been more concerned with social relations than the production of material objects by an individual artist. Such practices include the relational, participatory, dialogical and socially-engaged.[1] Despite this growing trend, art in schools has largely held on to a selective modernist model of art education, principally concerned with aesthetics and characterised by formalist and reproductive exercises that "effectively exclude the learners' voices, or learners as directors of their own learning" (Adams, 2013, p. 243). Adams and Owens (2016) argue that, in fact, the "practice of education has many parallels with relational art practices" (p. 55), suggesting that an art education beyond aesthetics might offer new, and more productive, ways of thinking about learning through the arts. The Village Project can be conceptualised as a relational art practice; one that privileges the social and views art as an encounter or an event rather than the production of easily assessed or commodifiable objects.

Crucially, the Village Project is also an outdoor learning experience. When we leave the classroom, we leave behind many of the perceptions associated with artistic activity, and the dominance of individual self-expression can give way to more open-ended opportunities. The natural environment in this context makes for a wonderfully unlevel playing field, one in which:

> Learners are engaged intellectually, emotionally, socially, politically, spiritually, and physically in an uncertain environment where the learner may experience success, failure, adventure, and risk taking. The learning usually involves interaction between learners, learner and educator, and learner and environment.
>
> (Itin, 1999, p. 93)

The inclusivity relational creative practices provide is arguably beneficial for wellbeing, but so too is the environment in which it takes place. Hoad, Deed, and Lugg (2013) argues that working in the natural environment "increases the potential for building awareness of different perspectives on the world" (p. 43). The Village has always been concerned with working in and with nature. The creative practitioners invited to take a residency all have expertise in nature-based materials and processes. However, it has largely been the relationship between the agents within the Village that has been the primary area of research. What has become apparent, particularly following the pandemic, is the significance of the natural environment; not just as a setting for the learning that takes place but as an active agent within that dynamic social process.

Latour's Actor-Network Theory (ANT) (1999) provides an alternative social structure of the Village Project, one in which both human and non-human actants have the same amount of agency. In this conceptualisation, diverse elements such as the practitioner, the tools they are using, and the woods in which they are situated have social roles within the network, and each has a script to be enacted (Latour, 1999, p. 177). The theory is often applied to social contexts concerning technology, such as a hospital, where the relationship and interactions between disparate elements, such as medical and non-medical professionals, equipment, and technology are analysed to understand the function of the system better. The entanglement of human and non-human social actants that constitute the Village presents an array of relations and opportunities for dialogue and participation in which the non-human elements of the natural environment are understood as actors and not "hapless bearers of symbolic projection" (Latour, 2005, p. 10). This is a useful approach when we consider creativity as a relational activity, its impact on the young people engaging in that activity, and the role nature plays in those relations. It reveals a dialogic relationship in which learning events are determined just as much by the natural environment as by the student or the teacher and an understanding for the students that these events also "affect or change the environment" (Itin, 1999, p. 95).

The Village Project 2022

While the first day of the Village is loaded with anticipation and perhaps a little anxiety, the students have not arrived unprepared. They have spent the previous half-term preparing for the week. Most subject areas have oriented their curriculum to support and inform the project. In Design and Technology, the students have been experimenting with modular hut building designs using sustainable materials. In Geography, they have been learning about sustainability practices that may be applied throughout the week. In History, they have been learning about forms of government in preparation for their own society. In Art, they have been working with ceramics, ready to be fired in the Village raku kiln. In English, they have been studying relevant texts and developing public speaking skills. They have also had PSHE and extra-curricular time dedicated to practicalities such as personal hygiene, fire safety, and food preparation, as well as an introduction to more complex skills such as conflict resolution strategies. The students have spent a substantial amount of time learning how to communicate as a large group and practise various forms of representation that will constitute the politics of the Village.

The project is staffed by a core team of eight teachers from different departments and several sixth form students who camp just outside the main Village area. All other members of staff are also invited to work with the students at any time, but like everything in the Village, this is optional. This is often used as an opportunity for teachers to share a passion or interest that is not necessarily their subject area. Previously, we have had scientists teach painting, mathematicians build pizza ovens, and members of the estates team facilitate guided meditation.

Additional creative practitioners were invited to participate, including bushcrafters, blacksmiths, a storyteller, martial artists, a sculptor, and a ceramicist.

On Monday morning, the students enter the empty strip of woodland with their belongings and will not leave until Friday evening. We have our first morning meeting, which takes the shape of a large circle around a communal fire in a clearing in the middle of the site; a ritual that is repeated every day. A talking stick is passed around, and each person introduces themselves, revealing something they are looking forward to and something they are worried about. The external practitioners are also introduced, explaining what they will be doing throughout the week and inviting participation. When the meeting closes, the individual groups get together and start building their huts for the week. The students are now familiar with the tools and materials provided and are encouraged to work independently to construct their huts. Some groups work remarkably well together – others less so, but by the end of the day, they will sleep in whatever they build.

The first day of the Village is about establishing the space. While the students are building their huts, the blacksmiths are setting up a forge, the sculptor is constructing an outdoor studio, and the bushcrafters are creating their own space for nature-based activities. Lunch is a relatively quick affair consisting of sandwiches and fruit so as not to disrupt the momentum of the day. By late afternoon, all the huts have been constructed and the students have settled into their new homes. It is a day of intense activity in which the small strip of woodland is quickly transformed into a thriving village of 12 huts and various communal spaces.

The evening meal is cooked in open fire pits. The Villagers retrieve food from the Village pantry and prepare and cook their own dinner. For many, this is the first time they will have prepared a meal, and the experience of sharing food together under the trees can leave a lasting impression. After the evening meal has been cleared up, there is a campfire sing-along around the communal fire and an opportunity to get everyone together and reflect on the day.

The only other rule of the Village is bedtime. Students are in their own huts by 10 and lights out by 10:30 p.m. This is a necessary expectation to maintain positive relations with the neighbouring houses, something the students understand and largely respect. The first night can be unpredictable, and sleep can be elusive for both students and staff. Some students are excited to be sleeping outside with their friends; others are very anxious.

Tuesday is the first proper day of the Village. Logs are split and fires are lit for breakfasts of varying ambition. Our morning circle begins at 9:30 a.m., and while it is not mandatory to attend, everyone does. The talking stick is passed around, and we discuss the previous night and the day ahead. A large blackboard is populated with activities that are taking place – some of these are facilitated by external practitioners, while others are student-led. There is no timetable for the day and no formal lessons as such. The realisation that they will be leading their own learning can be a difficult proposition for many students. The blacksmiths, sculptors, and bushcrafters will not be delivering 'lessons' but performing their identities as creative practitioners and inviting collaboration. Some students make their way to the forge and ask if they can make axes. Some join the bushcrafters in whittling and making cookies from foraged nettles. Some hang a slackline between two trees to practise tightrope walking. Some find a foot-operated pottery wheel and take turns throwing pots of varying success. On the first day, however, many use this new freedom to do nothing. They will simply hang out with their hut mates.

During lunch, there is a council meeting, where a representative from each hut meets to discuss life in the Village. Issues such as stolen firewood, noisy neighbours, or untidy hut members often come up, and the Villagers are encouraged to deal with these issues independently but can ask for guidance when necessary. Conducting effective meetings can be a difficult task, so the early meetings are often facilitated by sixth form students who have previous experience with the project. By the end of the week, it is hoped that these meetings will be entirely student-led. After lunch, there is a whole Village meeting, this time delivered by the council, where they give feedback on any issues raised. After the meeting, the afternoon activities continue. In addition to the practitioners, a collection of resources is made available to the Villagers, including musical instruments, tools, and materials. There are also printed instructions and the necessary resources for a range of activities, such as how to build a trebuchet or how to make a kite. These activities can be undertaken at any time without adult supervision or guidance. Throughout the week, students form groups, work collaboratively to decipher instructions, try things out, and make a lot of mistakes. However, every year, without fail, a pizza oven made from kitty litter will appear somewhere in the Village.

The Village demon

As the week progresses, the Village takes on a life of its own, taking on an identity that distinguishes it from previous years. With increasingly less adult intervention, the students become more confident in exercising autonomy, making decisions, and taking responsibility. With each conflict, there is growth and new understandings. During this time, the practitioners continue building their communities of practice. Two martial artists run a series of Japanese Jujutsu workshops, a storyteller spends Wednesday collecting and sharing stories, and on Thursday, a ceramicist installs a raku kiln in the heart of the Village.

Throughout the entire week, the resident sculptor has been collaborating with the students on a huge Village demon. The idea is loosely based on the Balinese ritual of purification, where individual villages build giant demonic puppets and burn them the day before the New Year. The Village demon is a large installation situated between trees; its form is dictated by the space it occupies. The sculpture changes every day, growing with the Village. Skills that have been learnt in other situations, such as knot-tying, lashing, and whittling have been brought to the sculpture. It is adorned by found objects, foraged foliage, and wrought iron forms forged with the blacksmiths. It is an assemblage of the many narratives of this year's Village. The condition of its construction is in constant negotiation between the participants – both past and present – the materials and processes employed, and the space in which it is situated.

These relations create a highly discursive environment requiring questioning, reflection, and critical thinking. Importantly, it creates a safe space for dialogue. Although the Village Project is underpinned by notions of democracy and political engagement, it seems the space cultivated through a shared creative practice can be a particularly fertile one. The students bring their identities to this social encounter; they share their experiences and demonstrate a level of vulnerability that is perhaps more difficult in other environments. There is no ownership over the sculpture and no sense of completion until its ritualistic burning on the last night. It is art as a social process, inviting encounters with both human and non-human actants. It resists authorship, classification, and assessment, elements of more formal educational practices that are all too often exclusionary. The collaborative nature of the work facilitates a civic ethic, a safe space where the many voices and the inherent conflicts are able to play out through the sculpture and the social bond it has generated. The relationship with the natural environment fosters an ethics of sustainability where the active role that the site, the trees, and the materials play have also contributed to the co-construction of meaning and a reconfiguration of the social network the sculpture has provided.

At four o'clock on Friday afternoon, the small, wooded area behind the tennis courts has been returned to its original condition. The huts have been dismantled, and the materials will be carefully stored for next year. The site has been thoroughly cleared by the students so they can leave it in the same state they found it. Even the pizza oven has disappeared. It is once again a quiet place, bearing little trace of the events and transformative experiences of the previous week.

A laboratory for learning

The Village Project is a "laboratory for learning" (de Brett, 2022) and, as such, undergoes a substantial amount of analysis and reflection. Adults contribute through participant action research, while the students are encouraged to maintain reflective journals, complete surveys, and take part in small focus groups. For example, last year, the students were asked to reflect on the impact of being outdoors without their mobile devices for a sustained amount of time. Responses included:

> I think living outdoors had a massive impact on creativity and increased productivity and the will to get up in the morning.
> It made me think about how much we rely on screens and how we don't really need them.
> I felt like it was a bit calmer.
> I felt more myself because I didn't spend all my time on my phone; I could spend more time with people, and I'm trying to continue.
> I felt very peaceful during the day, and it was a great change of pace from regular school.

In addition to this, the project has benefitted from the analysis of external researchers. For example, in 2016, Professor Bill Lucas and Dr Ellen Spencer from the Centre for Real-World Learning at the University of Winchester worked with Village staff to conduct research into how the project might lead to "enhanced understanding by students of themselves as learners and better staff-student relationships" and how the project might develop five specific capabilities: creativity, independence, resilience, social responsibility and sustainability (Lucas & Spencer, 2016).

The Village Project 2022 continued to build on findings and recommendations from the research, particularly around ideas of sustainability. It aimed to understand better the specific role nature plays in relation to teaching and learning through the arts and its impact on wellbeing. Unsurprisingly, this year further supported the idea that young people might benefit from the digital detox the Village provides. Having no access to portable electronic devices or social media highlighted the pressure it exerts and the passivity it creates. Student feedback consistently reports how this absence led to a more social environment and much more engagement in alternative activities.

Another recurring observation is the importance of the natural environment to this experience. The opportunity to spend a sustained amount of time in nature has clearly had a positive impact on the wellbeing of the Villagers, many of them discussing and comparing it to their experiences during the lockdown. The creative practices have provided opportunities for reflection, risk-taking, and developing self-confidence and resilience. What is noteworthy from the Village is the potential of such activities when understood as a relational practice. It cultivates the conditions for a community of practice as defined by Lave (1991) and Wenger (2008). The collaborative and transient nature of many of the activities, such as the Village demon, invited participation from students who may not otherwise have chosen to engage in an art practice more typical of the school setting. Free from predetermined lesson outcomes or assessments, it provided an inclusive invitation for students in which "the event and their participation in it constituted the purpose, the meaning, and the material of the work" (Adams, 2013, p. 252). This relational understanding of creative practice suggests that much rich learning occurs through the dialogue it generates and directly implicates the natural environment within this discourse.

Implications for practice and research

The Village Project is an example of how engagement with the arts in nature can have a positive impact on the wellbeing of young people. The reflections gathered over the years clearly show how this experience supports the social, physical, and mental health of the students who take part. However, it also worryingly highlights the health inequalities at play as not all young people have access to such opportunities. King Alfred School is a particular type of institution. As an independent progressive school, it has the support and resources for endeavours such as the Village Project. While this is undoubtedly a privilege, it is hoped that the learning from the project can be applied to a range of settings by demonstrating how immersive learning experiences, less didactic pedagogies, and a sustained encounter with nature can provide the conditions for developing capabilities that might benefit young people beyond the school setting. It also reveals rich cross-curricular opportunities through an arts-in-nature practice that can make meaningful links across the school curriculum. Crucially, the project highlights the importance of relationships with regards to pedagogy and how having the courage to really trust students can have a profound impact on the learning that occurs. However, cultivating these relationships is not without its challenges, particularly in more mainstream settings. Teachers, arguably more than most, can find it difficult to reconceptualise their own identities and to act less 'teacherly', but embracing the position of a participating co-learner can be transformative for everyone in the relationship. The Village Project has shown that even small changes in one's approach to teaching can have a significant impact. Taking the time to listen, admitting you don't know something, and agreeing to find out together can be the first steps in an exciting new journey.

Conclusion

The Village Project provides a much-needed opportunity for young people to immerse themselves in nature, to take responsibility for themselves, each other, and their environment, and to direct their own learning. The activities and the relationships they foster have a positive impact on students' wellbeing by developing not only a sense of independence but also an understanding of interdependence, one that includes nature. The community of practice the Village establishes provides a social and inclusive learning experience. In an increasingly accountable and assessment-driven regime, this relational approach to creativity is not only good for our students' health but also good for the health of art education in the UK. The extensive planning, preparation, and resourcing of the project is not insignificant. However, it has become clear that the educational value is not in the site, resources, or external practitioners but in the space carefully cultivated to explore, challenge, and disrupt how we learn in a social context and to recognise and value the active role nature plays in the process.

Note

1 The dematerialisation of the art object was an idea that characterised conceptual art practices of the 1960s that turned away from traditional notions of art production, exchange, and distribution. This trend continued through Futurist, Situationist, and Dada performances and can be found in more recent participatory and socially-engaged art practices, in which artists act as facilitators of social events, rather than producers.

References

Adams, J. (2013). The artful dodger: Creative resistance to neoliberalism in education. *Review of Education, Pedagogy, and Cultural Studies, 35*(4), 242–255. doi: 10.1080/10714413.2013.819726

Adams, J., & Owens, A. (2016). *Creativity and democracy in education: Practices and politics of learning through the arts*. London and New York: Routledge.

Anderman, E. M., & Maehr, M. L. (1994). Motivation and schooling in the middle grades. *Review of Educational Research, 64*(2), 287–309. doi: 10.3102/00346543064002287

de Brett, S. (2022). *The village project* [Unpublished Manuscript]. London: King Alfred School.

Eccles, J. S., Wigfield, A., Midgley, C., Reuman, D., Iver, D. M., & Feldlaufer, H. (1993). Negative effects of traditional middle schools on students' motivation. *The Elementary School Journal, 93*(5), 553–574. doi: 10.1086/461740

Galton, M., Gray, J., & Rudduck, J. (2003). Transfer and transitions in the middle years of schooling (7–14). In *Continuities and discontinuities in learning*. London: DfES.

Gielen, P., & de Bruyne, P. (Eds.). (2012). *Teaching art in the neoliberal realm: Realism versus cynicism*. Amsterdam, New York: Valiz; USA distribution, D.A.P. (Antennae series).

Hoad, C., Deed, C., & Lugg, A. (2013). The potential of humor as a trigger for emotional engagement in outdoor education. *Journal of Experiential Education, 36*(1), 37–50. doi: 10.1177/1053825913481583

Itin, C. M. (1999). Reasserting the philosophy of experiential education as a vehicle for change in the 21st century. *Journal of Experiential Education, 22*(2), 91–98. doi: 10.1177/105382599902200206

Latour, B. (1999). *Pandora's hope: Essays on the reality of science studies*. Cambridge, MA: Harvard University Press.

Latour, B. (2005). *Reassembling the social: An introduction to actor-network-theory*. Oxford and New York: Oxford University Press.

Lave, J. (1991). Situating learning in communities of practice. In L. B. Resnick, J. M. Levine, & S. D. Teasley (Eds.), *Perspectives on socially shared cognition* (pp. 63–82). Washington, DC: American Psychological Association. doi: 10.1037/10096-003

Lucas, B., & Spencer, E. (2016). *The village a week of community living and experiential learning*. Winchester: University of Winchester.

OFSTED. (2015). *Key stage 3: The wasted years?* 150106. Retrieved from www.gov.uk/government/publications/key-stage-3-the-wasted-years

Rogers, C. R. (1954). Toward a theory of creativity. *ETC: A Review of General Semantics, 11*(4), 249–260.

Rogers, C. R. (1995). *On becoming a person: A therapist's view of psychotherapy*. Boston, MA: Houghton Mifflin.

Wenger, É. (2008). *Communities of practice: Learning, meaning, and identity* (18th printing). Cambridge: Cambridge University Press.

Chapter 8

An outdoor therapy service offering art therapy for young people and adults

Katarina Horrox

Introduction

This chapter explores an art therapy practice delivered as part of an Outdoor Therapy Service. It begins by situating the Outdoor Therapy Service in its organisational and social context. It explains the rationale that underpins the Service, drawing on research and theory, and explores practical and ethical considerations. The practice of art therapy with this client group is illustrated through a composite case study. The chapter illustrates how art therapy can be applied in a specific milieu and suggests that outdoor therapy services may be effective in wider contexts, such as public health services.

Venture Trust Outdoor Therapy Service

The Outdoor Therapy Service is part of the charity Venture Trust. Venture Trust has provided personal development work in outdoor and community settings in Scotland since 1982. As an organisation it has focused on working with marginalised groups. Consequently, the charity has amassed extensive experience of working safely and reflectively in the outdoors with clients who have experienced adversity and trauma. Venture Trust began this work because it believed that offering an 'alternative' route to personal development, via outdoor experiential learning, could assist engagement for certain clients (Gass, Gillis, & Russell, 2020).

In 2016, Venture Trust began offering psychodynamic wilderness therapy programmes with clinical practitioners embedded in service design and delivery. Building on this experience, the Outdoor Therapy Service was launched in 2020. This work has been developed, monitored and refined over the years, with results published in magazines, journals and newspapers (e.g., Lloyd, 2018; Hildmann, Higgins, White, Strang, & Hardie, 2019; Horrox & Hardie, 2020; Paquette & Vitaro, 2014). In this chapter, the term *therapy* refers to counselling, psychotherapy and art therapy and the term *outdoor therapy* includes outdoor art therapy.

The Outdoor Therapy Service offers therapy in outdoor settings. Accredited counsellors and therapists work one-to-one with clients for up to 20 sessions in green spaces within the client's local community. Green spaces may be woodlands,

DOI: 10.4324/9781003357308-8

inner-city parks or country estates. The therapeutic work is referred to as 'out-door therapy', rather than 'ecotherapy', because it does not always take place in a nature-based environment. On occasion, the work will take place in an urban environment, such as a football pitch or a housing estate. This depends on the needs of the client and where they feel able to meet. The Service operates in Edinburgh, the Lothians, Glasgow, Fife, Clackmannanshire and Falkirk. Within these local authority areas, it focusses on areas defined as 'deprived' on the Scottish Index of Multiple Deprivation (SIMD). SIMD areas generally have lower incomes, less resources and fewer opportunities. They may also have higher instances of mental health issues (Scottish Government, 2020). The Outdoor Therapy Service was developed as a response to the dearth of service provision available in SIMD areas and the obstacles experienced by clients in accessing traditional clinical services.

Clients of the Outdoor Therapy Service include young people aged 16–24 and ex-service personnel of any age. They have commonly experienced multiple adverse childhood events, including relational and/or shock trauma. Clients may have received diagnoses such as borderline personality disorder, post-traumatic stress disorder, anxiety and depression. Clients self-refer or are referred through third parties, such as specialist third-sector organisations, social work and Child and Adolescent Mental Health Services (CAMHS). The criteria for accessing the service is that the person has faced or is facing some form of adversity. The service is free to its users.

The multi-modality clinical team is comprised of an art psychotherapist (clinical manager and author of this chapter), a psychodynamic counsellor, an integrative counsellor, a person-centred counsellor, a transactional analyst, a pluralistic counsellor and two counselling student placements.

Rationale for outdoor therapy in this social context

The Service practises therapy outdoors for a variety of reasons. Firstly, because there is compelling evidence that practising outdoors may increase access to therapy; this has been identified through client feedback, monitoring and professional experience (Venture Trust, 2022). One reason for this seems to be that sessions occur in a 'neutral' non-clinical setting. For clients who have experienced institutional power dynamics, such as being taken into care or encounters with the police, there may be an understandable resistance to engaging with institutional settings or statutory services, because they may have felt unsafe in such contexts. Meeting in a setting where clients choose the location can add a degree of autonomy to the process. Additionally, clients may choose a place already familiar to them, such as a local park, and this may encourage a greater sense of safety. This arrangement also alters the therapist-client power dynamic because the therapist meets the clients more on their own terms, literally stepping into their environments.

Outdoor therapy may be doubly relevant because, after several years of people being confined to their homes during the COVID-19 pandemic, many clients have described an increase in social anxiety (Gray et al., 2022). For clients without private access to gardens, such as those living in housing estates, we might reasonably

expect an increase in instances of anxiety. By meeting clients close to home, sometimes at the end of their street, therapists are able to accompany clients into the
community. Clients are able to access therapy in a way that could be more difficult
if they were obliged to attend a doctor's surgery. Anxiety is often accompanied by
internal bodily dysregulation, such as increased heart rate or shortness of breath,
which may feel to be beyond the client's immediate control. By accompanying
clients into public spaces, they may feel safe enough to experience autonomic nervous system regulation. This can be integrated into the therapeutic work, helping
clients to feel more at ease again in public. In going back into their community, the
client may re-develop a link with local spaces, potentially fostering a wider sense
of connection. In larger rural council areas, such as Fife, services can be hard to
access if the client lives remotely or has difficulty with public transport, so working
in this way can allow therapy to reach more people.

Rationale for outdoor therapy

Outdoor therapy has a range of benefits related to an encounter with the natural
world. These are further explored in what follows. For clarity, the terms 'nature'
and 'natural' will be used to describe environments or objects that are not made by
humans, such as plants, trees and landscapes. The author acknowledges that this
term nonetheless remains problematic.

Theoretical rationale

The theoretical premise for working therapeutically outdoors begins with the recognition that environments have a profound impact on us (Clayton & Saunders, 2012;
Searles, 1960); they can shape us, just as we can shape them. We exist in relation
to our environments (Bennett, 2010; Deleuze & Guattari, 1987; Heidegger, 1996).
A person's experience in any environment will impact how they might engage with or
relate to someone or something. In this context, the environment of the therapeutic setting inevitably has an impact on the work (Takkal, Horrox, & Rubio-Garrido, 2017).
This observation applies, whether it is a therapist's consulting room with its carefully
chosen furniture and decor or an ancient woodland with trees many centuries old. In
the outdoor context, a person may learn a lot about themselves through their encounter
with the environment, when they engage with it as a live, dynamic space full of information. By means of this encounter with the place, accompanied by another person
(the therapist), the client may be able to find themselves in relation to a wider world,
which can encourage a sense of 'being-in-the-world' (Heidegger, 1996).

Research rationale

The effectiveness of practising therapeutically outdoors is supported by a growing
body of research. Clinical studies and empirical evidence indicate positive outcomes related to psychological and physical wellbeing, though further research

is needed (Cooley, Jones, Kurtz, & Robertson, 2020; Ewert, Mitten, & Overholt, 2014; Harper & Dobud, 2021; Mygind et al., 2019; Naor & Mayseless, 2021a; Stier-Jarmer et al., 2021). To summarise key themes arising from these studies, nature-based therapies may encourage insight and growth. They may also foster an embodied and ecological sense of self which support the client to feel connected with and part of nature. This can develop through the therapeutic process in the live, natural setting which engenders a sense of interconnectedness and perspective.

The practice of outdoor therapy is also supported by evidence that time simply *spent* in natural environments has mental and physical health benefits (Kuo, 2015). Research has shown that it can encourage emotional regulation and decrease stress, which can lead to attention restoration (Kaplan, 1995; Yao, Zhang, & Gong, 2021). Similarly, research suggests a genetic tendency to affiliate with the natural world, and, as such, people often experience nature as a benevolent and restorative environment that encourages cooperation and bonding (Frumkin, 2001; Roszak, 1995; Wilson, 1984). If we consider this in the context of neuroscientific research by Damasio (2019), evidencing that we integrate our experiences via the senses, it is reasonable to imagine that time spent in nature encourages growth and regeneration.

Outdoor art therapy rationale

The practice of art therapy outdoors, sometimes known as 'eco-art therapy', is supported by a small but growing body of literature (Berger, 2017). Some recent contributions have been made by clinicians in the UK, Russia and Israel, which have pointed to varied benefits in different populations (Heginworth & Nash, 2019; Kopytin & Rugh, 2017; Bourassa, 2021). Some of the value of eco-art therapy overlaps with the benefit of outdoor therapy, but there are aspects that make it distinctly different. An example would be working with natural materials, which permits clients to have a symbolic, sensory or visual experience in the therapeutic process. This means that processing may be undertaken, not just through verbal or cognitive means, but experientially, on an embodied or unconscious level.

Practice rationale

The practice is rooted in the idea that the outdoor environment is a live setting which contains animate experiences (Rust, 2020). It can, therefore, play an active role in the therapeutic process. The environment may be described as a co-therapist, offering information and insights. Client, therapist and natural environment have a reciprocal and triangular relationship, rather than a dyadic relationship (Jordan & Marshall, 2010). If the natural environment is considered an active participant, we may also have a transferential relationship with it ('transference' is understood as the redirection of feelings from one being to another and a key element of therapeutic work). In this case, the natural setting becomes not just a context in which things occur but a part of the transference exchange. An example would be a client experiencing a grey sky as frightening or persecutory, when speaking about an abusive experience.

If we presume that a person's psychological and physical wellbeing is inherently connected with the natural world, we may reasonably imagine that outdoor therapy might help to foster a healthy, reciprocal relationship with it (Segal, Harper, & Rose, 2020). This experience of developing an ecological sensibility has the potential to impact and shape a person's response to the ecological and climate crisis, a response which is more engaged and less prone to being overwhelmed by anxiety or disavowal (Weintrobe, 2022).

When working with art materials, the therapist might invite the client to work with natural objects in the vicinity of the session. These are found in situ and often left behind once the session ends. This generates an ephemeral and cyclical element to the work because something is created and then returned. The materials also offer clients a means of understanding themselves symbolically in natural forms, implicitly reminding clients that they themselves are part of nature. Using found objects as art materials may be helpful with some clients because it is a way to connect with and contemplate the outer world. These materials can symbolically bridge psychological barriers to allow clients to identify with something beyond themselves. Brooker (2010) describes how found objects may offer a cognitive process that assists in thinking beyond the self, addressing issues such as isolation and social inclusion.

When there is movement in the session, the therapist will often follow the physical rhythm of the client in pace and direction. This mirroring may encourage a sense of attunement (Siegel, 2010). The therapist may work with the client's embodied experience, noting that their pace is unusually erratic or slowed down or that a walking route has changed significantly. This can hint at the client's psychological state and can offer material to work with (Marshall, 2016). Clients also comment on the importance of not holding eye contact when walking side-by-side. With clients that have experienced significant trauma, eye contact can sometimes prompt dysregulation, as the client seeks and over-interprets information from the face of the therapist.

The openness of the outdoor location may also generate feelings of space and distance, which can encourage a sense of perspective. Clients can feel awe in the natural environment and this can promote a desire for self-exploration (Jiang & Sedikides, 2022). These aspects of working outdoors contribute towards a non-verbal, experiential, embodied and unconscious therapeutic process.

Practical and ethical considerations in outdoor therapy

The Outdoor Therapy Service is built on the rationale that when therapy is practised outdoors, it must take place safely and ethically (Richards, Hardie, & Anderson, 2020). Careful consideration is given to the work, just as in an indoor setting, with particular attention to additional elements pertaining to: clients; therapeutic work; therapists, service and organisation; and natural environment. These are considered separately in what follows.

Clients

The assessment process for a client to access outdoor therapy is adapted to include an exploration of the client's motivation for *outdoor* therapy. There will be a discussion about how the client relates to the natural environment and their previous experiences in natural settings, both positive and negative. This is relevant because, although there is evidence that time spent in nature is positive for many people, this is not always the case. A person's experiences in any environment will be shaped largely by early life experiences with caregivers in different environments (Santostefano, 2008). It is possible that natural environments are not always experienced as safe or benevolent, and this must be given consideration. Traumatic events in particular settings might also mean that these places are not suited to therapeutic work. The information collected at assessment helps inform whether outdoor therapy is regarded as appropriate for that client and which environment the therapy might take place in.

Particular attention will also be paid to a client's physical health, including any accessibility issues, which will be considered regarding the location, terrain and movement within the session. Any risks related to the client's physical or mental health will be thought about and the therapist will decide whether a specific risk assessment is necessary. The service works primarily with clients experiencing mild to moderate mental health issues. People presenting with severe mental health issues will be given due consideration before outdoor therapy is offered.

Therapeutic work

Consideration is also given to managing boundaries. Observers sometimes question outdoor therapy in regard to the unpredictability of the therapeutic environment, where the context appears more fluid and challenging (Jordan & Marshall, 2010). However, as Jordan and Marshall suggest, boundaries can be thought about and what is gained from working outdoors often outweighs the perceived challenges. In the Outdoor Therapy Service, much thought is given to how to maintain the therapeutic frame. This will include thinking about elements, such as, how psychological and physical safety can be maintained, how the sessions can be kept confidential, how time is managed and how to work with unexpected events. For example, client and therapist may agree to remain in silence if someone comes within earshot or to walk a particular route for a certain length of time. The therapist may manage the nebulousness of the physical boundaries by inviting the client to define a symbolic 'threshold', such as a gate, which marks the start and end of the session.

Therapist and client may also anticipate what can be done if the client begins to feel more emotional. For example, they may agree on where they can go that feels safe. A challenge to outdoor therapy can be that a client might feel more exposed in the outdoor setting. However, the consulting room may not necessarily be experienced as safe either. Naturally, not everything can be contracted for, but with sufficient care, the more difficult situations can be managed in a good enough way.

Therapists, service and organisation

For the Service to operate safely and ethically in the outdoor context, therapists must be professionally trained, accredited and practising within clearly established ethical guidelines (Richards et al., 2020). The staff team are supervised individually in their modality, whilst also undertaking monthly group supervision with a psychodynamically oriented supervisor. In group supervision, the therapists are invited to reflect on themselves, their client work, the staff team, the wider organisation and the socio-political and environmental context. Therapists in the Service have a commitment to reflective practice and continued professional development, particularly in relation to outdoor therapy.

Therapists have also spent time exploring their personal relationship with the natural world. This may include studying ecopsychology, ecotherapy, deep ecology, conservation, adventure therapy or wilderness therapy. Therapists must hold the relevant outdoor qualification for the environment in which they practise (Mountain Training, 2023). Additionally, they must hold a valid Outdoor First Aid Certificate. In short, therapists must feel fully competent to work in the natural environments they enter into.

Jordan (2015) has written about the need for therapists to feel proficient when practising outdoors to be able to carry the setting internally. This requires both professional expertise from the individual therapist and responsibility from the organisation as a whole. The organisation needs to provide attentive line management, clear guidance on lone working, an on-call system for emergencies and a commitment to protect the practitioner as well as the client. The therapist's clinical supervisor and accrediting body also carry a degree of responsibility for the work undertaken. With appropriate support, the therapist can experience this as a secondary container, holding the therapist, both consciously and unconsciously, when undertaking challenging therapeutic work (Stokoe, 2015).

Natural environment

Working in this environment raises fundamental questions about how nature is engaged with. The Service works from the premise of respect and relation to the natural environment rather than its use for consumption. This is fundamental, given the current societal model based on the exploitation of this finite resource. As such, the Service is committed to minimising its impact on the environment, and it seeks to 'leave no trace'. During art activities, clients are invited to work with available materials, such as fallen leaves and sticks, rather than picking something that is living or part of an active ecosystem. When working with a group, attention is paid to the trail not being over-used. The biggest impact that the Service currently makes is from driving between sessions. The Service attempts to minimise this by seeing clients in a similar area on the same day, but this issue remains a concern.

Case illustration of an outdoor art therapy practice

This composite case illustrates some aspects of an outdoor art therapy practice with a young person. The therapy lasted for six months, during which time 20 weekly sessions of 50 minutes took place. The following summary focuses on certain moments that illustrate elements of the practice.

The young person

The young person, aged 19, was referred by a social worker. She was having difficulty managing her close relationships and was engaged in risky behaviours. She had been adopted as a toddler after being taken into care. Her biological parents had been unable to care for her because of their substance use. The adoptive experience had been acrimonious, and in adolescence, the young person had withdrawn from school and began relations with an older person. The client had a close but fraught relationship with her biological mother. At the point when therapy began, she was living independently in homeless accommodation, having broken contact with her adoptive family. Her motivation for coming to therapy was to think about these relationships.

The art therapist

The work was undertaken by a psychodynamic art therapist who had training and experience in outdoor therapy and working with vulnerable young people.

The location, materials and process

The work took place in the public grounds of a quiet walled garden near Edinburgh. The location was familiar to both client and therapist because the client had visited the grounds as a young person and the therapist had worked there previously. The therapist had assessed risks associated with the site.

The art materials worked with were items available in the vicinity of the garden. These included leaves, seeds, earth, logs, water, etc. The client chose a number of different locations to work over the 20 sessions and the elements changed slightly according to the place.

The art therapy was non-directive, meaning there was an open invitation for the client to make something that was relevant to herself related to issues that preoccupied her. The client would sometimes work in silence, and at other times the creation would be developed in dialogue. Once the creating was finished, the therapist and client would take time to observe what had emerged and think about it together.

In the first session, the therapist contracted with the client around the therapeutic work, including added outdoor considerations. At the sixth session and in the final sessions, they reviewed the work together. The client also completed weekly questionnaires that gave feedback on the sessions [Session Rating Scale

(Duncan et al., 2003)] and measured her wellbeing [Clinical Outcomes in Routine Evaluation (Evans et al., 2000)], which at certain points helped to inform the therapy.

The sessions

The initial sessions centred on developing psychological and physical safety. In the first session, it appeared that the client experienced some dysregulation. Her discomfort was manifested somatically through shallow breathing, tightly held posture and a fast gait. The client walked chaotically through the park and, when invited to create something with the natural materials, she chose a location that was beyond the sight of the therapist while still being nearby. The client concentrated on her creative process whilst also paying close attention to what the therapist was doing. The countertransference experienced by the therapist was characterised by a sense of anxiety. She was reminded of a sense of being a watchful parent caring for a young child that needs attention whilst worrying that the child might feel easily invaded or overwhelmed. When the client had finished working, the therapist asked if she might approach the client, only observing the artwork with the client's consent. Through the client's somatic experience, physical distancing and positioning, the therapist and client could think together about the difficulty experienced by the client in trusting this new relationship. At the same time, the client seemingly wanted the therapist to be present and, in some sense, desired her interest and care. The therapist could begin to touch on what it may have meant for the client not to have been cared for by her biological parents. The client could consider the value of having someone with whom to mentalise this experience. She could reflect on her desire to have an adult available to her while worrying deeply about the adult's reaction.

In these early sessions, the client explained that the artworks she made were meant to be introductions to herself. She worked with various materials but focused primarily on 'damaged' objects, such as torn leaves or broken twigs, which she felt represented different parts of herself. At the end of each session, the therapist would take a photograph of the artwork as part of the records of the session. For the client, this became an important moment. Perhaps the photograph served as a shared recognition of the injury she had experienced in her internal world. After taking a photograph, the client would carefully collect the objects and take them to an area of the park that she had identified as 'safe'. Over time, some of these objects were retrieved and developed into other artworks. The client and therapist were able to reflect on the symbolic meaning of these damaged parts that represented the client's internal world and the importance of them later being reintegrated into the client's self-image once her sense of self had developed and felt a bit more solid.

From the fifth session onwards, the client started returning to the same location each week, choosing a position at the foot of a large chestnut tree on the edge of the garden. The client still worked at a slight distance from the therapist but was now clearly in view, perhaps because the therapeutic alliance was now more firmly established. These sessions were characterised by themes of family and relationships. The materials that the client chose were a combination of natural materials, as well as human-made objects, such as scraps of metal and plastic bags, seemingly rubbish.

In session eight, the client built a nest from these mixed materials, weaving together plastic shreds with branches, metal and long-dried grass. She described it as a representation of the network that sustained her, referring to her biological mother, partner, friends and professional workers. She said that the plastic represented her partner, and the metal stood for her biological mother. The therapist and client observed that the natural and human-made materials seemed incongruous together, that they were not well connected and that the nest appeared to be collapsing. This induced a conversation about the client's sense of fragility about what sustained her and the complexity of her various relationships. Seeing her biological mother represented in metal, she reflected on the ambivalence that she felt towards her. On the one hand, she valued that her mother was solid and tough, but on the other hand, her mother could be cutting and destructive. The client reflected on the weight and size of 'the metal', that appeared to be causing the nest to collapse. The client suggested that 'the metal' needed to take up less space and other 'twigs' were needed in the network to sustain it. She linked this to her mother's impact on her own sense of identity, with whom she felt closely enmeshed. She suggested that perhaps she needed greater separation from her mother. Prior to this, the client had only felt able to talk about her biological mother in positive terms, indicating that she had split off negative feelings associated with her, perhaps because these feelings were intolerable and needed to be projected outwards (or inwards). Perhaps working in this symbolic way allowed the client to identify and re-think some (previously unconscious) negative associations, permitting a re-working of her internal objects.

In the fifteenth session, the client reflected on the way that she returned to the chestnut tree. She noted that initially, she had experienced it as a safe place but now it gave her some sense of sustenance. She experienced it as she might imagine a kind grandmother. It was sturdy and constant, offering fruits and shielding her from the rain. The client and therapist could reflect on this metaphor in a visceral way. Together, they looked at the breadth of the branches and touched the trunk. They could think about the benevolent caregiver that the young person had been deprived of in her early years but that she was now able to imagine and perhaps begin to internalise. The client was also able to reflect on her adoptive family. Just as the tree had been absent from the dialogue in the sessions, so had the thought of her adoptive family. It had been hard for the client to bring this aspect into the therapy. Now, she suggested that one branch of this tree might represent her adoptive family. This was notable because it spoke directly to her capacity to recognise and internalise something nurturing. The somatic experience of looking, touching and feeling the tree perhaps helped to enhance the metaphor and permit free-associative thoughts to emerge.

One might also wonder whether the client had developed a greater sense of herself in relation to other beings and a more distinct relationship with the natural world. In this way, perhaps she was developing an ecological sense of self in relation to something wider than herself.

The brief moments described previously help to illustrate a small part of what can materialise in an outdoor art therapy practice.

Outcomes and feedback

The Outdoor Therapy Service monitors its impact through clinical measures, as well as client and referrer feedback. The measure used to capture client wellbeing is the Clinical Outcomes in Routine Evaluation (Evans et al., 2000). This is collected each week throughout the therapy. The 2021–2022 Outdoor Therapy Impact Report showed that, following outdoor therapy, 59% of clients showed a significant improvement, 23% a small improvement and 18% stayed the same or deteriorated (Venture Trust, 2022). This was measured in a sample size of 54 clients. The Nature Connection Index (Richardson et al., 2019) is also collected weekly. Reporting has shown a 64% increase in nature connection in a sample of 31 clients.

Anonymous feedback is also collected from the client when therapy ends. This provides detailed information about what was useful or not about outdoor therapy. The main points that clients identify as valuable are the sense of space, feeling at ease in nature, movement in sessions and being able to manage eye contact. Nothing has been identified as unhelpful thus far. On average, clients have rated the importance of therapy being outdoors as 4.8 out of 5. Feedback from referrers has also been promising. Third-sector organisations and statutory services have pointed to varied benefits, including that the Service is felt to suit clients that have been reluctant to engage with other services.

Implications for policy and research

Outdoor therapy appears to improve wellbeing and access to therapy. It would be beneficial for trials to take place at a statutory level, but hitherto organisational barriers have prevented this (Cooley et al., 2020) Objections seem to arise in statutory bodies due to perceptions of risk and from the prevalence of a medicalised national healthcare approach. Given the varied potential benefits of this practice, it would be valuable for statutory services to evaluate effectiveness on a broader basis.

Research is needed to evaluate outdoor therapy, both for its efficacy and *what* is efficacious about it. It would be helpful to study *who* is more likely to benefit and *why* that might be. It could also clarify whether outdoor therapy impacts nature connection. Research could explore outdoor therapy's impact on the development of an ecological sensibility and how this impacts on a person's capacity to engage with the climate crisis. The Outdoor Therapy Service is currently exploring collaborations with researchers and welcomes further such discussions.

Conclusion

To conclude, experience and research suggest that outdoor therapy is an effective and meaningful practice when organised thoughtfully, safely and ethically. It can open up access to therapy and harness non-verbal elements inaccessible to other therapies. In addition, it has the potential to offer a unique stimulus to the development of an ecological sense of self.

References

Bennett, J. (2010). *Vibrant matter: A political ecology of things*. Durham, NC and London: Duke University Press.

Berger, R. (2017). Nature therapy – Highlighting steps for professional development. In A. Kopytin & M. Rugh (Eds.), *Environmental expressive therapies: Nature-assisted theory and practice* (pp. 48–60). New York: Routledge and Taylor & Francis Group. doi: 10.4324/9781315310459-4

Brooker, J. (2010). Found objects in art therapy. *International Journal or Art Therapy*, *15*(1), 25–35. doi: 10.1080/17454831003752386

Bourassa, T. (2021). The secret garden: An eco-art therapy retreat for youth struggling with mental health issues. *Canadian Art Therapy Association Journal*, *34*(2), 72–82. doi: 10.1080/26907240.2021.1976367

Clayton, S., & Saunders, C. (2012). Introduction: Environmental and conservation psychology. In S. Clayton (Ed.), *Oxford handbook of environmental and conservation psychology* (pp. 1–6). Oxford: Oxford University Press. doi: 10.1080/21711976.2013.10773870

Cooley, S. J., Jones, C. R., Kurtz, A., & Robertson, N. (2020). Into the wild: A meta-synthesis of talking therapy in natural outdoor spaces. *Clinical Psychology Review*, *77*(101841). doi: 10.1016/j.cpr.2020.101841

Damasio, A. R. (2019). *The strange order of things: Life, feelior the making of cultures*. London: Robinson.

Deleuze, G., & Guattari, F. (1987). *A thousand plateaus: Capitalism and schizophrenia*. Minneapolis, MN: University of Minnesota Press.

Duncan, B., Miller, S., Sparks, J., Claud, D., Reynolds, L., Brown, J., & Johnson, L. (2003). The session rating scale: Preliminary psychometric properties of a "working" alliance measure. *Journal of Brief Therapy*, *3*(1), 3–12.

Evans, C., Mellor-Clark, J., Margison, F., Barkham, M., Audin, K., Connell, J., & McGrath, G. (2000). Clinical outcomes in routine evaluation: The CORE-OM. *Journal of Mental Health*, *9*, 247–255.

Ewert, A. W., Mitten, D. S., & Overholt, J. R. (2014). *Natural environments and human health*. Wallingford: Cabi Publishing. doi: 10.1079/9781845939199.0000

Frumkin, H. (2001). Beyond toxicity: Human health and the natural environment. *American Journal of Preventive Medicine*, *20*(3), 234–240. doi: 10.1016/S0749-3797(00)00317-2

Gass, M. A., Gillis, H. L., & Russell, K. C. (2020). *Adventure therapy: Theory, research, and practice* (2nd ed.). New York: Routledge and Taylor & Francis Group. doi: 10.4324/9781003016618

Gray, B., van Ommeren, M., Lewis, S., Akhtar, A., Hanna, F., Fleischmann, A., Chisholm, D., & Kestel, D. (2022). *Mental health and COVID-19: Early evidence of the pandemic's impact scientific brief*. World Health Organization. Retrieved from www.who.int/publications/i/item/WHO-2019-nCoV-Sci_Brief-Mental_health-2022.1 [Accessed October 1, 2022]

Harper, N. J., & Dobud, W. (Eds.). (2021). *Outdoor therapies: An introduction to practices, possibilities, and critical perspectives*. New York: Routledge.

Heginworth, I. S., & Nash, G. (Eds.). (2019). *Environmental arts therapy: The wild frontiers of the heart*. New York: Routledge and Taylor & Francis Group. '

Heidegger, M. (1996). *The principle of reason*. Bloomington: Indiana University Press.

Hildmann, J., Higgins, P., White, S., Strang, M., & Hardie, A. (2019). Empowerment and transformative competencies through socio-emotional learning in the outdoors – the Edinburgh Model. *Zenodo*. doi: 10.5281/zenodo.5828465

Horrox, K., & Hardie, A. (2020). Wondering in the wilderness. *Therapy Today, 31*(2). Retrieved from www.bacp.co.uk/bacp-journals/therapy-today/2020/march-2020/wondering-in-the-wilderness/

Jiang, T., & Sedikides, C. (2022). Awe motivates authentic-self pursuit via self-transcendence: Implications for prosociality. *Journal of Personality and Social Psychology, 123*(3), 576–596. doi: 10.1037/pspi0000381

Jordan, M. (2015). *Nature and therapy: Understanding counselling and psychotherapy in outdoor spaces*. New York: Routledge and Taylor & Francis Group.

Jordan, M., & Marshall, H. (2010). Taking counselling and psychotherapy outside: Destruction or enrichment of the therapeutic frame? *European Journal of Psychotherapy and Counselling, 12*(4), 345–359. doi: 10.1080/13642537.2010.530105

Kaplan, S. (1995). The restorative benefits of nature: Toward an integrative framework. *Journal of Environmental Psychology, 15*(3), 169–182. doi: 10.1016/0272-4944(95)90001-2

Kopytin, A., & Rugh, M. (Eds.). (2017). *Environmental expressive therapies: Nature-assisted theory and practice*. New York: Routledge and Taylor & Francis Group.

Kuo, M. (2015). How might contact with nature promote human health? Promising mechanisms and a possible central pathway. *Frontiers in Psychology, 6*, 1093. doi: 10.3389/fpsyg.2015.01093.

Lloyd, J. (2018). Evaluation of the positive futures programme 2016–2018: Independent research report. *GAP, Filling the Knowledge GAP*. Retrieved from www.venturetrust.org.uk/wp-content/uploads/2021/01/Positive-Futures-evaluation.pdf

Marshall, H. (2016). A vital protocol – Embodied-relational depth in nature-based psychotherapy. In *Ecotherapy: Theory, research and practice* (pp. 148–160). London: Palgrave.

Mountain Training. (2023). *Mountain training qualifications*. Retrieved from www.mountain-training.org/qualifications [Accessed February 7, 2023]

Mygind, L., Kjeldsted, E., Hartmeyer, R. D., Mygind, E., Bølling, M., & Bentsen, P. (2019). Immersive nature-experiences as health promotion interventions for healthy, vulnerable, and sick populations? A systematic review and appraisal of controlled studies. *Frontiers in Psychology, 10*, 943. doi: 10.3389/fpsyg.2019.00943

Naor, L., & Mayseless, O. (2021a). Therapeutic factors in nature-based therapies: Unraveling the therapeutic benefits of integrating nature in psychotherapy. *Psychotherapy, 58*(4), 576–590. doi: 10.1037/pst0000396

Paquette, J., & Vitaro, F. (2014). Wilderness therapy, interpersonal skills and accomplishment motivation: Impact analysis on antisocial behaviour and socio-professional status. *Residential Treatment for Children & Youth, 31*(3), 230–252.

Richards, K., Hardie, A., & Anderson, N. (2020). *Outdoor mental health interventions and outdoor therapy* (Institute for Outdoor Learning statement of good practice). Carlisle: Institute for Outdoor Learning.

Richardson, M., Hunt, A., Hinds, J., Bragg, R., Fido, D., Petronzi, D., Barbett, L., Clitherow, T., & White, M. (2019). A measure of nature connectedness for children and adults: Validation, performance, and insights. *Sustainability, 11*(12). doi: 10.3390/su11123250

Roszak, T., Gomes, M. E., & Kanner, A. D. (Eds.). (1995). *Ecopsychology: Restoring the earth, healing the mind*. San Francisco, CA: Sierra Club Books.

Rust, M. J. (2020). *Towards an ecopsychotherapy*. Woodbridge: Confer Books.

Santostefano, S. (2008). The sense of self inside and environments outside: How the two grow together and become one in healthy psychological development. *Psychoanalytic Dialogues, 18*(4), 513–535.

Scottish Government. (2020). *Scottish index of multiple deprivation 2020*. Retrieved from www.gov.scot/collections/scottish-index-of-multiple-deprivation-2020/?utm_source= redirect&utm_medium=shorturl&utm_campaign=simd [Accessed October 2, 2022]

Searles, H. (1960). *The non-human environment in normal development and in schizophrenia*. New York: International Universities Press.

Segal, D., Harper, N., & Rose, K. (2020). Nature-based therapy. In N. Harper & W. Dobud (Eds.), *Outdoor therapies: An introduction to practices, possibilities, and critical perspectives* (pp. 95–107). New York: Routledge and Taylor & Francis Group. doi: 10.4324/9780429352027-10

Siegel, D. (2010). *The mindful therapist: A clinician's guide to mindsight and neural integration*. New York: W. W. Norton and Company.

Stier-Jarmer, M., Throner, V., Kirschneck, M., Immich, G., Frisch, D., & Schuh, A. (2021). The psychological and physical effects of forests on human health: A systematic review of systematic reviews and meta-analyses. *International Journal of Environmental Research and Public Health, 18*(4). doi: 10.3390/ijerph18041770

Stokoe, P. (2015). Ethics and complaints procedures for psychoanalytic organisations: Some thoughts about principles. *Couple and Family Psychoanalysis, 5*(2), 188–204.

Takkal, A., Horrox, K., & Rubio-Garrido, A. (2017). The issue of space in a prison art therapy group: A reflection through Martin Heidegger's conceptual frame. *International Journal of Art Therapy, 23*(3), 136–142. doi: 10.1080/17454832.2017.1384031

Venture Trust. (2022). *Outdoor therapy 2021–2022: Year one impact report*. London: Venture Trust Charity. Retrieved from www.venturetrust.org.uk/wp-content/uploads/2022/07/ Venture-TrustOutdoor-Therapy-Report-21-22.pdf [Accessed September 29, 2022]

Weintrobe, S. (2022). The new bold imagination needed to repair the ecological self. In W. Hollway, P. Hoggett, C. Robertson, & S. Weintrobe (Eds.), *Climate psychology: A matter of life and death* (pp. 98–144). Quezon City: Phoenix Publishing House.

Wilson, E. O. (1984). *Biophilia*. Cambridge, MA: Harvard University Press.

Yao, W., Zhang, X., & Gong, Q. (2021). The effect of exposure to the natural environment on stress reduction: A meta-analysis. *Urban Forestry & Urban Greening, 57*. doi: 10.1016/j.ufug.2020.126932

Chapter 9

Learning to live well together

Art and ecological research with young children

Debi Keyte-Hartland and Louise Lowings

Introduction

Madeley Nursery School is a place for young children aged two to five years, with an ecological curriculum based on contextual relationships between children, their ideas, and their encounters with the world. The school is situated in Telford and Wrekin, at the edge of the UNESCO World Heritage Site of Ironbridge Gorge. The current nursery school building was opened in 1976; however, the school was established in the prefabricated premises of a wartime nursery in 1946. It has a front lawn and gated garden space with a central tree at the front, as well as a larger rear garden that has been developed for play and exploration of wildlife, as well as spaces for growing produce and composting.

The nursery school is a place of research (for children and adults), and educators have been involved with two international Erasmus + projects linked to early childhood that explored the creative and expressive potentialities of digital technology and media (Keyte-Hartland, 2016) and ways of evaluating and assessing transdisciplinary learning which both amplified ways of working in and with nature. The nursery school offers government-funded education and is a place that celebrates a community of learning based on deeply held principles that are continually being explored, questioned, and developed as understanding grows and practice is reflected upon. One of the children said of the nursery: "We look after all the creatures in our nursery, and they look after us all, and all the plants in the world" (Phillip).

This chapter is written by Debi Keyte-Hartland, an independent artist-educator and early childhood pedagogical consultant who has worked with the school on research projects and professional development with the educators and by Louise Lowings, the Headteacher of Madeley Nursery School, which has been graded "Outstanding" by Ofsted, the national regulator of schools in England on four consecutive occasions. The authors met in Reggio Emilia, Italy, in 2000 when they each came across the work of the infant-toddler centres and preschools and continue to be inspired and enriched by the Reggio Emilia Approach and thinking of Loris Malaguzzi (2011).

DOI: 10.4324/9781003357308-9

In this chapter, we will set out the culture and ethos of the school as it relates to children's learning and use examples of children's engagement with nature to explore how the pedagogy based on ecological ideas and creative modalities builds reciprocity, empathy, and wellness amongst the school community. We end with a consideration of implications for wider practice, which promotes the centrality of an ecological approach and curriculum in early childhood education and beyond that uses the arts as an activator of relational and mutual learning.

Practice description

As a research school with a creative, ecological curriculum, Madeley Nursery School promotes collaboration and active participation from everyone in the school community. Here, learning and teaching are considered a cyclical process, a journey that is built on children's funds of knowledge and working theories (Hedges, 2022). It is a vibrant and friendly school that places wellbeing for all at its centre, including the woodlice, snails, worms, trees, grasses, and more residing in its gardens and outdoor spaces. Madeley's approach to teaching and learning has been inspired by the preschools of Reggio Emilia, Italy, regarding its use of the arts as languages of learning and expression (Malaguzzi, 2011; Vecchi, 2010). It is also inspired by Gregory Bateson (1972), an English ecological anthropologist, social scientist, and cyberneticist whose interest in systems theory ran as a thread throughout his work that intersected fields such as environmentalism, sustainability, and learning. Bateson influenced the development of the preschools and infant-toddler centres in Reggio Emilia, particularly through its founder Loris Malaguzzi and its first atelierista Vea Vecchi who described the pedagogy of Reggio Emilia approach as being a sort of "transdisciplinary fertilizer, full of vitality, capable of welcoming different ways of thinking" (Vecchi, 2010, p. 6). These qualities of vitality or liveliness are cultivated and exist in the children's ideas and experiences that are expressed through their 100 languages (Malaguzzi, 2011).

The focus of the school is an ecological perspective on learning, which enables young children to engage in long-term research where they observe natural phenomena directly, investigating subjects and matter they can see, touch, listen to, move with, and smell. Educators design contexts which activate the curiosity, care, and solidarity of the children with the natural world, and amongst everyone in the school community, by focusing on the immediate environment and developing a deep understanding and respect for it. The belief is that this attitude and value will help the children build their ecological identities (Pelo, 2014). However, as a school, it is important not to treat environmental sustainability or forest school approaches as separate subjects or add-on activities that can become just another part of an already full and mandated curriculum; instead, the aim is to activate each day the ecological curriculum and to build it through the daily life of the school. Building this sustainable, ecological education paradigm has meant seeing wellbeing not just as pertinent to children but pertinent to all, including the multiple species that live and learn together as a transversal value running throughout curriculum, policy, and pedagogy. This way of working is the heartbeat of the school and is enacted as a way of building a curriculum *with* children, which emerges through living and learning together *with* nature and expressing their own understanding of what matters for them through languages of the arts (Sellers, 2013). The work featured in this chapter focuses on the children's curiosity and how they represented their ideas about the nursery garden, a place of entangled living systems which offered opportunities for relational and mutual learning (Bateson, 2016). The enquiry began when a small group of children asked the Local Authority gardeners to stop cutting the lawn and poisoning the weeds, enabling wild grasses and flowers to flourish along with the wildlife it encouraged. Their resulting investigations and discoveries included different varieties of grass and the many different species of insects, spiders, worms, slugs, and snails that returned when the grass was not mown, resulting in the children producing a guidebook about the garden and what lived there. The process of constructing this guidebook revealed children's ways of expressing their solidarity with nature and each other, as well as representing their ecological knowledge using languages of graphics, photography, story, and curated collections of ideas about what lived together in the nursery garden.

What has been, and continues to be, important is that this approach to learning is one based on ecological and systemic perspectives that are not only applicable to educational contexts but to any ecologies in nature or complex human systems. It situates the arts and creativity as co-existing with logic and science as an interrelated whole (Nachmanovitch, 2007) in which diversity and multiple perspectives are sought and considered essential qualities for learning. This challenges fixed notions of education in which children's learning is mapped out in advance through carefully sequenced, high-level plans (Ofsted, 2023). Learning instead was seen occurring in the reciprocal relational entanglements of children, educators, families, gardens, and living and non-living things that dwelled in togetherness as part of the learning community. The children's and adults' learning, which occurred through these intra-actions and entanglements, was considered dynamic, vibrant, interconnected, and flowing in a continual state of elaboration.

The garden and its central tree at the front of the nursery school (the site of the enquiry) was a space where the children played and noticed the plants and creatures that lived in its constantly transforming context. The enquiry involved 19 young children, together with two educators and the headteacher, who explored this small garden over the course of an academic year through the games the children played together, and from the representations made by the children of the community of mutual living systems that caught their attention and curiosity. Children used this garden to run and chase, play hide and seek, and find ways that enabled them to feel connected socially, physically, and emotionally as part of a group. This was learning full of joy and vitality, and the children identified the games they played as being "good to play with friends". All children's names used are pseudonyms, and their dialogue was collected as part of the open and daily pedagogical documentation that informs teaching and learning, which was shared with both families and children.

The traces of pedagogical documentation, such as photographs, films, transcripts of conversations, drawings, and artefacts were critically reflected on by the educators collectively as they looked to grow their insights of changes in children's understanding. Reflection on documentation makes visible educators' interpretation of how the children develop and elaborate their knowledge of ecology and of what lives together in the garden.

Pedagogical documentation is an ongoing form of professional learning for the school; this makes it possible for the educators to test and make theories related to the strategies and processes of children's thinking as expressed and as it unfolds in the daily experiences of learning together (Rinaldi, 2021). This process can lead to transformations in educators' thinking, and the shared analysis builds the listening attitude which enables educators to co-design future learning contexts based on what they have understood about the children's knowledge and motivations (Filippini & Ruozzi, 2021). The different forms of documentation and group reflection make visible to the children, too, the connections they make in their understanding as they learn together as part of a social group. This establishes a metacognitive awareness of how their ideas, feelings, and emotions contaminate, pollinate, and inform each other in the development of their understanding of the garden and its inhabitants, materials, and environments.

An understanding of an intra-active pedagogy challenged the idea that interaction only occurred between the human subjects in the garden (Lenz-Taguchi, 2010). The soil, worms, ants, leaves, bark, seeds, air, water, words, sounds, and drawings all possessed an agentic and dynamic force which was "constantly exchanging and diffracting, influencing and working inseparably" (Barad, 2007, p. 141). We theorised that learning was a relational and mutual act to be extended to the complexity of all evolving living systems present in the garden, all learning to live amiably together. As Bateson asks, what is the difference between learning and life, and "When is something living not learning? Never" (2016, p. 170).

An example of the recognition of mutual learning occurred when the children recalled what they had discovered at the bottom of the tree. Amber thought back to her experiences when watching the woodlice at the rock that sat at the base of the tree in the garden: "They [the woodlice] were finding out what's going on under the rock. . . . I think you found some worms under the rock".

Amber described here how learning was a process of finding something out in which the woodlice were not just there to be observed by a human but were engaged themselves in learning to live together well with the multiple species that co-existed at the base of the tree. Amber seemed to be stating the possibility that the woodlice were engaged in learning too, through an active enquiry of their own, in trying to discover what was going on under the rock. Amber then suggested that the woodlice might acquire the knowledge that worms live underneath the rock. This was a thought that drew on her prior knowledge gained in previous encounters with finding a multiplicity of species, such as worms, woodlice, snails, hoverflies, and butterflies, all living together in and around the tree in the nursery garden. The tree drew the children to it throughout the year in different ways. It stood at the centre of the circle when the children gathered round for stories or joined together for their games. Children would climb around it and, in doing so, would get to know the tree better, in more detail than just looking at it from the ground, which enabled new insights to emerge. Pelo (2014) considers how living in a place over time can breed a sense of over-familiarity in which we believe we already know and understand. In her description of developing children's ecological identities, she describes the 'jolt' of new ways of seeing when we become "detached to the vitality of a place" (Pelo, 2014, p. 45). The children's climbing, games, and observational drawings forged with the tree with pedagogical actions such as inviting the children to lie on their backs to look again at the tree from new perspectives and in imagining what the tree looked like at night, were the 'jolts of vitality' that enabled new ways of coming to know and understand the ecology of this tree (Pelo, 2014).

This aesthetic dimension and way of approaching art is a central aspect of how learning is activated through developing empathy and is a way in which we all relate, connect, and build knowledge (Vecchi, 2010). Through experiencing and representing the vitality of the garden, it affects all those who encounter and inhabit it. When we become aware of and open to both this affect and vitality, they become the base for connecting and relating between other human beings and nature and to art and aesthetics (Hay, 2020). In creating and attending to the aesthetic dimension, we recognise it as an activator of learning in which the children sense, relate, and take care of the vitality within the garden in which wellbeing is considered as an outcome for all multispecies and matter dwelling in the space.

The language of graphics and the use of different drawing media are explored as a way of engaging and encountering the subjects of the garden. The revisiting of previous drawings and the return to drawing the creatures and plants of the garden throughout the seasons and on multiple occasions enabled evolutions in representational skills and ideas. Educators looked for changes occurring through these tangled processes of looking, looking again, drawing again, and sharing ideas as a community of learners. As the children drew directly from life, they narrated not just what they perceived but also exchanged their working theories and ideas (Hedges, 2022). The act of observational drawing went beyond the search for realism and instead paid attention to the story and ideas that emerged (Brookes, 2022).

In cultivating children's ecological identities, both art and the senses played a key role in learning about the ecology of the nursery garden and the place of the tree as a living system bursting with vitality. The senses are to be embraced as a process of learning, especially in a culture that can value intellect and the remembering of facts more so than processes of intuition, emotion, and sensing (Pelo, 2014). We observed how children constructed knowledge that required a polysensorial engagement; they were learning about the world through feeling the cold of the frost on their skin, they smelt the freshness of rain on a warm and sunny day, they heard the birds singing in the trees and tasted the sweetness of strawberries they had grown in pots. These polysensorial experiences were also activating factors in developing an understanding of and with nature, as they described grass seed as being tickly and recognised that climbing a tree for a snail can be prickly.

Figure 9.1 The Blossom Tree, by Kim and Amber

During the summer term, Kim and Amber drew the central ornamental cherry tree in the garden. Over several days, their drawing increased in complexity as Kim and Amber adapted their ideas, explaining, negotiating, and redefining in continuous loops of engagement. Amber suggested that they should add the blossom that had adorned the tree earlier in the year to their drawing because "it would make the tree its best beautiful again". The drawing began to transform from something observational in form to something that reflected their ideas and memories about the vitality of the tree and of what lived together with it. As they painted the blossom back on, they discussed what could happen if they were able to really put the blossom back onto the real tree, saying that the bees and butterflies would have food and a more beautiful home. This wider understanding and empathy for the connectedness of life brought vitality to their thinking, learning, and wellbeing (Bateson, 1972).

When Kim and Amber were drawing, we think they were making intuitive choices and judgements that were driven by their polysensorial perception of the tree, their experiences of it, memories, and observations; this was a response to what they saw and understood about the tree (Brooks, 2022). It was not that they were drawing an exact replica of it at a specific moment in time. The language of drawing was a way of producing an image that sought to pursue the ideas, theories, and questions that they had about that tree as a living system (Brookes, 2022). They were telling their stories about the tree, which helped to cultivate their ecological identities by fostering an intimate relationship between themselves and the cherry tree (Pelo, 2014). This was achieved through their imagination and conjecture of theory that was elaborated through their shared representational experiences. As they made propositions to each other (as seen in what follows), they gave value to each evolving idea, mirroring vocabulary and using affirmation. They gathered ideas of love, beauty, health, and desire that had emerged over time amongst the group and attributed them to their drawing, the tree, and its wider network of wildlife. It was a dance between all protagonists that contributed to this culture of mutuality in which learning and wellness thrived for all, including the bees and the butterflies.

Kim: This tree wants to be pink again.
Amber: Yeah, it wants to be beautiful again.
Kim: Yeah, it's beautiful.
Amber: It will love it, and the bees.
Kim: All the bees will love it and the butterflies. It's food for the bees.
Amber: They will love it, their beautiful home.

How the children perceived the world involved thinking about how the world perceived them. For example, in the search for the field poppies that came and went each day, the children engaged in a kind of game, looking for their anticipated appearances.

Max: That's a poppy.
Sofia: There's another one round there.
Wanda: That looks like a poppy because of the red.
Saul: The poppy is looking at us Lou; it's peeping out.

For these children, their narrative commentary acknowledged that it was not just themselves observing the living elements of the garden but that the living things in the garden could observe them, too. In an interview, Tonino Kimmerer said of plants' intelligences that they have "the ability to perceive, sense, respond to, and communicate about the environment. They create and maintain relationships with other beings. And they adjust their behaviour in ways that benefit survival and reproduction" (Tonino, 2016). Therefore, it is not a naïve idea of the children that plants can 'peep' or perceive. Instead, it underlines how young children are open to sensing and seeing the world in relational ways, actively hypothesising about what is co-dwelling, and receptive to seeing the world in more-than-human ways in which plants can observe and give their attention to what they glimpse from between the fence panels. There is also a creative element to this wondering and thinking *with* the world that brings great satisfaction to the children in their collaborative encounters with nature and natural subjects. These were dynamic and authentic interactions amongst the children and adults that included opportunities for agreeing and disagreeing with each other. Educators listened to the children to find the tension and rubs in their ideas where one way of thinking contested another. It was in these moments of friction that there was creative energy and potential for new ideas and ways of thinking to emerge. These dynamic qualities of seeking multiple perspectives sat at the heart of the democratic practice of the school and related to ways of working with children who could find different ways of thinking where ideas could clash, converge, or become positively infected with others, which brought a nourishing sense of vitality that enriched learning together in a group (Vecchi, 2010).

Outcomes

Learning *with* the flowers, plants, grasses, and creatures of the garden was far more than just learning *about* nature or learning *in* nature. Learning *with* nature was about creating a foundation for action and developing a strong sense of empathy between the multiple species, co-dwelling and co-learning in mutuality together in the garden. It was an approach that was critical for acting *with* the world in which children were learning to care and take responsibility for its wellbeing, as much as the garden gave to the children's sense of wellbeing. The two relations of the wellbeing of the garden and of the children were inseparable. We drew on Kimmerer's (2020) metaphor of mutual and collective flourishing, in which she describes the mass fruiting of nut trees which spend years making sugar and hoarding starch in their roots so that when their stores overflow, the crop of nuts appears, but, when one nut tree in the forest begins to produce its nuts, they all do, as the trees act collectively. It is an example of mutual flourishing, which we liken to a meshing of shared prosperity in health and wellbeing within the ecology of a place in the same way a mycorrhizal fungal network also works collectively with tree roots within a forest.

Implications for policy, practice, and research

This approach was the collective daily practice and engine of learning and participation at the school in which a coherent classroom culture was built on group enquiry, collaboration, and solidarity with each other and *with* nature. The arts enabled deeper enquiry, greater autonomy, and routes to increased critical and creative competencies with insights and understanding across all statutory educational programmes of the Early Years Foundation Stage (DfE, 2023). By being attentive to ecological systems and using creative and expressive modalities, we developed healthier environments for both children and the natural subjects they encountered in which a learning culture of vitality was sustained. Children and educators, as part of nature, learnt together *with* nature, expressed their ideas, and listened to others, and their differences of opinion were experienced as acts of caring, new learning, and mutual support. These small acts of mutual compassion had wider effects on establishing a sense of belonging and self-worth. The sustained research by children and adults *with* the immediate natural environments around the school generated great respect and curiosity for the good health of the plants and creatures that inhabited it as well as themselves, and we hope that this stays and transitions to wider nature and ecosystems beyond the life of the nursery school.

Conclusion

As authors, we question if it is enough to tag learning *about* the environment and sustainability onto an already full curriculum of schools and argue instead for an ecological pedagogical approach to be at the centre, influencing the culture, contexts, leadership, and educational practices of the whole school. In creating a researchful, ecological, and creative culture and ethos at Madeley Nursery School, we have set out how learning can be full of vitality and mutuality, and how difference can be cultivated as a positive value and as an asset within the classroom and wider school. Through examples of children's engagement *with* nature, we have explored how pedagogy based on ecological ideas and creative modalities builds reciprocity, empathy, and wellness amongst the school community and across species. In this approach, nature, children, and their ideas all flourish and highlight the significance of collective responsibility, care, and attention to the health, wellbeing, and sustainability of the human and more-than-human world. As Kimmerer (2020, p. 16) reminds us that "We make a grave error if we try to separate individual well-being from the health of the whole".

We recommend that other early years settings and primary schools develop this practice in their own contexts by considering the development of their children's ecological identities (Pelo, 2014) through exploring, representing, and telling the stories (both real and imagined) of their immediate environments using the arts and aesthetics as activators of relational and mutual learning *with* nature. We also propose that in considering children's health and wellbeing, the health and wellbeing of the locality are simultaneously taken into consideration and acted upon. And finally, we must take seriously listening, responding to, and acting, on children's authentic ecological enquiries as ways of ensuring this mutual learning and relational flourishing.

References

Barad, K. (2007). *Meeting the universe halfway: Quantum physics and the entanglement of matter and meaning*. Durham, NC: Duke University Press.

Bateson, G. (1972). *Steps to an ecology of mind: Collected essays in anthropology, psychiatry, evolution, and epistemology*. Chicago, IL: The University of Chicago Press.

Bateson, N. (2016). *Small arcs of larger circles: Framing through other patterns*. Axminster: Triarchy Press.

Brookes, M. (2022). *Drawing to learn*. Jamberoo: Pademelon Press.

Department of Education. (2023). *Statutory framework of the early years foundation stage*. Retrieved from https://assets.publishing.service.gov.uk/government/uploads/system/uploads/attachment_data/file/1170108/EYFS_framework_from_September_2023.pdf [Accessed July 31, 2023]

Filippini, T., & Ruozzi, M. (2021). *Analysis, interpretation, and relaunching: Building an open, flexible, and listening attitude.* North American Reggio Emilia Alliance Winter Conference. Retrieved from www.reggioalliance.org/conference-archive/ [Accessed July 7, 2023]

Fox, H., Gessler, M., Higgins, A., Meade, A., Warden, C., & Ridge, S. W. (2022). *Children's environmental kinship guide.* Retrieved from https://environmentalkinship.org/ [Accessed June 5, 2023]

Hay, P. (2020). *If the eye leaps over the wall – Researching new paradigms for education.* Retrieved from https://houseofimagination.org/if-the-eye-leaps-over-the-wall-researching-new-paradigms-for-education/ [Accessed November 14, 2022]

Hedges, H. (2022). *Children's interests, inquiries and identities: Curriculum, pedagogy, learning and outcomes in the early years.* Oxon: Routledge.

Keyte-Hartland, D. (2016). *Digital media and technology and its relations to learning in and with nature.* Retrieved from https://wethinkeverywhere.wordpress.com/2016/09/30/digital-media-and-technology-and-its-relations-to-learning-in-and-with-nature/ [Accessed June 5, 2023]

Kimmerer, R. W. (2020). *Braiding sweetgrass: Indigenous wisdom, scientific knowledge, and the teachings of plants.* London: Penguin Books.

Lenz-Taguchi, H. (2010). *Going beyond the theory/practice divide in early childhood education: Introducing an intra-active pedagogy.* Oxen: Routledge.

Malaguzzi, L. (2011). No way the hundred is there. In C. Edwards, L. Gandini, & G. Forman (Eds.), *The hundred languages of children: The Reggio Emilia experience in transformation* (p. 3). CA: Praeger.

Nachmanovitch, S. (2007). Bateson and the arts. *Kybernetes, 36*(7/8). Retrieved from www.emerald.com/insight/content/doi/10.1108/03684920710777919/full/html. doi: 10.1108/03684920710777919 [Accessed June 5, 2023]

Ofsted. (2023). *Education inspection framework.* Retrieved from www.gov.uk/government/publications/education-inspection-framework [Accessed September 10, 2024]

Pelo, A. (2014). A pedagogy for ecology. In B. Bigelow & T. Swinehart (Eds.), *A peoples curriculum for the earth: Teaching climate change and environmental crisis* (pp. 42–47). Milwaukee: Rethinking Schools Publishers.

Rinaldi, C. (2021). *In dialogue with Reggio Emilia: Listening, researching and learning.* Oxon: Routledge.

Sellers, M. (2013). *Young children becoming curriculum: Deleuze, te whàriki and curricular understandings.* Oxen: Routledge.

Tonino, L. (2016). *Two ways of knowing: Robin Wall Kimmerer on scientific and native American views of the natural world.* Retrieved from www.thesunmagazine.org/issues/484/two-ways-of-knowing [Accessed November 14, 2022]

Vecchi, V. (2010). *Art and creativity in Reggio Emilia: Exploring the role and potential of ateliers in early childhood education.* Oxen: Routledge.

Chapter 10

Forest of Imagination

Reimagining familiar spaces through creativity and nature awareness

Penny Hay

Introduction

> Forest of Imagination is a place where everyone can explore their own creativity. It offers a re-imagining of a familiar space into a fantastical world to inspire intuitive play, imaginative thought and to heighten a sense of nature in the city. The Forest is a wild place, a metaphorical retreat from the everyday urban world, to share the innate creativity of human nature.
>
> (Andrew Grant, Co-founder of Forest of Imagination and Founding Director of Grant Associates; cited in the House of Imagination, 2023)

Forest of Imagination is an annual participatory contemporary arts and architecture event in Bath, UK. It is free and open to all, with a creative learning programme that has been developed in partnership between Bath Spa University, House of Imagination (a creative education charity), schools, and cultural organisations. The impact of arts-in-nature practice on wellbeing, mental health, and sustainability is central to Forest of Imagination as it reimagines familiar spaces, inspiring creativity and heightening awareness of nature in an urban context.

Forest of Imagination is a metaphor for our collective imagination; it brings art, creativity, imagination, and nature into the heart of a city with sublime natural and immersive interventions, such as artistic and architectural installations, that connect the natural and urban landscapes with creative experiences. It also brings nature and creativity to the heart of the public realm and highlights the urgency of climate change. Co-founded by the House of Imagination and Grant Associates, this research and public engagement project is a unique collaboration between the creative and cultural industries and the community of Bath. The Founding Director of Grant Associates, Andrew Grant, is famous for the Super Trees, Gardens by the Bay in Singapore, which have inspired the Forest of Imagination.

In the Forest of Imagination, spaces in the city are reinvented to inspire spontaneous play, unleash imagination, and deepen our engagement with nature. It shines a light on the importance of global forests and the capacity of forests to inspire creativity in everyone. Our partners have significant track records delivering world-class cultural and creative learning programmes for all ages and encouraging

DOI: 10.4324/9781003357308-10

seldom-heard community members to engage through active interaction. This has been achieved by developing dedicated outreach programmes and working with local schools in marginalised areas. This chapter considers the impact of the Forest of Imagination on children's wellbeing and sustainability through a multi-modal case study, the Living Tree Mirror Maze.

Practice description

House of Imagination offers a creative approach to research and learning alongside artists. This creative methodology, where everyone becomes an artist, aims to make creativity visible through an arts-based participatory action research enquiry (McNiff, 2007), including transformative "glow moments" (MacLure, 2010) that informed this case study (Stake, 1994). This research was conducted in line with the BERA code of ethics (BERA, 2018) and gained ethical approval by Bath Spa University.

Throughout the project, House of Imagination collaborated with the St Andrews Primary School in Bath, working in particular with Year 5 children. Consent was given from children, parents, and teachers to take part in a multi-modal case study using photography, film, and written documentation. Children's responses, enquiries, dialogue, and processes of artmaking were observed and documented in this in-depth case study. The case study also addressed the artists' design and intent for the Living Tree Mirror Maze, as well as children's interpretation, debate, thoughts, and theories developed in collaboration with artists. Learning outside the classroom, with the city as a campus for learning, created a new space for children's collective imagination and celebrated the power of imagining a different world.

The aims of Living Tree Mirror Gaze were, therefore, to create a space that elicits children's imaginative thinking and creative engagement and to invite children to be good stewards of planet Earth.

Living Tree Mirror Maze 2022 case study (with thanks to Liz Elders' documentation)

Living Tree Mirror Maze was an installation at the Egg Theatre in 2022 designed by Berlin-based artist and filmmaker Andrew Amondson. It was also co-designed alongside mathematician Professor Alf Coles from the University of Bristol and Marcus Rothnie, architect at Feilden Clegg Bradley Studios. In this installation, we invited visitors and participants to walk through a geometric maze of mirrors into a living forest full of sound, light, and sensory experiences. The sound installation was created by musician Cosmo Sheldrake. Designer Matthew Leece created a FUNgal network of connecting and communicating tubes to represent the concept of a mycelium network in the Egg café.

Living Forest Mirror Maze invited enquiry into the natural world and agency for action in response to the climate emergency through a series of creative workshops for local schools facilitated by artists. The Living Forest Mirror Maze installation provided a 'living classroom', an experimental site of learning that deliberately brought the inspirational experience and sensations of nature and wildness to children's doorsteps. Children were invited to find and follow their fascinations, ask powerful ecological questions, and immerse themselves in self-directed enquiry following their 'flow' (Csikszentmihalyi, 2014). In total, 16 classes of children and over 800 families visited the installation over a period of three weeks.

Collaboration of artists, children, and teachers

The Year 5 class was invited to consider the ideas of a Living Tree and Mirror Maze a week before their visit to the installation. The aim was to document the classroom discussion and share their thoughts with the artists. The teacher worked with the artists' sketchbooks of ideas for the design of the Living Tree Mirror Maze and collaborated with the artists to co-lead the session at the theatre.

The artists and educators collaborated before and during the sessions in school and at the theatre. The teacher was an integral part, acting as a conduit for the flow of conversation and exchange of ideas. With his knowledge of the children, understanding of pedagogy, and the culture of enquiry the children were familiar with in his classroom, he was able to frame the sessions and questions and co-construct a dialogue with them. The teacher structured the sessions with the children around these key questions:

- How can we reflect on the nature of responsibility and our responsibility to nature?
- How can we reflect in the forest and hold a mirror up to nature?
- How does the forest and our connection to nature nurture our wellbeing?

Artists' design and intent for Living Tree Mirror Maze

Living Tree Mirror Maze was a delicately balanced natural sculpture. Ferns, mosses, and plants had been borrowed from a local forest (to which they returned), providing a living forest for the children and families to explore and interact with; the conical tree had a circular pool of water inside (Figure 10.1). Andrew Amondson explained that the intent behind the initial concept was that the forest could become a space where we would all learn something about ourselves and nature: "These mirrors give us the opportunity to reflect upon ourselves, in nature, in the theatre".

Matt Leece also installed yellow connecting tubes, which were designed to represent a mycelium network. These 'talking-tubes' were used to represent mushrooms and the underground, extensive network of tubes that bring information and sugars to the trees, referred to as the 'wood-wide-web'. Professor Alf Coles explained to children that scientists have discovered that these networks, which produce mushrooms, are how the trees communicate with each other. For example, if there is a particular kind of insect, a predator, they will communicate that they need to put out a particular kind of scent to deter them.

Figure 10.1 Forest of Imagination

Children were invited to explore the network of talking-tube mushrooms through questions such as: What would the trees say to each other? What if we could talk through a tree? What would you say if you were a tree?

A special soundtrack was created for the installation to accompany the conversations with children by musician Cosmo Sheldrake, including recordings of rare birds threatened with extinction. Artists used the soundtrack in different ways throughout the week to create a space for listening and reflection. This added another layer to the atmosphere and experience of the Forest.

Outcomes of practice

> Without the forest, rivers and trees, I would be a different person.
>
> (Lily, aged 15 years)

Key themes that emerged during the conversations with children and young people included the importance of creative and inclusive placemaking, everyday creativity, co-design, and co-creation, and how these can lead to a higher sense of belonging, engagement, wellbeing, connection to nature, sustainability, and active citizenship.

Learning in, about, for, with, and through nature is vital in children's development and wellbeing. Forest of Imagination and Living Tree Mirror Maze invited children to become stewards of the environment through observing, noticing, feeling, choosing, and acting in social connection. Imagination, creativity, agency, wellbeing, and shared compassionate values elicited hopeful action, envisioning change, and transformation. The following dialogue illustrated children's reflections on hope for their own future as well as for the future of our planet, both of which are intertwined.

Andrew Amondson gave the following provocation to support children's reflections:

> Imagine that you can plant a tree that can save the world. Imagine if you could plant an idea that can save the world, plant it in the ground so that everyone can experience it. Plant an idea, maybe an amazing idea that could save the world.

In response to that, children described their thoughts and discussed how even the smallest changes have the potential to change the world:

> If you have an idea, then that idea grows and grows like a tree, and it can change the world.
>   I kind of think, like, when you plant a tree, what does that tree symbolise? Does it symbolise a forest, or does it symbolise just this lone tree? And I thought about what if it was me . . . and you could show that you can change the world, you don't need a whole country, you don't need a whole continent . . . you can change the world.

Many recent articles (Kuo, Barnes, & Jordan, 2019; Moula, Palmer, & Walshe, 2022; Monbiot, 2013; Griffiths, 2013, 2014) advocate those experiences of nature boost learning, personal development, and environmental stewardship, playing a key role in the development of pro-environmental behaviour, particularly by fostering an emotional connection to nature. For example, Kuo's research implies that nature can promote learning by improving children's attention, interest, and enjoyment in learning and providing a calmer context for learning (Kuo et al., 2019). This study also revealed several engagement outcomes: children were more interested in learning in nature than inside, they were better able to concentrate, and they showed improved self-discipline. This was especially evident with children living in areas of socio-economic deprivation, which echoes the results of another arts-in-nature approach, 'Artscaping', which was delivered to children in areas of high deprivation and explored changes in children's eco-capabilities (Walshe, Moula, & Lee, 2022; Moula, Walshe, & Lee, 2023).

A recent systematic review on the impact of arts-in-nature for children and young people's nature connectedness found that "arts-in-nature offered inclusive medium to engage all children and young people, especially those who might otherwise remain disinterested about environmental issues and disengaged with educational programs" (Moula et al., 2022, p. 1). As such, through arts-in-nature, we have the opportunity to reconceptualise how we nurture children's natural drive to learn (Lee, Walshe, Sapsed, & Holland, 2020). This intention is set against an education system in England that is increasingly narrow, instrumental, and technical, obsessed with targets and testing. Yet if education is about being in the world, then a pedagogy of enquiry is essential to make sense of the world as a rich tapestry of nature-connectedness.

Forest of Imagination and Living Tree Mirror Maze aimed to exemplify 'nature-culture' (Haraway, 2003, 2016) in direct response to the United Nations Sustainable Development Goals (UN, 2023) through vibrant public engagement. This was achieved by encouraging children, young people, and their families to rethink their own relationship with nature and to co-create responses, experiences, and exchanges that open up a space of dialogue around the role of creativity and imagination to invite change. Our priority was to demonstrate the importance of nature by integrating creative, inclusive, and interdisciplinary pedagogic approaches (Capra & Luisi, 2014, p. 13). As Andrew Grant stated:

> We need to rewild ourselves before we can rewild the planet. We need to create places in cities that inspire and feed the future creativity of our children.
>
> (Cited in Hay, 2018)

Implications for practice, research, and policy

Forest of Imagination demonstrates a significant shift in thinking in relation to children and young people's wellbeing, health inequities, and sustainability. The children and young people who participated shared how nature within the Living Tree Mirror Maze made them feel, as well as the sense of calm and wellbeing they experienced. Furthermore, the Living Tree Mirror Maze invited them to be "good stewards of planet Earth", to share their ideas about rewilding cities and bringing nature into homes, and how this would make places better to live. As such, the Forest of Imagination shines a light on the capacity of forests to inspire creativity, which in turn can enhance wellbeing and transform lives, communities, and economies.

There is an urgent and critical need for pedagogy and curricula worldwide to demonstrate how an understanding of biodiversity is central to surviving the climate crisis. We can learn from the indigenous wisdom of forests and pay attention to the opportunities that forests offer for learning, for being well, for belonging, and for taking hopeful action in response to climate change. Living Tree Mirror Maze sought to elicit the children's thoughts and feelings on climate change, sustainability, and positive actions for change. The documentation of the children's immersive learning experience in this 'living classroom' demonstrated the value of such experimental sites of learning. Working alongside artists, teachers, and co-designers supported the children's imaginative thinking, creative engagement, and co-enquiry. The analysis shows the different ways in which the children engaged in self-directed enquiry through the sensory nature of the Living Tree Mirror Maze; their kinaesthetic ways of learning and how they used their imagination to reflect on 'what if' and 'as if'. This effective exchange and dialogue between children, artists, and teachers in a democratic and authentic way of decision-making where everyone's ideas are valued is especially important for children's sense of agency for action and hope in response to the climate emergency.

Based on Orr's (1992) notion of ecological literacy, our approach encouraged the recognition of connectedness between human and planetary wellbeing. Similar approaches, such as those adopted in the Forest of Imagination, have the potential to co-design eco-creative solutions for teaching and learning that empower young people and local communities to create positive change for future generations (Cutter-Mackenzie-Knowles, Malone, & Hacking, 2020). Echoing Bourn (2021a, 2021b), Forest of Imagination suggests that we need a pedagogy of hope for planetary citizenship, which recognises our connection to the planet (Louv, 2008). Young people as climate activists can be a powerful movement for hopeful futures for future generations.

Conclusions

The Forest of Imagination and Living Tree Mirror Maze highlighted five key areas in terms of the impact of arts-in-nature practice: connectedness to nature; creativity and imagination; mental health and wellbeing; community engagement; and a curriculum for sustainability. Working alongside artists showed the importance of the arts, culture, and the environment in feeding people's capacity to flourish in a world where imagination and creativity are central.

Forest of Imagination shines a light on the capacity of forests to inspire creativity, which in turn can enhance wellbeing and transform lives, communities, and economies. We need to learn like a forest, with everything connected, tending to the possible. The forest is a space of connection, belonging, and learning; tuning into it invites us to explore imaginative solutions for a more hopeful future, allowing both people and the planet to flourish.

References

British Educational Research Association (BERA). (2018). *Ethical guidelines for educational research*. Retrieved from www.bera.ac.uk [Accessed July 5, 2023]

Bourn, D. (2021a). Ecopedagogy: Critical environmental teaching for planetary justice and global sustainable development. *Policy and Practice, 32*, 147–149.

Bourn, D. (2021b). Pedagogy of hope: Global learning and the future of education. *International Journal of Development Education and Global Learning, 13*(2), 65–78. doi: 10.14324/IJDEGL.13.2.01

Capra, F., & Luisi, P. L. (2014). *The systems view of life*. Cambridge: Cambridge University Press.

Csikszentmihalyi, M. (2014). *Applications of flow in human development and education*. Claremont: Claremont University.

Cutter-Mackenzie-Knowles, A., Malone, K., & Hacking, E. B. (Eds.). (2020). *Research handbook on childhood nature: Assemblages of childhood and nature research*. Zurich: Springer; Switzerland: Nature.

Griffiths, J. (2013). *Kith: The riddle of the childscape*. London: Hamish Hamilton Ltd.

Griffiths, J. (2014). *Why green is good for you*. Retrieved from www.theguardian.com/commentisfree/2014/jan/08/green-space-combat-depression-mental-health [Accessed December 31, 2022]

Haraway, D. (2003). *The companion species manifesto: Dogs, people, and significant otherness*. Chicago, IL: Prickly Paradigm Press.

Haraway, D. (2016). *Staying with the trouble*. Durham, NC and London: Duke University Press.

Hay, P. (2018). Visions of childhood. *Interalia Magazine*. Retrieved from www.interaliamag.org/articles/penny-hay-visions-of-childhood/ [Accessed August 20, 2023]

House of Imagination. (2023). *Forest of imagination*. Retrieved from https://houseofimagination.org/forest-of-imagination-2014/ [Accessed August 20, 2023]

Kuo, M., Barnes, M., & Jordan, C. (2019). Do experiences with nature promote learning? Converging evidence of a cause-and-effect relationship. *Frontiers in Psychology, 10*, 305. doi: 10.3389%2Ffpsyg.2019.00305

Lee, E., Walshe, N., Sapsed, R., & Holland, J. (2020). Artists as emplaced pedagogues: How does thinking about children's nature relations influence pedagogy? In A. Cutter-Mackenzie-Knowles, K. Malone, & E. B. Hacking (Eds.), *International research handbook on childhood nature: Assemblages of childhood and nature research*. Zurich: Springer; Switzerland: Nature.

Louv, R. (2008). *Last child in the woods*. Chapel Hill, NC: Algonquin Books of Chapel Hill.

MacLure, M. (2010). The offence of theory. *Journal of Education Policy, 25*(2), 277–286.

Monbiot, G. (2013). *Rewild the child*. Retrieved from www.monbiot.com/2013/10/07/rewild-the-child/ [Accessed December 20, 2022]

Moula, Z., Palmer, K., & Walshe, N. (2022). A systematic review of arts-based interventions delivered to children and young people in nature or outdoor spaces: Impact on nature connectedness, health and wellbeing. *Frontiers in Psychology, 13*, 858781. doi: 10.3389/fpsyg.2022.858781

Moula, Z., Walshe, N., & Lee, E. (2023). "It was like I was not a person, it was like I was the nature": The impact of arts-in-nature experiences on the wellbeing of children living in areas of high deprivation'. *Journal of Environmental Psychology, 90*, 102072. doi: 10.1016/j.jenvp.2023.102072

Orr, D. W. (1992). *Ecological literacy*. New York: State University of New York Press.

United Nations. (2023). *United nations global sustainability report*. Retrieved from https://sdgs.un.org/gsdr/gsdr2023 [Accessed April 29, 2023]

Stake, R. E. (1994). Case study: Composition and performance. *Bulletin of the Council for Research in Music Education, 122*, 31–44.

Walshe, N., Moula, Z., & Lee, E. (2022). Eco-capabilities as a pathway to wellbeing and sustainability. *Sustainability, 14*(6), 3582. doi: 10.3390/su14063582

Chapter 11

Open spaces, open senses

On sensuous presence in eco-somatic practice of felt thinking and therapeutic walking with young people

Anna Dako

Introduction

In times hit by worldwide spreads of pandemics, crises in societal health, and increasing health inequities, the importance of access to outdoor spaces has become uncompromising. This is because regular access to natural environments is a basic prerequisite to health and wellbeing. As Chown (2014) points out, whether it is within the local forested areas, beaches, parks, or nature reserves, all human beings need access to nature as our own therapist that connects us to the vital energy of the earth; indeed, perhaps one of the most critical realisations of the post-COVID era is that health-related importance of walking outdoors is unquestionable, irrespective of age. However, I argue that nobody experiences the negative consequences of a lack of time spent in nature as much as children and young people.

At this crucial age, and until adolescence, young people grow in openness to the bigger sense of self through a healthy variety of psycho-somatic stimuli. Openness to being outdoors means being in touch with the real, the living, and the palpable world, as opposed to functioning within the technological virtualities of distanced communication subjugated to flat screens or indoor education only. Thinking long-term, it is important to notice that the 'button mentality', as I would call it, disconnects young people from the natural processes of being and coming into being, as well as the processes of the open-ended synergy of action. It thus impedes their natural capacities for physically engaged and explorative interaction with their living surroundings.

A proper balance between the time spent indoors and outdoors is crucial. While the societal life frames do resonate with the daily rhythms moderated by sunrise and sunset, many technologically overstimulated young people seem to be speeding up to a minute-by-minute tempo of both mental and physical operation. The multi-plane dissociation from the natural rhythms is an observable challenge of the fast-paced modern world which, as an eco-somatic therapist, I regularly notice. Processing over-exposure to information has become a new skill that the younger generation needs to tackle within ever shorter spans of time.

DOI: 10.4324/9781003357308-11

Nevertheless, I do not argue that we should become oblivious to the long-term demands of the societal factors of civil fulfilment. Myself included, most of us need to carry on relying on versatile types of software and phone apps, and looking back at the last 20 years of internet-driven developments in day-to-day activities, one needs to admit that the virtually connected world adds layered-ness, versatility, and complexity to the fabric of life; that virtual connectivity presents itself both as a challenge and a great opportunity.

Through my own practice of walking as a form of experiential therapy, I keep asking what openness to the living environment really means. What does being in touch with the natural environment bring to the healthy comprehension of the self in both human and more-than-human contexts, as well as to the world of therapy as a whole?

The practice of *felt thinking* (Dako, 2023), which I have been working with for many years now, is a body-based method of working with movement in the somatic experience of the self that addresses questions about the sense of care for ecologically-inclusive wellbeing. It is a deep self-inquiry journey which brings the lived connections between nature and the self to the fore and which offers new insights into how we are in the world and how to remedy multiple imbalances. For a number of years now, in my private practice, I have been developing ways of introducing co-creating with the natural world as the healthiest way of living; it is walking through versatile landscapes as an open inquiry about the unfolding interactions that is the best way for me to support young people in times of rapid change and cognitive overload.

Looking through the lens of developmental opportunities, walking outdoors can definitely be a life-long exploration. An exploration into the subtle adventures of embodied expansions happening somewhere between the inner and the outer worlds, and an exploration into how we can become more authentic and more true to what our senses are opening up to and to what they are communicating.

I often feel that, as a living kind at the top of the food chain, we do quiet our sensuous noticing because we do not value enough other forms of life around us. Our own human perspective is what always wins, keeping the natural world in the background. Technological dependency seems to be stressing our 'otherness' even further, yet our human predicament does not need to be so self-centred. It is during outdoor walking that we can expand on and re-educate our bodyminds about the openness we share and about the interconnectedness of all life that calls for our attention and appreciation.

The rich imagination that the majority of the young people I have been working with have supported the practice itself, and there is undoubtedly a lot of undiscovered freedom still to be explored. Most importantly, though, there are new ways to feel safe and secure within the outdoor environments to be included in the therapeutic outlook on health and wellbeing, as well as on how the young people are able to feel more whole within them. These are the grounding propositions within the practice of *felt thinking*.

Figure 11.1 Sensuous Presence in Practice, Aberdeenshire, Anna Dako

Felt thinking with nature/self – as an introductory framework for walking therapies

By introducing *felt thinking* here in relation to walking, I refer to the first stage of eco-somatic practice, which concentrates on the sensuous presence – or sensuous presence-ing rather – as walking itself helps us understand that 'being present' is not a static state but rather an ongoing and changeable process of active participation and active dialoguing. When contemplating walking as a practice of connection or re-connection with the natural rhythms within and around us, I perceive human nature as the nature of being in movement and acknowledge both differences and commonalities within the wider considerations for life on earth; i.e., life in earthy contexts of time and space shared reality that we, as a species, come to live and co-create in.

Contemplating walking involves actively reflecting on our place in all life on Earth and the historicity of how the activity of walking has been the primal movement of our species, as we, humanoids, have been evolving over millions of years on planet Earth. Our feet connect us to all the natural development of life; as we step on the surface of today, walking often becomes an entry point into more mindful pacing through landscapes and playfulness that children easily pick up on. Slowing down and noticing opens doors to curious explorations. At the same time, the freedom of changing the pacing and reacting to what calls their attention is also there to remind us that we keep evolving today, too, and that we continue to learn about ourselves in this wider life context with every step.

Our evolutionary story is very much alive in every cell of our body-minds; the embodied capacity to move, feel, and think in three dimensions, into the now, the past, and the future, is also a complex continuum of how we are able to move in/ with space and is where the value of time emerges. All body systems develop in relation to one another, and the body of nature is present for us all the time, with or without its therapeutic relevance. Both literally and imaginatively, children and young people are able to reflect upon the past, contemplate the present, and chase forward into their plans for the future. And while becoming more aware of the complexity of that motion in relation to the landscapes and their own physiology of constant instability, conscious walking means learning how to appreciate being in a constant mode of co-creating our own movement with the living ground, the Terra, alongside the weather conditions and the flora and the fauna.

We are indeed ongoingly giving in to the ground to be able to move away from it. Next to that, our physiology is intricately woven into our emotional and ethical considerations through care and receptivity, while our living body operates on all planes possible: vertical, horizontal, and diagonal. In my practice of walking with young people, I am continuously reminded that neglecting or taking functional movement for granted is the first mistake made in creating 'out of body' experience, which destabilises the healthy dynamics of the fast-developing psyche.

Our embodied physiology is also naturally expressive, and we move through our lives in constant dialogue with the changeable dynamics of time and space. Facilitating young people's capacities to feel into that dynamic and expanding on their connection to the versatile exchanges happening every single moment grounds them; it encourages them to follow the many freedoms of ongoing choices that they can tap into. I often remind my young clients that they are the choice themselves, and so is the constant movement within and around them. The right pacing in the process of familiarising themselves with such sensations is the key. Connective presence is all about one's wilful participation in what is actually happening, and this is exactly where the path to wellbeing begins.

To me, facilitating sensuous presence in the movement of walking with young people means being with what is unfolding for them with every step we take. Participation, as Andrea Olsen (2002) reminds us, is "a connective link to our embodied awareness and all-inclusive attention" (p. 3). The ultimate goal of balancing multiple imbalances in developmental challenges is to be able to explore the method of *felt thinking* in walking as a way of opening up to new possibilities of relating to themselves not only as human beings but as living beings and to remind them that movement connects all life in a healthy web of belonging through time and space.

This therapeutic context of doing more by doing less helps facilitate a more grounded sense of belonging to the living presence of the Earth and a more versatile and resilient self-reflection. Being in movement, as a form of engagement in both a physical activity and a sensuous experience like thinking a thought, cannot happen without its spatial-temporal relatedness to 'the where' and 'the when'. All movement happens through an engagement with time-space and, to me, the most extended version of such engagement in movement is in sensuous co-presence.

The practice of somatic receptivity in movement refers young people to deeper layers of relatedness that correspond to feeling through pacing, the frequencies of being, and other qualities of co-existence as opposed to picking on spatial bearings from occupying space only. It is important to keep in mind that we are not just walking through the landscape, but we are connecting in co-presence with the living agency of Terra, the Earth, which is a form of therapy itself.

Practice description

I have been working with children and young people (aged 6–18) over the last 15 years of my practice in movement education and therapy. The reflections on walking with sensuous presence as an introduction to the practice of *felt thinking* that I offer in this chapter do not concern any specific case study but rather concentrate on a description of this outdoor practice as offered to young people of versatile, often multi-cultural backgrounds.

In recent, post-COVID-19 pandemic years, I began to notice the importance of offering this new format of therapy sessions to my clients. I also realised that, unlike online or indoor therapy, this is a preferred method for parents of young people who struggle with the effects of indoor-life restrictions, including hyperactivity, irritability, anxiety disorders, depression, forms of withdrawal, instability of emotional states, excessive worrying, or eating disorders.

Before meeting a new client, I usually begin with extensive communication with their parents in the introductory consultation session so I can gather enough information on the day-to-day life of the young person. I also suggest, whenever possible, inviting young people to participate in all communication so they do not feel 'talked about' or excluded from the exchange of feedback. Once a child or a teenager feels comfortable accompanying me on a walking session, there are multiple entry points into getting to know their 'inner landscape', as I like to call it. My conversations with them and the activities we come up with are, for the most part, improvised, yet they are also strongly grounded in my close observations of how they move through the landscape.

Whether it is a forest, a hill, a beach, or a more accessible park area, the choice of the landscape is usually suggested by the young person, which itself is very telling in relation to their inner needs for connection. To me, as a facilitator, creating opportunities for engagement is the key. Walking outdoors is an opportunity to distract young people from behaviours they might be struggling with and to vent their accumulated energy. Following their tempo of walking before suggesting any changes or activities is my regular starting point. Only then, after being able to confront the landscapes physically for a while, can the real dialoguing about what resonates with their current sense of being begin.

To me, walking with a sensuous presence is all about arriving at the most authentic ways of whole-bodily dialoguing and being aware of the connection between the inner and the outer worlds. After the pace has been adjusted and engagement has been achieved, it is through touching different surfaces, listening to the sounds, or picking up on scents that we can connect with the grounds that we are walking at. Then, there is also the genuine curiosity. When curiosity is matched with youthful imagination and playfulness, it opens new doors to psycho-physical engagement in outdoor spaces, especially when the walk is slowed down and focused on a specific area or a path. The guidance to openness through senses happens when arriving at and meeting the time and space of the place itself.

The environment needs to shift its presence in the young client's awareness from the peripheral background to being here and now with it. That is also why the easiest way to arrive at being present in the moment is through addressing questions about when and where their attention is while encouraging them to reflect on what comes into their sensuous, visceral experience. It is also in the 'when and where' reflection, in *felt thinking* in movement, that the young movers become more aware of the dimensionality of their participatory being, and 'when and where' they sense that their own spatio-temporal presence co-exists in a multitude of other. Addressing versatile questions about time and space of being in movement and exploring opens ways for connecting to the living dynamic of the place. Somatic receptivity conveys an implicit co-presence of time and space in the experiential dimension; this includes tangible patterns, audible rhythms, sensed frequencies, and shapes in the making, both visible and invisible to the eye, that our embodied attention brings forth into the experience of movement and attentive dialoguing through observing, noticing and listening.

I often propose looking at embodied receptivity as a form of wit(h)-nessing, a way of 'being with' or relating to whatever enters the client's attention in the fullest way they can possibly experience, starting with the bipolar dynamics of the breath. Guiding young people through breathing exercises can vary, depending on their energy levels. Some exercises can be introduced through continuous walking, some through more playful explorations, while some clients require a bit more focussed, slow pace, or times of stand-still. Working with short attention spans and impatience, which is often the case with young people, can also be supported by attending to breathing in intervals between other activities; for example, by noticing reiterated characteristics of the trees, playing with the step games in sand or foliage, or by joining in sound-making with the forest.

Another example of connecting through breath is playing a give-and-take game, when I usually ask the young person to use as much imagination and emotion as they can. The game is an invitation to voice as many things as possible that they *need* from the living environment following the in-breath and then list as many things as possible that they *want to offer* to the environment while breathing out. Responding to what is offered and what is being received creates a playful ground for carrying on walking with an open and informed attitude thereafter, as well as for more playful responding in physical action or in reflective dialoguing. Young people also appreciate other creative activities, such as imagining the earth breathing along with them and carrying on reflecting on what they sense that might mean.

Accessing this resonating connection with the earth through breathing is also when young people begin to discover qualitative time-making. The pace of the natural world, irrespective of the landscape, is innately slower than the pace characteristic of the human race. Connecting to the sensed pace of the trees, rocks, the sea waves, or the breeze helps young people slow down as well. And when that change is realised, there is usually an opportunity to reflect upon the rhythm of the walk as part of their choice-making. Since young people rely on their instincts, this gentle reminder that they can influence the pace of walking themselves is a big shift in their attitude towards themselves. Feeling in charge of making a change helps them build confidence and trust in their own agency.

Furthermore, noticing different ways of being in time and space helps young people connect many experiential opposites and work towards balancing swinging emotions. 'Being here and now' can be practised by asking a young person to have an interactive conversation with a tree or a rock. I often encourage them to feel into the answers they might be receiving in a self-performed dialogue and have fun with creating different ways for explorative exchange in touch, smell, physical interaction, imagining, or sounding. What is it like to be a tree? How does the tree feel its own growth through the air, and how it interacts with the elements, the seasons, and the surrounding landscape? By letting playful movement answer these questions, young people have an opportunity to learn to be a bit more playful with themselves and soften their emotional guard that often keeps them disconnected and insecure.

Working towards the flowful channelling of emotions and learning about time and space as a shared landscape is usually where the dilution of many forms of inner stuck-ness or states of overwhelm can begin. Playful interaction with the opposites experienced outdoors, like hot and cold, shadow and light, solid and fluid, huge and minute, gentle and rough, fast and slow, and up and down, occurs seamlessly.

Outcomes and feedback

The biggest challenge that the practice of walking to wellbeing faces is related to communication with parents. As this practice and the ontological positioning of the role of the therapist widens to the ecological contexts of wellbeing, it is important that parents understand and support the implications of the therapeutic sessions in the everyday lives of their children and continue securing their continuous contact with the outdoors. Even though the regular feedback is generally very positive, I do occasionally meet parents who find it challenging to introduce long-term changes into the everyday lives of their children.

Gathered from the most recent three years of the practice, parents' feedback often mentions a positive influence on how their children perform at school and their child staying in a good mood throughout the week following the session. They also mention improved focus on tasks, being better able to tackle emotional challenges, and achieving stability in personal motivations for afterschool commitments. What is also mentioned is the improved communication patterns between the children and their parents, which may be an indicator of more stable parental support in the future.

In the last three years of offering outdoor sessions to children and teenagers, the practice has not received any negative feedback. Instead, a few cases of leaving the sequence of therapy appointments were supported by statements about the sessions being something different than expected or cut due to financial reasons, with hopes to return to therapy in due course.

Implications for practice and research

In further reflection on *felt thinking* as a therapeutic practice, it is important to underline the impact of the ongoing dialogue between the environment and the nervous system. The practice reminds us that the young people's sense organs record all interactions, such as with textures, sounds, sights, or light. The practice also helps to establish both perceptual and emotional networks of connection within the ever-learning nervous system.

The healthy mind relies on processing capacities that integrate ways of perceiving, feeling, reasoning, and initiating movement. Dynamics of being in movement with specific qualities of a place help to grow in understanding that movement itself is an "amodal sensory modality" (Stern, 2010, p. 26), based on the fact that our nervous system keeps learning and re-educating itself throughout our lives. There is little doubt that the intensive periods of growth in childhood and adolescence need to be supported by felt events of the natural world, which themselves undergo constant change.

In her chapter "Ecopsychology of Child Development", Barrows (1995) reminds us that, for the most part, mainstream developmental psychology has been ignoring the environmental contexts of early support and that new theories of healthy child development must be evolved. They must acknowledge, she continues, that "from the earliest moments of life, the infant has an awareness not only of human touch, but of the touch of the breeze on her skin, variations in light and colour, temperature, texture, sound" (Barrows, 1995, p. 103). What is needed to advance the field, I would suggest, is an integrative, interdisciplinary, and complementary approach, combining the insights of environmental psychology, eco-phenomenology, neuroscience, and the arts.

To me, as an eco-somatic arts education professional, reconnecting the fast-developing nervous system of children and young people with the most inherent extensions of caretaking relationships in ecological exposure is an ongoing priority in my therapeutic work. Instead of shielding ourselves away from the natural world, as the Western paradigm of 'being well' has been suggesting, in unprecedented times of today, the paradox definitely expands towards re-finding our connection back to nature as the only way forward.

The relationality of processes of integration through sensory and motor functions of the body engaged in movement should then be considered in developmental psychologies as fundamental to healthy growth and wellbeing. There are over five million sensory receptors in the human body that constantly inform the brain about the dialogue between the bodily peripheries and the living environment around us. Thus, losing touch with the palpable reality in engaged psycho-physical movement can have deeply damaging consequences on the development of a grounded sense of self, followed by a possible fragility of the immune system.

Thinking into the future of outdoor therapies then, the role of the therapist might further shift towards offering pathways to wellbeing as a facilitator, pointing and engaging the young people and their families to the natural processes of change rather than as a remedy provider. Trusting the innate wisdom of the natural processes occurring within the natural world should be the world we choose to raise our children within. In that respect, I would suggest that eco-somatic therapy makes a huge step towards a more integrative role of therapy, which sees the therapist as a guide, the clients as active agents in their own process of recovery, and the natural environment as a living extension to the living community that we all belong to.

In my book, *Dances with Sheep* (Dako, 2023), I describe those ontological stands in modern psychology that somatic work integrates and expands on in more detail, and I continue expanding my research work into the developmental patterns that intricately connect human beings to the living environment already at an embryonic level. Seeing life and health as a continuous flow of creative movement will continue to inspire my work with children and their parents, and life-long learning about our human contexts of being will continue to inform the practice of *felt thinking* and walking to wellbeing with sensuous presence.

References

Barrows, A. (1995). The ecopsychology in child development. In T. Roszak, M. E. Gomes, & A. Kanner (Eds.), *Ecopsychology – restoring the earth, healing the mind* (pp. 101–110). San Francisco, CA: Sierra Club Books.

Chown, A. (2014). *Play therapy in the outdoors*. London: Jessica Kingsley Publishers.

Dako, A. (2023). *Dances with sheep: On repairing human-nature condition in felt thinking and moving towards wellbeing*. Bristol: Intellect Books Ltd.

Olsen, A. (2002). *Body and earth: An experiential guide*. Hanover, NH: Middlebury College Press; University Press of New England.

Stern, D. N. (2010). *Forms of vitality: Exploring dynamic experience in psychology, the arts, psychotherapy, and development*. Oxford: Oxford University Press.

Chapter 12

Open studio in the greenhouse

Nature-connected expressive and therapeutic art experiences with vulnerable adolescents

Estella Guerrera

Introduction

The Open Studio experience has been implemented as a complementary mental health and psychosocial support intervention based on expressive and therapeutic arts with groups of vulnerable children and adolescents. According to the World Health Organization (2021), the term 'vulnerable' refers to "individuals or groups of individuals who are made vulnerable by the situations and environments that they are exposed to (as opposed to any inherent weakness or lack of capacity)" (p. 1). The Inter-Agency Standing Committee (2007) argues that some people and groups can be more vulnerable than others, such as: children and adolescents, in particular girls; people who experience poverty, migration, extremely stressful events, or trauma; people with neurological/mental disabilities or disorders; and people experiencing social stigma.

The beneficiaries of Open Studio were children and adolescents who experience vulnerability, psychosocial wellbeing, or mental health issues due to exposure to adverse experiences and increased risk factors (United Nations Children's Fund, 2022), such as lack of secure living environment and nurturing care; caregivers' lack of responsivity or parenting difficulties; maltreatment, abuse, violent punishment, and neglect in the home; exposure to domestic violence; experiences of displacement and migration (also for conflicts in the country of origin); isolation of the family and poor connection and inclusion within the community due to discrimination and stigma; poor access to primary care and services.

The two specific services described in this chapter involved:

- **a residential care service** for children with neglectful or abusive parents and families who have been taken care of by local social services; and
- **a semi-residential daily centre** for children with vulnerable and at-risk families who benefit from educational and psychosocial support activities to prevent institutionalisation.

Both of these were managed by the Santa Caterina Foundation, a charitable and not-for-profit organisation based in the town of Imola, Italy.

DOI: 10.4324/9781003357308-12

Figure 12.1 The Art Therapy Open Studio

Besides the family difficulties, some of the adolescents – in particular the ones with disabilities, neurodevelopmental disorders, and neurodiversities (Shah et al., 2022) or mental health issues – have experienced a lack of equal opportunities and/or stigma in their social environment. The difficulties faced while growing up impacted their rights to have access to nurturing, comforting, and trustful experiences and to be seen and validated in their identity, skills, and competencies. These experiences could have deepened conditions of vulnerability: disconnection from the living environment, interpersonal difficulties, emotional dysregulation, learning difficulties, and school-related problems.

In this context, group expressive and therapeutic arts were perceived as a means of promoting health as a fundamental human rights approach (United Nations General Assembly, 1989, 2006), promoting mental health as a basic human right (World Health Organization, 2013, 2022), and creating an enabling environment for being present, enjoying the moment, learning new skills and connecting with others. The mode of work chosen is rooted in two approaches:

- The concept of *restorative environment* (Kaplan, 1995) and the nature-based therapies framework. This approach underlines the beneficial effects of being immersed in natural areas, such as parks, gardens, and woods, on physical and mental health and is informed by the methodological frameworks of environmental arts therapies (Atkins & Snyder, 2017; Heginworth & Nash, 2019), and ecotherapy (Buzzell & Chalquist, 2009; Jordan & Hinds, 2016). Together, these disciplines identify a set of practices focused on creative experiences in connection with natural spaces through the use of different forms of arts. The value of this set of practices is connecting – or re-connecting – people with nature. The experience of practising creativity in green spaces helps rediscover a bond that has been lost or whose importance has been underacknowledged by not recognising the value of nature and respect for all living things. This approach has been chosen, considering the evidence of nature exposure on young people's cognitive functioning (Vella-Brodrick & Gilowska, 2022), mental health (Till-mann, Tobin, Avison, & Gilliland, 2018), restoration and consolidating resources to reduce and manage stress (Moll, Collado, Staats, & Corraliza, 2022).

- The *Open Studio approach to expressive and therapeutic arts*, which implies a "commitment to art made within a communal context" (Moon, 2015, p. 114). As the term implies, this approach embraces a certain amount of 'openness', including changes in the presence and group adherence; the unexpected as part of the experience; the freedom of choosing personal themes and art techniques; and the facilitating role of the art therapist, who is "going along with" and not guiding. In the Open Studio approach, sessions are open to the group, and the art therapist is present holding the space, facilitating the engagement, and estab-lishing a "welcoming and enabling atmosphere" (Finkel & Or, 2020, p. 2), but also leaving each person free to explore the evolving of their own creative flow and to enjoy the artmaking process at their own pace. Despite the presence and delivery of the sessions by a trained and qualified art therapist, the sessions have been described as expressive and therapeutic arts rather than art therapy; this is due to the difficulty of having a strictly "closed group" or a fixed number of participants. The presence of young users in care services is subject to changes due to a variety of conditions, such as school duties, health issues, temporary return to family, changes in the individual educational plan, or care leaving.

The core of this experience is, therefore, to enhance interpersonal relationships in small groups, as well as ecological relationships with the surrounding environment through spontaneous creativity outdoors; both of these are mediated by the use of artistic materials and respect for the environment. This approach also includes a focus on the sustainability of the project and activities; this is achieved through the use of resources already available in the settings, enhancing a minimal context that is easily replicable over time and over the course of different seasons, and choosing materials with low environmental impact.

Practice

The project was funded and managed by the Santa Caterina Foundation, a not-for-profit and charitable organisation that provides educational, psychosocial, and recreational services for vulnerable children and adolescents. The expres-sive and therapeutic art sessions at the greenhouse were facilitated by a qualified psychotherapist and art therapist with training in expressive psychotherapy and nature-based art therapy, as well as experience in group management.

One or two educators from the semi-residential or residential services participated in each session. Their role was to support children and adolescents directly; their presence in the sessions was, therefore, discussed from the beginning. The educators took part in the activities as participant-observers, adhering to the group rules concerning the non-judgemental approach and without commenting or evaluating the participants' work. The educators also facilitated the inclusion of vulnerable children (e.g., newly admitted users and participants with disabilities) and supported the management of the group. Participation was also open to trainees as participant-observers and to former young service users as peers, following the same rules. The presence of educators, trainees, and volunteers was agreed upon with the group of adolescents in advance, with a maximum of two adults per session.

Context

The activities took place in the countryside, both outdoors and indoors (Figure 12.1). Depending on the season and considering weather conditions, the Open Studio could take place outside, in a courtyard near a greenhouse used for growing plants, flowers, and vegetables, or inside using the premises of a rural house. The indoor spaces were used in case of rain, snow, wind, or very cold weather, particularly in autumn and winter.

With the aim of creating a sense of setting continuity for the groups, the set-up layout was similar for sessions held outside or inside the rural house (e.g., same furniture, similar placement of materials). During the outdoor sessions, a large table, chairs, and artistic materials were placed outside on the lawn next to the greenhouse. Participants had the opportunity to work freely with the artistic materials, take a break, and walk in the surrounding countryside. It was possible to collect natural materials to be used together with artistic materials, according to the group rules for respecting the environment: do not damage plants and trees; do not tear leaves, grass, and flowers; do not harm animals; do not throw waste; separate and recycle waste.

The indoor spaces comprised a larger room with a table, chairs, and sofas and a smaller room with a fireplace, a table, chairs, and couches. Artistic materials were set up on the table in the centre of the larger room (usually used for the activities). Participants worked seated at the table; they could take breaks, if needed, leaving the room or resting on the couches. Sometimes, the smaller room was used, particularly in the coldest days, due to the presence of the fireplace.

Delivery

The activities took place from 2020 until 2022. The Open Studio sessions were planned bimonthly with the staff in advance, with possible variations due to holidays or school calendars. In 2020, we held 17 sessions for each group; in 2021, 16 sessions per group; in 2022, nine sessions per group.

The Open Studio sessions were undertaken by two groups of young people aged 12 to 17; one group was from the residential care service, and one group was assisted in the semi-residential daily centre. To ensure a safe and comfortable environment, small groups were formed with a maximum of four or five participants. The participants were chosen by the educational team of each service based on the needs detected for each young person and their Individualised Education Plan.

The two groups tended to be stable, and the adolescents in the groups already knew each other; however, over time, there were some changes in the composition of the groups (particularly in one from the residential care service). On average, one new participant enrolled in the groups, and one left the activity during the year (for example, as a result of new admissions to the services, the inclusion of some young people in other groups or activities, or absences related to personal life). However, each participant was able to attend from one-half to two-thirds of the sessions over the year, with just a few exceptions where adolescents suddenly left the care program (e.g., they were reunited with their families, returned to home countries, or changed residence).

Each session took place in the early afternoon after school and was planned to last for one hour. However, the length of sessions sometimes varied in response to factors such as decreased attention, tiredness, or loss of interest on the part of the young people; a desire not to participate in the activity any longer; the need to take more breaks; and other contingent situations, such as interpersonal conflicts within the group, or interference of other people in the activity (e.g., parents who came and collected a participant before the end of the session, or sudden phone calls or messages from parents, friends or peers, that caused a change in mood and a loss of motivation).

Activities

The focus of the Open Studio sessions was placed on facilitating relationships within the small groups through experiences of spontaneous creativity, outdoors or indoors, mediated by the use of materials and artistic techniques. In this case, the natural space chosen for the activities was within a rural context; there were different types of trees, crops, plants, and flowers in the environment. The landscape nearby was typically agricultural; besides the greenhouse, there was a therapeutic garden used for rehabilitation activities, with medicinal and aromatic herbs and plants (e.g., calendula, lavender, sage, rosemary, thyme) and flowers (e.g., daisies, violets, roses, dog roses, sunflowers). In the surroundings, there were trees (e.g., plane trees, elms, birches, oaks, yews, horse chestnuts), vineyards, fields cultivated with forage and vegetables, a chicken coop, a carpentry workshop, and other rural infrastructures, such as barns and warehouses. It is a context that reminds us of and encourages caring for the natural environment, gardening, cultivation, and agriculture. The artistic activities were chosen with respect to the environment and considerations around seasonality and the skills and interests of the participants in the group.

The overarching objectives for the sessions were:

- to offer a relaxing space that enables calmness and decompression;
- to facilitate perception of and personal connection (bodily, sensory, emotional, cognitive) with the natural green space;
- to engage in an artistic practice following one's own rhythm and without feeling pressure with respect to the outcomes;
- to express emotions and personal experiences in verbal and creative/non-verbal forms;
- to help the group get to know each other better, relate and communicate;
- to promote the perception and acceptance of diversity, such as cultural or world-view differences; and
- to promote the ability of the group to understand, accept, and respect the rules during the activities.

The sessions were designed to be inclusive, fair, and accessible, providing a space open to the different skills and abilities of the young people. All activities were carried out in compliance with safety principles through an analysis of risks presented by the internal and external space, materials, tools, and equipment used, and respect for the environment.

Some basic rules were shared with the group, mainly with regards to mutual respect, such as respecting other participants and their artwork; suspending judgement of what has been achieved by oneself and by others; practising and respecting personal freedom of expression; and respecting the environment, space, and materials.

Each Open Studio session followed a simple structure for consistency. The phases of each session included:

1. **Preliminary set-up.** The whole group was involved in setting up the space, in the preparation and dismantling after the activity, as an act of care and respect towards the place.
2. **Welcoming the participants and opening of the session.** The rules were often repeated at this phase, especially in the case of new participants arriving or following difficulties and conflicts arising in the group.
3. **Expressive/creative activity, free or facilitated by the art therapist.** Each participant could dedicate themselves to a freely chosen artistic or technical project. Alternatively, the art therapist could present some artistic techniques to facilitate access and participation to the experience or to support participants who experienced difficulty in choosing what to do. The freedom of choice, and the absence of judgement, had the aim of accompanying each person to join the group at their own pace, to feel included, and to acquire confidence in their abilities. The intended purposes were to contribute to a progressive change in self-perception and to facilitate awareness of one's feelings and points of view through art. This could lead to a soothing transformation while improving the ability to stay in

social situations and cope with stress and difficulties, particularly for those who grew up in deprived and devalued families or social environments.

4. **Dialogue and communication.** During the activities, the group could speak freely, using respectful communication and avoiding judgement or criticism of other's work.

5. **Breaks.** Participants were allowed to take a break to rest. It was also possible to finish the activity earlier, for example, if a young person found it difficult to stay with the group for the entire time for any reason.

6. **Conclusion.** Participants were not required to present their artwork at the end of each activity, but they could share their experience with the group if they wished. At the end of each session, the group said goodbye, and the participants were reminded of the date for the following planned session.

Materials

A basic kit containing artistic materials, reused materials, and natural materials was made available (Table 12.1). The materials could be freely chosen and used for different artistic techniques, with the support of the art therapist and educators, if necessary.

The selection of materials was made in accordance with the following guidelines: they were **lightweight and portable**, allowing for easy transport and storage; **safe**, such that materials complied with safety regulations and guidelines (e.g., non-toxic, not risky, appropriate for age and specific use); **hypoallergenic**, as it was important to inquire on individual allergies or hypersensitivity (e.g., to substances, plants, animals); **multipurpose**, preferring less structured materials that can be used in different creative ways; **inclusive**, adapted to individual skills, and accommodated for use by participants with disabilities; and **sustainable**, to optimise resources, artistic materials already available at the services were preferably

Table 12.1 Art materials and tools used in the Open Studio sessions

Basic artistic materials	Natural materials	Recycled materials
Water-based tempera paints	Leaves	Books and magazines for collages
Pastels	Branches and pieces of wood	Wooden boards and blocks
Markers	Stones and pebbles	Resin blocks
White and coloured chalk	Sand	Wool
Wax crayons	Salt	Felt
Oil pastels	Natural chalk	Fabrics
White paper	White powdered clay	Linoleum
Paper in different colours	Natural charcoal	Cardboard boxes
Cardboard	Water	
Tissue paper		

Tools used for different techniques: brushes, scissors, rollers, sponges, clay scoops, glue, etc.

used. In the purchase of new materials, preference was given to artistic materials and products with low environmental impact; the materials (and the artworks) were stored in a closed cabinet and placed in internal spaces.

Different artistic techniques were chosen by the participants and proposed to the group during the sessions:

Visual arts included activities such as still-life drawing of flowers and plants; free-hand drawing; portraiture; tempera painting; watercolour painting; action painting and dripping; and linotyping and printing.

Plastic arts included activities such as modelling with natural clay and chalk.

Assemblage and installation arts included activities such as two-dimensional and three-dimensional collage; creation and decoration of objects with natural and recycled materials; and constructions with natural materials and recycled materials.

Storytelling and visual storytelling included activities such as inventing stories based on the participants' lives; poetry; and creative writing.

In each session, participants were reminded that the objective of the experience was not the result or to master a specific technique but the exploration of the creative process, the experience of learning something new, and, above all, feeling comfortable and experiencing a sense of wellbeing during the sessions.

Practice evaluation

To monitor the process, the activities, and the impact, each year, the following phases were planned.

1. Initial evaluation of the annual project for Open Studio activities (i.e., objectives, participants, methodology, inclusivity, artistic techniques and materials, timetable, monitoring practices).
2. Periodic meetings with the services' staff (e.g., ongoing briefings and final meeting) to ensure a comprehensive evaluation of the activities, the timely management of changes or critical issues; the monitoring of personal progress and difficulties of each participant, to be shared with the case managers of the Social Services, concerning the Individualised Education Plan.
3. Ongoing check-in with young people on how they felt during the activities in two ways: space for feedback at the end of each Open Studio session, with the possibility of sharing feelings, opinions, and suggestions, and through informal or planned briefings with the adolescents, carried out by the coordinator and educators of the service.
4. Follow-up group: to gather the perspectives of the beneficiaries a small focus group was conducted with some adolescents who previously took part in the Open Studio (at least half of the sessions attended) and who expressed interest in giving their feedback. Participants were asked about both the positive aspects

and difficulties of being involved in the activities and the perceived impact on their wellbeing.

5. Follow-up survey for educators: a short online survey was created to gather feedback about the main strengths and challenges of the experience and the perceived impact and changes for the adolescents who took part in it.

Outcomes

The experience of the Open Studio presented both positive outcomes, as well as presenting a range of complex challenges.

One particularly positive element recognised by the young people was that they were able to connect to the arts, particularly when they perceived the surrounding environment being a safe place. Dedicating oneself to creating art in a calm, free space enabled decompression, even by adolescents who generally struggle to relax, be present, and dedicate themselves to an activity for a long time. Young people highlighted that they were able to relax and express themselves freely without focusing on the result. They found their own way of using artistic materials to develop their 'personal style' and found gratification in the simple yet empowering process of artmaking. This was particularly important for adolescents who usually experience difficulties with emotional regulation and interpersonal relationships.

One of the main challenges was the increased exposure to being outdoors and a reduced sense of control as compared with working indoors in a well-defined space or room. While being in nature can be comfortable for many young people, some may experience difficulties being in an open space as they experience sensory overreactions (e.g., sensitivity to sounds, light, heat or cold, fear of noises or animals); this has to potential to lead to distress or discomfort for the young person. The activities were, therefore, planned to make natural spaces as safe, relaxing, and comfortable as possible in different seasons and climatic conditions. We were also open and flexible to changing the setting, where necessary; for example, staying in the shade on a hot day or taking natural shelter in the case of sudden rain. Finally, during the sessions, the group was asked if the setting layout was suitable and comfortable and if the participants had any specific needs.

Another challenge was related to the mitigation of the 'I can't draw' bias, which is linked to the internalisation of negative judgements that young people may have received about themselves (e.g., in school, sports, or other competitive and performative activities); this reduces the perception of one's creativity, abilities and internal resources. The lack of pressure towards 'good results' provided participants with the opportunity to feel increasingly comfortable in activities which were initially approached with distrust. Adolescents who experienced low self-esteem and fear of judgement were able to try new techniques which were complex and difficult to control (e.g., watercolours or linotype instead of pencils); they were able to focus on their 'creative microcosm' and carry out projects with calmness and commitment. Imperfections and 'errors' were not seen as personal failures but as a natural part of the learning and creative process.

In the follow-up focus group, participants reported that the group setting was perceived with ambivalence; being in a group could be rewarding and exhausting at the same time. Some difficulties that adolescents experienced included sharing the space and art materials; compromising; affirming their point of view in assertive and non-aggressive ways; exposing their artwork and themselves to the gaze of others; trusting others; and respecting limits and boundaries. Rules were, therefore, a fundamental part of the group process and were not always well-received, accepted, or respected. The aim of the Open Studio was to facilitate the consolidation of social skills, helping young people to find positive and respectful ways to stay in interpersonal and group interactions. Using the arts as an expressive medium allowed participants to resolve conflicts rather than acting them out aggressively, thereby protecting the most vulnerable. On several occasions, the drawing or painting space became a symbolic territory for peers, where they mediated and negotiated boundaries in a safe and reciprocally respectful way.

According to the feedback provided by the young people, a positive aspect of working within a group setting was that being together while making art had a positive impact on their sense of wellbeing. The flexibility offered by the Open Studio gave each person the opportunity to self-determine their level of participation; choosing to stay, staying as long as needed; leaving; recharging; and coming back. Furthermore, working in dyads or in groups allowed collaboration with others on the same work, exchanges of opinions, and observations of others' artwork that differs from one's own. The group art sessions allowed young people to reflect on issues concerning their identity; interpersonal boundaries; co-existence, inclusion, and belonging; mediating conflicts and divergences; knowing one's limits; and using personal and creative resources.

Implications for practice

Our practice recognises that situations of vulnerability can have an impact on existential dimensions, such as a sense of safety, self-esteem, perception of one's value, physical and mental health, psychosocial and emotional wellbeing, and relationships and connection with family or community. The support we provided aimed to enhance the sense of importance and preciousness of each individual, nurture a sense of being present, and give a chance to creatively imagine one's future by expressing desires and reaching personal goals.

Developing this practice over several cycles and years has highlighted some fundamental implications that could help other facilitators to create a safe and enabling environment for adolescents, using expressive and therapeutic arts as a practice to promote wellbeing, health, and human rights.

- **Ensure rights, accessibility, and equal opportunities** for each person, respecting their identity (e.g., gender; disability; language; culture; religion; opinions; social status) and meeting their needs throughout the project (e.g., planning; implementing; monitoring; consulting beneficiaries).

- **Always act towards the best interest of the children and young people,** and make sure your intervention does not negatively impact any of the persons involved or exacerbate inequities. Remember that *"Do no harm"* is a fundamental statement of psychosocial support and of the human rights approach to care for children and adolescents (United Nations Children's Fund, 2022).
- **Assess the adolescents' needs through direct consultation,** prior to and during each session in order to ensure that the intervention meets their real necessities, interests, and priorities.
- **Consider the perspectives of formal and informal caregivers,** such as parents, carers, educators, teachers, and social workers, and act together as a supportive community.
- **Involve all service staff in all phases of project design** and ensure that the social services are informed (where involved) to create cohesion around objectives, methodologies, and evaluation methods.
- **Try to ensure the presence of educators during the sessions** and ask them for support. A problem here could be the lack of resources (e.g., financial, human, transportation). Try to discuss these issues in the planning phase to make available forms of support for the Open Studio experience which are in line with the services' budget and resources.
- **Set a specific plan tailored to individual goals** for each adolescent that takes part in the intervention, in cooperation with the service staff and the case manager of the social services, connecting the objectives of the sessions to the Individualised Education Plan of each user, in order to create a coherent set of goals.
- **Accurately assess the outdoor and indoor spaces** using a checklist of the most important elements: safety, risks, accessibility, necessary accommodation, and comfort of spaces.
- **Create a safe, welcoming, and inclusive setting** to make each person feel seen, listened and validated in their identity. Consult and involve the whole group to define the shared rules and key principles for a safe environment.
- **Protect the natural environment** and ensure that all actions during the sessions respect nature and do not negatively impact the surroundings (e.g., biodiversity, places, and space layout and balance).
- **Ensure sustainability of the whole process** by designing and implementing the activities according to available resources and monitoring the intervention in collaboration with the service staff so that it lasts over time.
- **Be patient and adapt your methods and goals with flexibility.** Adolescence is a transitional period, so welcome the unexpected and complexities as a way to learn, improve, and tailor each session to the needs of the participants.

Conclusion

Following the creative flow at their own pace represented an opportunity for adolescents to find a moment of inner peace and contact with themselves and nature, and to experience acceptance and inclusion within the wider group. The absence of judgement on personal abilities, choices, and artworks created a precious space for adolescents, particularly for those who experience a sense of low self-esteem in other contexts, such as in their school, family or community. This was particularly important as it led to a sense of relief for young people who, in other situations, are used to being excluded, teased, or scolded for their behaviour.

Working in open natural spaces allowed the group to experience a unique and safely transforming 'emotional landscape'. It also gave them the opportunity to relax gradually, change their mood and perception, and sense the group as a growing habitat. Adolescents expressed that they perceived this place as safe, creative, and "good enough" for themselves and their own evolutionary trajectory.

This experience has been a small drop in a wide ocean of situations and events lived by the adolescents in their daily lives, and it aimed to complement other practices, such as educational and therapeutic interventions and other empowering opportunities. However, each drop that falls is generative and could have an impact whose size is unknown and whose shape is unexpected. In an enabling and supportive environment, even a single drop (or experience) can generate waves, which spread out to reach distant and isolated places (or persons) that may have long-term positive effects.

References

Atkins, S., & Snyder, M. (2017). *Nature-based expressive arts therapy: Integrating the expressive arts and ecotherapy*. London: Jessica Kingsley Publishers.

Buzzell, L., & Chalquist, C. (2009). *Ecotherapy: Healing with nature in mind*. Berkeley, CA: Counterpoint Press.

Finkel, D., & Bat Or, M. (2020). The open studio approach to art therapy: A systematic scoping review. *Frontiers in Psychology*, *11*(568042), 1–16. doi: 10.3389/fpsyg.2020.568042 [Accessed June 30, 2023]

Heginworth, I. S., & Nash, G. (2019). *Environmental arts therapy: The wild frontiers of the heart*. London: Routledge.

Inter-Agency Standing Committee. (2007). *Guidelines on mental health and psychosocial support in emergency settings*. Retrieved from https://hr.un.org/sites/hr.un.org/files/Guidelines%20IASC%20Mental%20Health%20Psychosocial_0.pdf [Accessed June 30, 2023]

Jordan, M., & Hinds, J. (2016). *Ecotherapy: Theory, research and practice*. London: Bloomsbury.

Kaplan, S. (1995). The restorative benefits of nature: Toward an integrative framework. *Journal of Environmental Psychology*, *15*(3), 169–182. doi: 10.1016/0272-4944(95)90001-2 [Accessed June 30, 2023]

Moll, A., Collado, S., Staats, H., & Corraliza, J. A. (2022). Restorative effects of exposure to nature on children and adolescents: A systematic review. *Journal of Environmental Psychology*, *84*. doi: 10.1016/j.jenvp.2022.101884 [Accessed June 30, 2023]

Moon, C. H. (2015). Open studio approach to art therapy. In D. E. Gussak & M. L. Rosal (Eds.), *The wiley handbook of art therapy (Wiley clinical psychology handbooks)* (pp. 112–121). Hoboken, NJ: Wiley-Blackwell.

Shah, P., Boilson, M., Rutherford, M., Prior, S., Johnston, L., Maciver, D., & Forsyth, K. (2022). Neurodevelopmental disorders and neurodiversity: Definition of terms from Scotland's national autism implementation team. *The British Journal of Psychiatry*, *221*(3), 577–579. doi: 10.1192/bjp.2022.43 [Accessed June 30, 2023]

Tillmann, S., Tobin, D., Avison, W., & Gilliland, J. (2018). Mental health benefits of interactions with nature in children and teenagers: A systematic review. *Journal of Epidemiology and Community Health, 72*(10), 958–966. doi: 10.1136/jech-2018-210436 [Accessed June 30, 2023]

United Nation General Assembly. (1989). *Convention on the rights of the child.* Retrieved from www.ohchr.org/en/instruments-mechanisms/instruments/convention-rights-child [Accessed June 30, 2023]

United Nation General Assembly. (2006). *Convention on the rights of persons with disabilities.* Retrieved from https://social.desa.un.org/issues/disability/crpd/convention-on-the-rights-of-persons-with-disabilities-crpd [Accessed June 30, 2023]

United Nations Children's Fund. (2022). *Global multisectoral operational framework for mental health and psychosocial support of children, adolescents and caregivers across settings, 2022.* Retrieved from www.unicef.org/media/109086/file/Global%20multisectorial%20operational%20framework.pdf [Accessed June 30, 2023]

Vella-Brodrick, D. A., & Gilowska, K. (2022). Effects of nature (Greenspace) on cognitive functioning in school children and adolescents: A systematic review. *Educational Psychology Review, 34*, 1217–1254. doi: 10.1007/s10648-022-09658-5 [Accessed June 30, 2023]

World Health Organization. (2013). *Comprehensive mental health action plan 2013–2030.* Retrieved from www.who.int/publications/i/item/9789240031029 [Accessed June 30, 2023]

World Health Organization. (2022). *Key facts on mental health.* Retrieved from www.who.int/news-room/fact-sheets/detail/mental-health-strengthening-our-response [Accessed June 30, 2023]

Chapter 13

What's beneath our feet? Cultivating cultural awareness through arts-in-nature with Australian children and young people

Melissa McDevitt Weston and Carla van Laar

Acknowledgements

We would like to acknowledge the Boon Wurrung/Bunurong Elders past and present, and Ancestors of this land where we have put this chapter together and created artwork. We especially acknowledge the Boon Wurrung/Bunurong People and their ancient living culture of care and creativity that continues today, and we honour this in our work.

Trigger warning

This chapter mentions atrocities that have occurred in Australia.

Introduction

Cultivating cultural awareness through arts-in-nature with children and young people can become a deeply healing and layered experience for the country, traditional owners, creative arts therapists, other arts and wellbeing practitioners, and communities.

Melissa, a proud Boon Wurrung/Bunurong woman and contemporary artist, provides cultural advice and training for creative arts therapist Carla, a non-Aboriginal woman who lives and works in Boon Wurrung/Bunurong Country. The content of this chapter is sensitive. The perspectives we share are our own, not a complete guide to cultural awareness in Australian arts-in-nature practices. By sharing some of our own stories, we hope others might connect through their own experiencing and cultivate practices that are culturally respectful and safe in their own contexts. Melissa draws on her cultural knowledge and experience as a Boon Wurrung/ Bunurong and Yorta Yorta woman living in the current state of Victoria, providing practical considerations for creative arts therapists and others working in the country. Carla shares some of the ways that she practises, emphasising relationships, deep listening, and respect. We see ourselves as co-authors, and others may read the text in this way. For our readers, it is very important that our voices are separate. Following cultural protocols, it would be inappropriate for Carla to comment on

DOI: 10.4324/9781003357308-13

some topics, which is why we have made it clear when we are quoting Melissa's words verbatim. Melissa would likewise feel uncomfortable commenting about creative arts therapies, so we have kept Carla's voice separate in those places.

In collaborating on this chapter, we met on many occasions to talk, or "yarn". We decided to adopt a practice-led approach and started by making an artwork together to inform the content of our chapter (Barrett, 2007). Through the collaborative art-making process, a structure organically took shape, and we developed the chapter subheadings (van Laar, 2020). This process is an example of self-determination, which has been described as "the ability of Aboriginal people to determine their own political, economic, social and Cultural development as an essential approach to overcoming Indigenous disadvantage" (State of Victoria, 2017, p. 20). Self-determination requires institutions to consciously give up some power and control so that Aboriginal people themselves make decisions about things like the content of publications. Melissa has a personal responsibility as a First Nations woman to offer some information in ways that support self-determination rather than conforming to colonial conventions. For these reasons, the structure of our chapter reflects our practice-led approach rather than a pre-determined format.

We made an ephemeral artwork in our local environment, using materials sourced onsite. Later, we saw the artwork photographed from above and realised we had made a tree. The bottom layer has roots going into the creek, and the top layer connects to the native bush above the stretch of sand that we worked on, creating a green canopy above our artwork. The middle layer reminds us of a tree trunk adorned with symbols that speak to layers of the environment, including

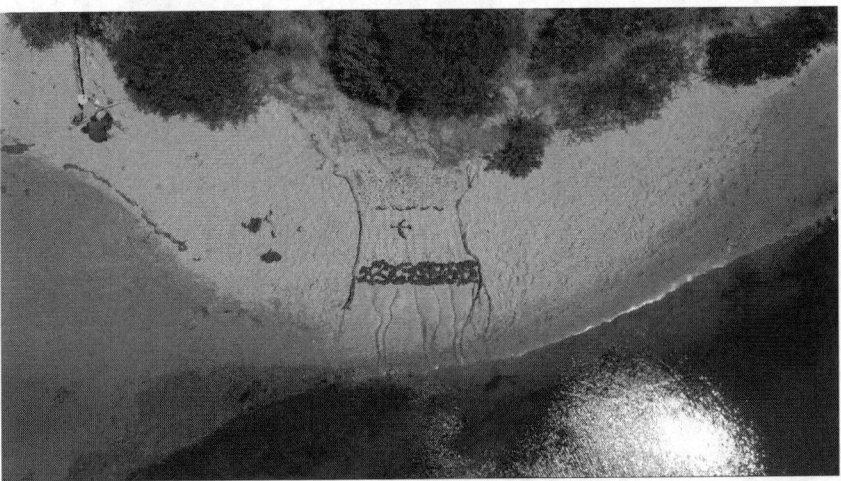

Figure 13.1 "What's beneath our feet?", created on Boon Wurrung/Bunurong (Bunurong) Country, 2022, Melissa McDevitt Weston and Carla van Laar: ephemeral artwork made of driftwood, seaweed, shells, feathers, mud and sand found on location

spirit, universe, sky, creatures, plants, Earth, waterways, and the depths beneath the Earth's surface.

These layers create a map for this chapter, working from the "bottom-up" and starting with our relationship. We move through the layers, looking at our context and the impacts of colonisation in Australia, before asking, "What's beneath our feet?" and talking about artefacts and Ancestors. Next, we explore cultural heritage and its relevance to arts-in-nature. We yarn about the ongoing connection of Aboriginal People to the country, which brings us to think about cultural awareness, healing the country, and forming relationships with traditional owners as part of the work of practitioners who work with arts-in-nature. We introduce acknowledging country as a practice that shows respect for the traditional owners and ancient cultural practices and consider how we can work in nature in culturally sensitive ways. Finally, we come back full circle to the mutuality of healing: healing the country, healing ourselves.

Our relationship

We made a connection when Carla was organising a "Creative Mental Health Forum" and asked Melissa about having a traditional owner facilitate a Welcome to Country. Melissa was the Chair of a local Aboriginal Corporation, the "Yowengerra Bun Wurrung Balug Clans" Association, and was an appropriate person to ask. Carla described the event to Melissa, how it was about creativity, the arts, healing, and wellbeing. Melissa was excited, enthusiastic, and keen to be involved. Carla learned that Melissa is a contemporary Aboriginal artist. Art is an important part of her own healing and community work. We kept talking and meeting. Melissa would patiently and generously offer Carla advice, helping Carla to be more culturally aware and culturally safe in planning the event and in working with others.

Working to become better at these things is important to Carla. She believes it is essential for all non-Aboriginal people living in this country [Australia] to take responsibility for contributing to the healing that needs to occur here. Not even 200 years ago, Carla's English ancestors were free settlers who came to "Australia" on a ship called "The China" in 1841. By the 1860s, they were farmers outside of Brisbane. This confirms that Carla's ancestors and their descendants, including herself, have benefitted from the lies, land theft, and acts of genocide that have occurred on this continent since colonisation. Carla knows she has a long way to go in developing her capacity to be culturally sensitive and safe. Despite Carla's frequent mistakes, Melissa is still Carla's friend and helps her. Our friendship is part of a bigger social story – the story of colonisation.

Impacts of colonisation

Two and a half billion Aboriginal people were born on this continent over the 60,000+ years before English colonisation began in 1788 (Smith, 2002). The English claimed they had discovered a vast, uninhabited land. It is now well known that more than 500 First Nations groups comprising 1,000,000 people inhabited the continent known as Australia (Australians Together, 2023). By 1930, as a direct result of English colonisation, there were only about 50,000 Aboriginal People living here (Pascoe, 2007).

Australia's multicultural population today is more aware than ever before of the ongoing harm from atrocities of attempted genocide that include massacres, rape, child theft, prohibiting traditional languages, forced removal of people from the country, deeply embedded racism against Aboriginal people, and the historical lies, that laid the foundation for English colonisation (Coleman, 2021). Growing numbers of Aboriginal and non-Aboriginal people actively support social justice and healing in this country, knowing that the wounds run so deep they will surely take generations to repair. Supportive activities include public actions such as political activism, participating in protests, attending First Nations Cultural events, purchasing, wearing, and displaying First Nations merchandise, and personal actions like relationship building, cultivating cultural sensitivity, and truth-telling.

Today, First Nations Peoples in Australia are celebrated as the contemporary custodians of the world's oldest living culture, and recognition that "First Nations peoples are clear leaders when it comes to understanding the links between arts, Culture and wellbeing" (Australia Council for the Arts, 2022, p. 17). Recognition, acknowledgement, respect, and celebration are part of what has been referred to as "Healing Country" (NAIDOC, 2021).

What's beneath our feet? The significance of cultural heritage in Australia

> Layers. It is really important that people understand there is Cultural Heritage in every foot and footprint on this Country, Australia.
>
> – *Melissa*

Renowned First Nations musician and songwriter Archie Roach, in his famous lyrics, urged us all to be mindful as we roam the land, reminding us that each environment we walk through is a place where a child was born (Roach, 2019).

Melissa recalls working on a cultural heritage site and looking into a hole that was about four feet deep. She asked the archaeologist on site, "How old is the soil at the bottom?" They replied, "About 10,000 years". This story has stuck with Melissa as an example of how "we are always so close to our Ancestors' artefacts", and "as long as you are digging into original soil, you will find artefacts anywhere because Aboriginal people have been everywhere".

The preservation of cultural heritage and the artefacts beneath our feet includes identifying places in the natural environment that would have been occupied by Aboriginal People many years ago. Traditional owners work in teams along with archaeologists who contribute their scientific knowledge to conducting cultural heritage assessments. Cultural heritage assessments are important for protecting significant areas, for example, an ancient "scar tree" that has a wound on the trunk showing where a section of the tree's surface has been carved out to make a timber artefact – maybe a boat, shield, or coolamon. The tree and surrounding areas can be listed as culturally sensitive areas, helping protect them from being destroyed.

Finding and registering artefacts beneath our feet is deeply important. It provides scientific and cultural proof of occupation by Aboriginal People. The depth at which artefacts are found can be used to determine their age. Artefacts tell stories of trading that occurred across thousands of years. When artefacts are found in one region that is made from a natural resource from another region, this tells the story of people from different areas meeting and trading. Artefacts and artworks are sacred objects and communicate intimate knowledge about the landscape of the country, ensuring the stories of the land will be handed down to future generations. These artefacts and artworks are evidence of the long and beautiful culture of creativity and care that has occurred on this land since time immemorial.

Before colonisation, the thousands of clans living on this continent belonged to particular areas. In Aboriginal Cultures, this belonging to the country is an ongoing and deep connection that includes responsibility for caring for the land and waterways as well as all the living creatures inhabiting it. The spiritual nature of the connection between Aboriginal people and the land is communicated in the following extract from the Uluru Statement from the Heart (First Nations National Constitutional Convention and Central Land Council, 2017):

> Our Aboriginal and Torres Strait Islander tribes were the first sovereign Nations of the Australian continent and its adjacent islands, and possessed it under our own laws and customs. This our ancestors did, according to the reckoning of our culture, from *the Creation, according to the common law from 'time immemorial', and according to science more than 60,000 years ago.*
>
> This sovereignty is a spiritual notion: the ancestral tie between the land, or 'mother nature', and the Aboriginal and Torres Strait Islander peoples who were born therefrom, remain attached thereto, and must one day return thither to be united with our ancestors. This link is the basis of the ownership of the soil, or better, of sovereignty. It has never been ceded or extinguished.

Arts-in-nature practitioners and the people we work alongside

Arts-in-nature practitioners can read literature and find information, ideas, and stories about Indigenous knowledge and healing. Ancient wisdom traditions predate and are the foundations of the eco-consciousness that is at the heart of nature-based healing (e.g., Atkins & Snyder, 2018). We can find resources about consciously working to avoid cultural appropriation and practising cultural humility when we work in ways that are connected with ancient practices (e.g., Arslanbek, Malhotra, & Kaimal, 2022; Kaimal & Arslanbek, 2020; Malchiodi, 2022). Some publications by Australian creative arts therapists describe how they have worked collaboratively with Aboriginal communities (e.g., Linnell, 2009). *Towards Indigenous*

Australian Knowing is a chapter by Aboriginal and creative arts therapist co-authors who "hold to the idea that art therapy with the use of traditional healing approaches alongside mainstream social and emotional wellbeing services should be envisioned" and that "art therapy services should be provided to Aboriginal people by Aboriginal people" (Lawson, Woods, & McKenna, 2019). We have not yet found any resources that address cultural safety when practising arts-in-nature with children and young people in Australian contexts.

Non-Aboriginal creative professionals often work with Aboriginal children and young people. Melissa cautions that it is not appropriate for non-Aboriginal therapists or other practitioners to facilitate cultural art-making with Aboriginal children and young people. Examples of cultural art-making could include painting, woodworking, weaving, and other cultural practices. Cultural art-making is the Aboriginal community and family's role, not a role for non-Aboriginal people. Aboriginal children and young people will sometimes initiate cultural art-making because they know it and choose to do it. In these situations, creative practitioners can let the child lead rather than try to extend them and refrain from attempting to create meaning in the artwork. If the child does choose to make cultural art while working with us, we can simply hold a supportive and interested space.

Cultural awareness and healing the country: knowing whose country we are on

Knowing whose country we are on is the foundation that can inform everything else we do when working in the environment. This knowledge can help us to remember we are always on the country, whether we are outdoors under a tree, canoeing on a river, or sitting in a room. For non-Aboriginal arts-in-nature practitioners living and working in Australia, it is simple to find out whose country we are on. This information is freely available on local government websites, and the Australian Institute of Aboriginal and Torres Strait Islander Studies (AIATSIS, 1996) has a map of Aboriginal language groups that provides guidelines. This is important so we can acknowledge the traditional owners and know who to approach to ask permission to work in protected areas, such as national parks, or to collect or work with natural materials. When there is an absence or lack of cultural sensitivity it can be harmful. Melissa says, "It can make an Aboriginal person feel that everything that they are doesn't exist. Because so much has been taken, it feels like another layer of that hurt. It makes Aboriginal people feel invisible".

Invisible layers exist within the landscape, too. Atkinson (2002) describes these in her book *Trauma Trails: Recreating Song Lines*, stating that "country can hold healing or traumatic memory and energy, by the human activity or ceremony that has made a place unique, sacred or profane" (p. 30). When we are working in and with the environment, layers of hurt and healing are always present but not always visible or acknowledged. The notion of making the invisible visible is inherent to creative practice (Lawson et al., 2019). Creative practitioners can help to make energetic layers visible by researching the Aboriginal origins of the areas they are working in, consulting with traditional owners, and creating relationships. Without developing cultural awareness and sensitivity, there will always be something missing from the layers of healing that we seek to facilitate.

Communicating with traditional owners

Building a relationship shows respect and reciprocity. It's not just about ticking a box. People don't want to feel used or manipulated or as though consultation is a token gesture.

– *Melissa*

As arts-in-nature practitioners who are interested in working in the environment, building a relationship with traditional owners is important. Reach out to the local Aboriginal Corporation, gathering place (building for the community to meet), health service, or community centre as a starting point. Attend events that are open to the public or events that you are invited to. This will strengthen the process of building a trusting relationship.

Going to a local Aboriginal organisation can be a sensitive thing. There are different community protocols and cultural lore in every community. Trusting relationships grow over time, and traditional owners may say "no", or might not be interested in developing a relationship with you. Keep in mind that for Aboriginal people, grief and trauma are always present in everyday life. Be aware that "sorry business" is when a family and community are grieving the loss of a loved one, and it takes priority over everything else. During sorry business, you will need to wait until you have been told it is appropriate to make contact again. This is when a third party like an Aboriginal Corporation or local Elders can be helpful because they will guide you.

Melissa says, "When you do have this trusting relationship you will be amazed how much Aboriginal people will give you, share with you and help you, but it needs to be on their terms". Melissa describes cultural safety as simply respecting the emotional and spiritual wellbeing of First Nations People on their country:

Ways of respecting wellbeing include from negotiating first contact with a community or individual, and asking "would it be alright if I go out and work on your Country?". Before you have even asked anything, showing respect by thanking them for the meeting, or the time they are making to spend with you. In my experience, as a child of the stolen generations, there has been so much time lost from spending with family members. Any time an Aboriginal person spends with you is time away from catching up with their family. You are one of many people who want their time and Cultural knowledge.

Be aware that Western customs, such as making eye contact, might not be shared by Aboriginal people. This does not necessarily indicate an absence of connection and respect. There are cultural customs and ways of doing things that are unfamiliar to us, and we need to learn about them and understand them.

Acknowledging the country creates respect and cultural safety

Acknowledging the country is part of creating cultural safety for Aboriginal People on their lands. By doing this, we acknowledge that Aboriginal People have occupied these lands and cared for them for thousands of years (Reconciliation Australia, 2023). For Melissa, being present at an acknowledgement at an event on her country supports her identity, connection to country, and sense of belonging.

Melissa says, "There are assumptions that Aboriginal People were and are not very structured in their day-to-day living. In fact, they were and still are very structured in Cultural lores and community protocols. Part of those lores and community protocols are being always aware of whose Country you are on, and respectful to the Traditional Owners of the land you are visiting. Smoking ceremony is about this too. If you have an opportunity to participate in one this is highly recommended, for your spiritual protection and ours. It is about cleansing spiritually".

Acknowledging the country when working with children and young people

Creative practitioners facilitating arts-in-nature with children and young people can use their own creativity to make Acknowledgements that are age-appropriate, personal, and inclusive. For example, Carla might go for a walk down to the creek with a child who needs to work with lots of water. When they decide together on a place to stop, Carla can ask, "Before we start, do you know whose country we are on?". Many children already know the answer. "Yes! That's right, we are on Boon Wurrung/Bunurong country. Shall we pay our respects together and ask the Ancestors to help us?" Then, together, Carla and the child might place their hands on the sand and either say or think some words to acknowledge the country and pay respect to the Elders and Ancestors of this land.

When working with a group of children and young people, Carla might include movements so that gestures become part of acknowledging the country, and a familiar ritual to start each session. We can place our hands on the ground and say, "We pay our respects and honour the beautiful Boon Wurrung/Bunurong Country, the Boon Wurrung/Bunurong People, their Ancestors and Elders", then hug our arms around ourselves, saying, "We pay respect and honour ourselves", and finally, extend our arms out towards the other group members, saying "We pay respect and honour each other".

In our local community, there is a child-care/kindergarten whose non-Aboriginal teachers are actively committed to enabling self-determination for the community's First Nations children who attend the centre. As part of this commitment, they commissioned Melissa and another First Nations artist to paint a permanent mural for the exterior building. They have also implemented a daily acknowledgement of the country with the children. Ways to do this might include a special large rug where all the children sit in a circle each morning and learn to say or even sing an acknowledgement together. The environment of the kindergarten includes many resources that help to acknowledge the country in multi-modal ways, such as toys, games, and books that reference Aboriginal stories, traditional language names for animals, and traditional instruments such as clap sticks. The centre regularly engages Aboriginal facilitators to bring cultural workshops for the children. This commitment to supporting self-determination for First Nations children by creating a culturally safe environment has had a flow-on effect on the whole kindergarten community.

Including children, young people, and their family members in acknowledging the country helps to create cultural, interpersonal, energetic, and spiritual safety for everyone in the group, especially First Nations People. As facilitators, we can practise acknowledging the country and asking Ancestors for their guidance and safe passage when we work on their country. We can do this simply in our minds, silently, or through symbolic healing gestures on the country, making a small offering such as a sand drawing, interlaced sticks, or fallen leaves arranged in a meaningful way. We can also acknowledge the country wherever we are, whether it is out in the natural environment or in the context of a centre such as a school or a kindergarten.

Working in nature in culturally sensitive ways

When working in the natural environment, there are ecological and cultural considerations of which creative practitioners should be conscious.

Culturally significant places

Many different places have cultural significance, including shell middens, rock art, ceremonial grounds, ochre quarries, fish traps, stone arrangements, water holes, burial sites, artefacts, and others (Aboriginal Heritage, 2023).

Carla remembers the feeling she experienced when she first saw "Uluru", the stunning red rock in the heart of the continent, and the unmistakeable sensation that this was a sacred place. She heard many stories about former visitors who had taken pieces of the famous red rock as souvenirs and later returned them by post. This is now known as "The sorry rock phenomenon at Uluru-Kata Tjuta National Park" (Australian Government, 2017). A fact sheet published by the Director of National Parks describes how:

> Anangu, the Aboriginal traditional owners of Uluru, believe that rocks and sand belong at Uluru, not in the homes or pockets of visitors. Under Tjukurpa, the Anangu law governing life and land, there are consequences for disobeying the law of the land . . . (and) respect that should be shown to the land, especially as a visitor.
>
> (Australian Government, 2017)

We suggest that it does not matter where we are; we can apply this same sensitivity and respect to all lands and waterways.

Waterways

All waterways in Australia have cultural significance as the "veins of Mother Earth", food sources, and gathering places. Many river and creek beds are also burial grounds, either known or unknown. Some of these burial grounds are traditional sites. Others are the unmarked graves of the thousands of Aboriginal people killed in massacres during the early days of colonisation when settlers were claiming and clearing land for farming. All waterways are sites of very sensitive cultural significance. Cultural heritage protects all waterways and the land around them that extends 200 metres from the bank or shoreline (Victorian Government, 2023).

Finding an artefact

If you suspect you have found an Aboriginal artefact, like a stone that has been worked to make a blade, axe head, or painting, leave it where it is, and mark where you have left it for reference. Contact your local Aboriginal Corporation or Cultural Heritage Officers to let them know you have found something of potential cultural significance. Your report could lead to the protection of a culturally significant place.

Working with natural materials

Cultural lore tells us "never take the first one of anything that you find, because it might be the last one", for example, plant life like a medicinal plant, or some kind of "bush tucker".

– *Melissa*

In this section, Melissa shares her cultural knowledge to help practitioners make respectful choices when working in Australian environments.

Seeds – in keeping with cultural lore, you can't harvest the first one you find; you have to find another one and leave the first one so it can shed its seeds and grow again. This is our sustainable environmental cultural protocol. For creative practitioners, you can't just incorporate seeds into your artwork. Even if they are dead on the ground, you can't take them because they are part of a whole cycle. They are a food source for birds, and then the bird poo replants them.

A lot of the plant life tells us when we can hunt certain animals to eat. If a certain tree is flowering, that means you can go and get fresh-water crays because it is not their breeding season. Looking after the trees and their seeds is looking after the wildlife too, as well as their babies and offspring.

Rocks – are an absolute no-no. Our cultural beliefs are that rocks have their own spirit and connection to the country. If you remove them, it can be "not good" for your spiritual wellbeing. It is disrespectful to the land and the traditional owners from that area. There is an environmental impact as well. People might think, "It is only one rock", but when you have a thousand people who think that it changes the landscape, changes the habitat for the animals, and changes the flow of the water, as environmentally, rocks are the filter for water.

Soil – certain plants can only grow in their specific soil environment. An example of this is a medicinal plant that grows along the banks of a large river. People have removed the plant and tried to grow it elsewhere, which has failed more than not. This shows us the relationship between the soil and the plant and the importance of preserving the original environment for plants without disturbing the process. You might be unaware that there were seeds in that soil that you were moving.

Sand – is like rocks but smaller. It is about energy. It is inappropriate to remove sand from anywhere. Even bought sand has come from somewhere. There are currently protests about the sand mine not far from here. Sand plays a big part in filtering water, whether it is rain, a spring, or a water table. When you disturb the sand, you are disturbing many other things. There is a lot of mining near water tables. Like quartz for concrete, the quartz is the filtering system for the water table. After the quartz was mined, the water was contaminated. It doesn't just affect the area that has been mined. It affects the whole flow, the fish that live in the rivers, and everything else. You can see this where water flow has been diverted.

Ochre and clay – all ochre comes from somewhere. Traditional owners use it for cultural ceremonies and events, and it should not be gathered or used by non-Aboriginal people at any point unless gathered and offered as a gift by a traditional owner to a non-Aboriginal person. Ochre is very special and significant to all Aboriginal People on the continent. Part of ochre's role is to connect that individual to land and to the Ancestors. In its natural environment, clay provides natural minerals for everything else. It is like a food for the environment.

Conclusion – growth: mutual healing – healing the country, healing ourselves

Cultivating cultural awareness in working with children and young people in Australian environments contributes to wellness and healing for First Nations People, their Ancestors, the country we are on, all the life that it sustains, and supports safe passage on this country for us and the people we work alongside. The process of becoming friends, sharing stories, and co-authoring this chapter has also been healing for both of us.

For Melissa, "It's been an absolute joy working with Carla and experiencing her passion towards caring for the environment and her drive to ensure Cultural safety for First Nations People. Collaborating has also been a healing process for myself in sharing some of my lived experiences as an Aboriginal woman".

For Carla, "Through this work, and my friendship with Melissa, I am coming closer to a sense of belonging in this Country than I have ever yet had. I hope that one day I will have earned the privilege I have to call this place home".

We invite you to reflect on your experience of reading our chapter and what this might mean for you in your life, your own community context, your ways of acknowledging the country, respecting culture, and making arts-in-nature with children and young people. We hope that opening up this conversation about "What's beneath our feet?" adds another layer of depth to your practice and becomes part of the healing that is needed in this country and everywhere on Earth.

In closing, we reflect on the well-known statement by Martin Luther King, Jnr (1967), which emphasises that the silence of the many can be more troubling than the actions of the few.

References

Aboriginal Heritage. (2023). *Identifying aboriginal sites*. Retrieved from www.aboriginal-heritage.org/sites/identification/ [Accessed February 28, 2023]

Arslanbek, A., Malhotra, B., & Kaimal, G. (2022). Indigenous and traditional arts in art therapy: Value, meaning, and clinical implications. *The Arts in Psychotherapy, 77*, 101879.

Atkins, S., & Snyder, M. (2018). *Nature-based expressive arts therapy: Integrating the expressive arts and ecotherapy*. London: Jessica Kingsley.

Atkinson, J. (2002). *Trauma trails, recreating song lines: The transgenerational effects of trauma in indigenous Australia*. North Geelong: Spinifex Press.

Australia Council for the Arts. (2022). *Connected lives: Creative solutions to the mental health crisis*. Retrieved from https://australiacouncil.gov.au/advocacy-and-research/arts-creativity-and-mental-wellbeing-policy-development-program/ [Accessed February 28, 2023]

Australian Government. (2017). *The sorry rock phenomenon at Uluru-Kata Tjuta national park*. Retrieved from https://sacredland.org/wp-content/uploads/2017/10/Media-Fact-Sheet-Sorry-Rocks-2.pdf [Accessed February 28, 2023]

Australian Institute of Aboriginal and Torres Strait Islander Studies. (1996). *The AIAT-SIS map of indigenous Australia*. Retrieved from https://aiatsis.gov.au/explore/map-indigenous-australia [Accessed February 28, 2023]

Australians Together. (2023). *Colonisation: Dispossession, disease and conflict*. Retrieved from https://australianstogether.org.au/discover-and-learn/our-history/colonisation/ [Accessed August 17, 2023]

Barrett, E. (2007). Introduction. In E. Barrett & B. Bolt (Eds.), *Practice as research: Approaches to creative arts enquiry* (pp. 1–14). London: I. B. Tauris & Co.

Coleman, C. G. (2021). *Lies, damned lies: A personal exploration of the impact of colonisation*. Melbourne: Hardie Grant Publishing.

First Nations National Constitutional Convention & Central Land Council (Australia), issuing body. (2017). *Uluru: Statement from the heart*. Central Land Council Library, Alice Springs, Northern Territory. Retrieved from http://nla.gov.au/nla.obj-484035616 [Accessed June 6, 2023]

Kaimal, G., & Arslanbek, A. (2020). Indigenous and traditional visual artistic practices: Implications for art therapy clinical practice and research. *Frontiers in Psychology, 11*, 1320.

King, M. L. (1967). *The three evils of society*. Retrieved from www.youtube.com/watch?v=j8d-IYSM-08&t=14s [Accessed February 28, 2023]

Lawson, C., Woods, D., & McKenna, T. (2019). *Towards indigenous Australian knowing*. In A. J. Gilroy, S. Linnell, T. McKenna, & J. Westwood (Eds.), *Art therapy in Australia: Taking a postcolonial, aesthetic turn* (pp. 77–105). Leiden: Brill.

Linnell, S. (2009). Becoming "otherwise": A story of a collaborative and narrative approach to art therapy with indigenous kids "in care". *Australian and New Zealand Journal of Art Therapy, 41*, 15–26.

Malchiodi, C. (2022). *Cultural appropriation, cultural humility, and expressive arts therapy*. Retrieved from www.youtube.com/watch?v=MXHadPXFUKI [Accessed February 28, 2023]

National Aborigines and Islanders Day Observance Committee (NAIDOC). (2021). *2021 Theme announced: Heal Country!* Retrieved from www.naidoc.org.au/news/2 021-naidoc-week-theme-announced-heal-country [Accessed February 28, 2023]

Pascoe, B. (2007). *Convincing ground: Learning to fall in love with your Country*. Canberra: Aboriginal Studies Press.

Reconciliation Australia. (2023). *Acknowledgement of country and welcome to country*. Retrieved from www.reconciliation.org.au/reconciliation/acknowledgement-of-country-and-welcome-to-country/ [Accessed February 28, 2023]

Roach, A. (2019). *Tell me why: The story of my life and my music*. Cammeray: Simon and Schuster.

Smith, L. (2002). How many people had lived in Australia before it was annexed by the English in 1788. In G. Briscoe & L. R. Smith (Eds.), *The Aboriginal population revisited: Seventy thousand years to the present* (pp. 9–15). Canberra: Aboriginal History Inc.

State of Victoria. (2017). *Korin Korin Balit-Djak: Aboriginal health, wellbeing and safety strategic plan 2017–2027*. Melbourne: Victorian Government. Retrieved from www.dffh.vic.gov.au/publications/korin-korin-balit-djak [Accessed February 28, 2023]

van Laar, C. (2020). *Seeing her stories*. Brunswick. Available from carlavanlaar.com

Victorian Government. (2023). *Cultural heritage sensitivity*. Retrieved from www.firstpeoplesrelations.vic.gov.au/cultural-heritage-sensitivity [Accessed February 28, 2023]

Chapter 14

Concluding reflections

The potential of arts-in-nature

Zoe Moula and Nicola Walshe

The aim of this book was to explore the potential of arts-in-nature practice for supporting the mental health and wellbeing of children and young people, potentially mitigating health inequalities and contributing to environmental sustainability. Building on our own research on the impact of arts-in-nature experiences through the Eco-Capabilities project, the book presents a range of examples of practice from academics, therapists, teachers, and practitioners. The work described draws on a varying approaches, incorporating visual arts, music, movement, drama, and poetry in a range of natural environments, including forests, woodlands, beaches, parks, school playgrounds, greenhouses, and community areas. However, despite this rich tapestry of projects, what is clear throughout the book is the passion with which authors describe the impact of the practice on the children and young people involved, the way that creativity and the arts provide a vehicle through which children and young people notice nature and become more connected to it, in doing so supporting their wellbeing. Whilst each project described set out with different aims, whether that be to develop or restore children's connections to nature (e.g., Adams & Beauchamp, 2024), to provide art therapy (e.g., Horrox, 2024), or to facilitate broader learning (e.g., Keyte-Harland & Lowings, 2024), each reports benefits of contact with the natural environment through and with the arts. These are wide-ranging, but echo the changes observed in children within our own eco-capabilities project, enhancing relationships by providing a space within which to voice emotions and safely confront differences (e.g., Guerrera, 2024; Cusack, 2024), developing children's capacity for play (e.g., Kurian & Sapsed, 2024), and demonstrating the importance of the arts, culture, and the environment in feeding young people's capacity to flourish (e.g., Hay, 2024).

Through the rich description of their practice, authors further emphasised the calming and grounding effects of arts-in-nature, achieved by immersion in the process of artmaking in nature alongside embodied participation through listening, smelling, touching, and noticing elements of nature. This echoes research from neuroscientists which suggests that even a gentle breeze against our skin can relax our nervous system, and that being in nature increases the production of serotonin in our body (e.g., Park et al., 2020); this is how many antidepressant

DOI: 10.4324/9781003357308-14

medications in Western medicine work. Some authors (e.g., Adams & Beauchamp, 2024) explicitly linked these effects to theories of 'optimal' states of mind, such as flow (Csíkszentmihályi, 1975) and experiences of transcendence which provide absorbing moments of lightness and freedom in which one experiences a sense of harmony with the world (Williams & Harvey, 2001). Arts-in-nature practice was also described as offering a plethora of opportunities to explore existential themes of life, allowing children and young people to process difficult life changes through symbols and metaphors inspired by nature. For example, dead plants and decomposed natural materials can offer creative opportunities to navigate loss or death, with nature as a partner in this process. Seasonal changes can also be seen as symbolic representations of life's changes, which can support children and young people to reflect upon and process the inevitable and unpredictable changes in their own lives. However, ultimately, the practices described in this book encourage us to focus on being and learning 'with' – rather than simply 'about' or 'in' – nature. Examples presented throughout the chapters illustrate that creating new nature through the arts and intertwining physical landscapes with real or imagined stories can foster children's and young people's connection with natural spaces. This is achieved by being exposed to the beauty of nature and the arts; the emotions that arise from engaging with the arts and nature; and with sustained contact with both arts and nature combined.

Alongside the wealth of benefits of arts-in-nature described across the book, authors have also highlighted a range of practical, ethical, and safeguarding challenges that arise when facilitating experiences with children and young people outdoors; this is perhaps particularly the case when working explicitly in therapeutic contexts. For example, some children and young people might feel unwelcome or out of place in certain outdoor spaces, whilst others might have previous experiences or memories of discrimination or forced displacement. Others might avoid mixed-gendered outdoor spaces for cultural reasons, while some children and young people may feel uncomfortable in spaces that lack proximity, maintenance, and essential facilities. Despite this, the involvement of children and young people who rarely have the opportunity to engage with the arts (Ashton & Ashton, 2022) and/or nature (e.g., Chen, Yue, & La Rosa, 2020) is of crucial importance. Every child and young person should have an equal right to connect with their local outdoor spaces, reimagine these through creativity and imagination, and feel an active part of their local communities. Examples such as the *Forest of Imagination* (Hay, 2024) and the *Village Project* (Cusack, 2024) are excellent initiatives for inclusive placemaking and artmaking that can lead to a sense of belonging, community engagement, and active citizenship. These projects illustrate how arts-in-nature experiences can move beyond interventions for small groups or individuals towards a preventative approach to supporting the mental health and wellbeing of children and young people, alongside empowering them to have a positive impact on their local environment and, thereby, broader planetary health.

Figure 14.1 'Artscaping', Cambridge Curiosity and Imagination

References

Adams, D., & Beauchamp, G. (2024). Immersion and transcendence through music making in the more-than-human world. In Z. Moula & N. Walshe (Eds.), *Arts in nature with children and young people: A guide towards health equality, wellbeing and sustainability* (pp. 12–23). Abingdon: Routledge.

Ashton, H., & Ashton, D. (2022). Creativity and the curriculum: Educational apartheid in 21st century England, a European outlier? *International Journal of Cultural Policy, 29*(4), 484–499. doi: 10.1080/10286632.2022.2058497

Chen, Y., Yue, W., & La Rosa, D. (2020). Which communities have better accessibility to green space? An investigation into environmental inequality using big data. *Landscape and Urban Planning, 204*, 103919. doi: 10.1016/j.landurbplan.2020.103919

Csikszentmihalyi, M. (1975). *Beyond boredom and anxiety.* San Francisco, CA: Jossey-Bass.

Cusack, A. (2024). The village project: A community of relational creativity. In Z. Moula & N. Walshe (Eds.), *Arts in nature with children and young people: A guide towards health equality, wellbeing and sustainability* (pp. 73–83). Abingdon: Routledge.

Guerrera, E. (2024). Open studio in the greenhouse: Nature-connected expressive and therapeutic art experiences with vulnerable adolescents. In Z. Moula & N. Walshe (Eds.), *Arts in nature with children and young people: A guide towards health equality, wellbeing and sustainability* (pp. 125–137). Abingdon: Routledge.

Hay, P. (2024). Forest of imagination: Reimagining familiar spaces through creativity and nature awareness. In Z. Moula & N. Walshe (Eds.), *Arts in nature with children and young people: A guide towards health equality, wellbeing and sustainability* (pp. 108–115). Abingdon: Routledge.

Horrox, K. (2024). An outdoor therapy service offering art therapy for young people and adults. In Z. Moula & N. Walshe (Eds.), *Arts in nature with children and young people: A guide towards health equality, wellbeing and sustainability* (pp. 84–97). Abingdon: Routledge.

Keyte-Harland, D., & Lowings, L. (2024). Learning to live well together: Art and ecological research with young children. In Z. Moula & N. Walshe (Eds.), *Arts in nature with children and young people: A guide towards health equality, wellbeing and sustainability* (pp. 98–107). Abingdon: Routledge.

Kurian, N., & Sapsed, R. (2024). "Pocket adventures": Nurturing young children's creativity and wellbeing through art-in-nature education. In Z. Moula & N. Walshe (Eds.), *Arts in nature with children and young people: A guide towards health equality, wellbeing and sustainability* (pp. 60–72). Abingdon: Routledge.

Park, B.-J., Shin, C.-S., Shin, W.-S., Chung, C.-Y., Lee, S.-H., Kim, D.-J., Kim, Y.-H., & Park, C.-E. (2020). Effects of forest therapy on health promotion among middle-aged women: Focusing on physiological indicators. *International Journal of Environmental Research and Public Health*, *17*(12), 4348. doi: 10.3390/ijerph17124348

Williams, K., & Harvey, D. (2001). Transcendent experience in forest environments. *Journal of Environmental Psychology*, *21*(3), 249–260.

Index

Note: page numbers in *italics* indicate figures, page numbers in **bold** indicate tables in the on the corresponding page and references following "n" refer notes.